THE HOOT
OWL MAN

THE HOOT OWL MAN

Roy M. Philp, Jr.

ISBN: 10: 1518737625
ISBN 13: 9781518737626
Cover design by Tom Bell
Printed in the United States of America by CreateSpace, an Amazon Company

This book is dedicated to Albert and Mable Shepherd who were my grandparents on my mother's side of the family whom we all called Papa and Bobbie. My book is also dedicated to their three daughters, Aunt Jane, Aunt Marjorie, and Mary Louise, my mom, as well as to my sisters, Jane and Catherine and to cousins Albert, Sherrill and David.
It is also dedicated to my dad and Uncle Moodye who taught us how to swim, fish, set trotlines, skin catfish, play horseshoes and gin rummy, run the boats, use fly rods and all about Hawaiian wigglers and Peck's poppers.
Thanks to all for the twenty plus summer vacations we spent together at Camp Clark on the Neches River at the mouth of Village Creek. The old camp house is gone but the memories will never be forgotten. The pristine sandbars on the creek are still there as is Belrow. The floods have also claimed Mr. Sweatman's house at the bend on the river. The sugarplum tree is gone but the hoot owls are still there and seem to be doing well. Last I heard, no one ever found Captain Clark's treasure nor has anyone seen a wampus cat in quite some time.
My book is also dedicated to Sue, my wife and best friend.
Love you guys. Thanks for the memories and thank you, Papa for Mary Ellen and for calling the owls.

TABLE OF CONTENTS

CHAPTER 1

TA DAAH

After about an hour ride in the truck and a thirty-minute ride in the boat they arrived at their secret camp spot. Everything was going according to plan. A little front had blown in and it was cooler than they had expected, but the weatherman promised sunny weather for tomorrow and Sunday. The cool was invigorating. Dave and Jim had the tent up and all the bedding inside. While Jim was getting the campfire going Dave busied himself loading the chuck box. The latrine had been dug, the trotlines had been set, and Jim had set his perch traps. After they set up the dining fly they pulled up their chairs to the fire and decided to take a break. Their dog, Slick had done recognizance of the area and marked all the appropriate boundaries to claim their spot. Having done so, he came to the fire for a little attention now that his first official job had been done.

"Good job!" said Dave and the yellow lab gave a "Woof!" in agreement.

Jim said, "I saw a good oak log a while ago that I'll get for firewood. It was dry and will probably be enough for tonight. I'll drag it over in a minute

"I'll help you cut it up." Dave answered. "Did you get your traps set?"

"Yes sir! I baited them with some dog chow. I'll check them in about an hour."

All of a sudden their dog ran to the edge of the creek and started barking and was looking at something. When they looked up they saw another yellow lab across the creek that was looking at them and then both dogs were barking. The dog on the other side looked nervous and scared at the same time and jumped in the creek and started swimming toward the campsite. The dog kept looking up stream as it swam toward them. Jim spotted the canoe first and said, "Look! Something's wrong!"

The current was bringing the canoe toward them but there was no one paddling. As it got closer they saw that there was a person slumped down and there were a few inches of water in the canoe. Dave knew immediately that something was wrong. He waded in the water about knee deep and grabbed the front of the canoe and pulled it alongside their boat.

The person in the boat was a girl wearing shorts and a sweater. She was barely conscious and a shade of blue. She was shivering uncontrollably and her fingers were wrinkled from being in the water a long time.

"What's wrong with her?" Jim asked. "Is she going to die?"

Dave said, "I'm not sure but I think it's hypothermia. We've got to act fast. Let's get her in the tent and try to warm her up." He picked her up and carried her into the tent. He took her shoes and socks off as well as her shorts. Next he propped her up and took her sweater off. He instructed Jim to get his long underwear and help him get it on her. He told Jim to close his eyes as he took off her bra. Dave quickly got the long underwear top on and told Jim he could open his eyes now. "Help me get these bottoms on now."

"What about her panties?"

"We'll leave them on."

Dave gave her a brisk rub down starting with her calves and working his way up to her back. He then placed her in his bedroll and took off his own wet jeans and socks and climbed in the bedroll with her. He instructed Jim to heat some water and put it in zip lock bags and Jim hopped to the task. Dave kept rubbing her back and tried to wake her up, but she was out like a light. In a little while Jim was back with the hot water bags. Dave wrapped a towel around one and placed it behind her neck and the other he wrapped a shirt around and placed it over her heart.

"How is she?" asked Jim.

"Well, she's stopped shivering but I can't wake her up."

"I'm scared, dad! What should we do?"

"I'm scared too. Hypothermia is serious. We should take her to a hospital but we don't have time. I believe we're doing about all we can right now. A little prayer might help. Why don't you look in the chuck box and get the first aid book and read what it says about hypothermia. See if you see anything else that we could be doing."

"OK" he replied and he left to get the book. He returned in a few minutes and said, "It looks like we're doing all the right things. It says we should try to get her to drink something hot like coffee or tea. I'll go make some coffee. I said a prayer already."

"That's my boy! Think positive."

About this time she opened her eyes and was looking face to face with Dave whose eyes were closed and he was still softly rubbing her back.

"God! He's handsome," she thought and she tried to access her new surroundings and put some thoughts together. "Have I died and gone to heaven?" she thought.

All of a sudden Dave started to pray. "Lord, please let this young lady be OK. I believe she has a lot of living left in her. She has a beautiful dog and anybody that canoes has got to have a lot of good in them. I feel she is a Christian but if she isn't I baptize her in Christ's name. Please don't let her die, especially in front of Jim. He's already lost his mom and I don't think he can stand more sadness. Please Lord, let her be OK. We ask this in Christ's name. Amen."

She kept her eyes closed trying to get her thinking straight. Was she in the bedroll with a preacher? Did he really baptize her? Did his wife die? Was she having a bad dream? Her mind was racing. "Here goes!" she thought and she opened her eyes. He was staring straight into hers. He smiled and said, "Hello!"

"Where am I?" she asked.

"We found you floating down the creek in a canoe. You were going into hypothermia and you were unconscious. We brought you into the tent to try and warm you up."

"Did you find my dog?"

"Yes!"

"Did you take advantage of me?"

"No!"

"Are you going to take advantage of me?"

"No!" he answered startled by this conversation.

"Shucks" she said.

"What did you say!" he said with astonishment.

"I said my chest is cold."

"You know what?" he said, "I think you're going to be OK. I don't know about me but you're going to be OK" as he got out of the bedroll and quickly put on some dry jeans.

"Jim!" he hollered, "How's that coffee coming?"

"Did she wake up?"

"Yeah, buddy" he answered.

"Look!" Dave said as he put his shirt on, "There are plenty of warm clothes in this bag. Probably all the wrong sizes but the price is right. My dopp kit has a brush and comb and if you need anything in it, help yourself."

"Thanks!" she said and as Dave left the tent she said, "Cluck, Cluck" and giggled.

"Did you get her all warmed up?" Jim asked.

"Smoking hot man, smoking hot! Got her so hot she almost caught me on fire" he said with a rigor.

"I thought I heard a chicken in the tent."

"You did!" Dave said as he poured himself a cup of coffee.

All of a sudden from inside the tent they hear, "Pudd'n! Are you out there?"

Her dog was ecstatic at the sound of her voice and darted into the tent and started jumping up and down. They heard laughter and then out of the tent she stepped and said, "Ta Daah!"

The boys were stunned. She looked like a million dollars. Bright eyed, rosy cheeks, dimples, smiling and an impish look on her face that would make men's hearts melt. The clothes she was wearing which should have been baggy were all tied in the right way that one could tell she had been reading all the right catalogs. The old Eddie Bauer chamois shirt never looked better.

Jim's eyes were about to pop and he said, "Wow!"

"And what are you "Wowing" young man?" she asked.

"You!" he sighed. "You're so pretty! My dad said you looked like a wet rat when we found you."

She glanced at Dave who had put his hands over his face at Jim's last comment.

"I don't think we've been properly introduced. I'm Molly and this is my dog, Pudd'n Tane."

Jim stuck out his hand and said, "I'm Jim."

Molly took his hand and said, "Well Jim, I'm glad to meet you."

Jim added, "This is my dog, Slick. Slick saw your canoe first and started barking like crazy. Uncle Dave said if he hadn't seen you that you probably would have died. Hypothermia is real serious."

"Thanks Slick!" she responded and stuck out her hand to Slick who quickly lifted his paw and wagged his tail in glee.

"Oh! He does tricks does he?"

"Yes ma'am! Uncle Dave taught him."

Molly looked at the campfire and saw a large limb that had been dragged over to the fire and was being used as a make shift clothesline. She recognized most of her clothes drying and walked over to the limb and asked, "whose idea was this?'

"Mine!" said Jim proudly.

She went over to the bra and picked it up. She turned to Dave and asked, "Is this yours?"

Dave wagged his head no. Then she looked at Jim and asked, "Is it yours?"

"No!" he giggled. "It's yours. Uncle Dave made me close my eyes when he took it off."

"Well, it's nice to know that chivalry is not dead" and then asked, "Where are my panties?"

"You're wearing them!" Jim answered "They're pink!"

Molly snapped back, "Thought you had your eyes closed."

Jim kind of cooed which was a habit he had when he felt anxiety. He jumped up and said, "Come on Slick!" and Slick and Pudd'n both jumped up and followed him into the woods.

She turned to Dave and asked, "What about you? Did you have your eyes closed?"

"No!" he said, "But I was behind you and believe it or not, I didn't look" and he gave her the Scout Sign.

"What's that mean?" she asked.

"That's the Scout Sign. That's my word."

"You were a Boy Scout?"

"I was."

"What rank?"

"Eagle."

"I'm impressed! My father is an Eagle Scout and so is my brother. That where you learned about hypothermia?"

"Matter of fact, I think it is, how about a cup of coffee?"

"I'd love some" she said and then said, "Thanks for saving my life. I've shaken hands with your dog but not with you."

They shook hands but it turned into a hug. "I'm glad you're OK. You gave us a pretty good scare."

"I'm sorry about that scene in the bedroll. I haven't been in a man's arms in a long time. I guess I got a little carried away. It won't happen again."

"Shucks!" he said, laughing as he led her to the campfire. "It's important that you stay warm," and he added more wood to the fire.

"Thanks" she said, "This feels good."

"How about some eggs and sausage to warm your insides up?"

"Sounds great, do you want me to help?

"No, you just stay warm."

Dave had the sausage sizzling in no time and was buttering the English muffins as Jim returned from the woods. The dogs were beside themselves with their new friendship and the smell of sausage in the air held promise.

Jim went to Molly and told her that he was glad she was OK.

"I said a prayer for you" he said, "I knew God was going to make you better."

Molly reached out and gave him a hug. "Thanks" she said, "I'm indebted to you two and to Slick. I'm sure you saved my life. I'm going to try and think of a way to repay you. I'll have to think on it."

Dave handed Molly a plate of scrambled eggs, sausage, toasted English muffins and a dab of jelly on the side. Molly started eating and there were eight eyes watching her as she ate each bite. The dogs were probably hoping she might drop a morsel of some type, but the men were admiring this beautiful and charming treasure that had fallen their way. This was like no other camping trip either of them had ever been on. A girl in the woods! They were mesmerized.

Molly could almost feel their stares and liked the feeling. After a while she asked, "Cat got your tongue, boys?"

Dave asked, "What happened in the creek? Were you by yourself? Should we be out looking for someone else?"

"I was by myself, just Pudd'n and me. The morning started out kind of chilly but then the sun came out and it started to warm up. I took off my warm ups to catch a few rays. There was a large limb about this high off the water. The creek was kind of narrow which made the current faster. There was no way to go around it so I ducked my head and under we went. Pudd'n got nervous and started barking. Right when the bow went under the limb. I guess her barking woke up a big black water moccasin that was sunning on the limb and he dropped off in the canoe. The snake went toward Pudd'n and she bailed out of the canoe."

"How long was the water moccasin?" Jim asked and Molly held up her arms about four feet apart.

"How'd you know it was a water moccasin?" Dave asked.

"Well, as far as I'm concerned, any snake that falls in my canoe is a water moccasin."

"Then what happened?" Jim asked.

"Well, the snake turned and started coming at me. I hit him with the paddle but he kept on coming. I tried to jump out of the canoe but when I did, it turned over. I lost everything. Almost lost the canoe but I finally got it over to a sandbar and got the water out. I lost the paddle. The water was freezing. The north wind picked up, and I've never been so cold. I found a long stick and started polling my way down stream thinking I'd find my paddle. I never did find it. I believe I hit every logjam and limb in the creek. I screamed so loud that I scared off any snake that might have been around. I fell in a couple more times. I started shivering and couldn't stop. Next thing I know I wake up in a strange tent in somebody's bedroll face to face with a wooly booger that had a slight case of peanut breath looking me straight in the eye. I thought that ole water moccasin was going to bite me yet."

Jim started laughing and Dave started feeling his whiskers. "Darn!" he thought, "I must look a mess and I need to brush my teeth."

Dave passed the last two sausages to Molly who took them and gave one to each of the dogs.

Molly added the last bit of jelly to the muffin and commented, "I believe this is the best jelly I've ever tasted. What kind is it?"

"It's mayhaw," Jim replied. "We made it. That's one of the reasons we camped here. We're going to pick some in the morning. Want to go with us?"

"Yes! I'd love to and since I've got no paddle, no car keys, no tent and no food, I guess I'd better earn my keep. I bet I can pick more than you!"

Jim loved a challenge and replied, "No way!"

"I'm embarrassed to ask this but I need to potty. Do you have a potty area?"

"Yes ma'am! I'll show you. We call it a latrine. I'm in charge of it each time we go camping," and he led her to it. It was located about 50 yards from the camp behind a giant pine tree. A blue folding potty seat was set over a narrow trench that had been dug with a sharpshooter shovel. Jim said, "You sit there, do your business and when you're through you add a little dirt. No smell and no flies. Pretty neat huh?"

"I'm impressed," she replied.

"Here's the paper and a book if you like to read. We keep it in a zip lock bag in case it rains."

Molly noticed that there was a Reader's Digest in the bag. She was not believing this.

"Know what? One time I was sitting on the throne (That's what Uncle Dave calls it) reading and when I looked up there was a doe and her fawn about 50 feet away staring at me. I kept real still and we just stared at each other and finally they just walked away.

She didn't even flag me. It was pretty neat."

"Sounds like it" Molly answered and said, "Now if you'd skedaddle, I would like to try out your blue potty."

As Jim started to leave she asked, "Please take the dogs with you if you don't mind. I don't want them watching me."

Back at the camp Dave had boiled water and was in the midst of shaving. As Jim approached he said, "I like her a lot! I wish she would come on all our camping trips. Do you like her?"

"You bet!" Dave answered, "She took my breath away when she stepped out of that tent. She's got class and has a lot of step in her get along, kind of spunky too!"

Molly reappeared in camp and walked by Dave just as he was slapping on some aftershave. She reached up and ran her fingers over the side of his face "No more wooly booger," she said smiling.

"Say!" Dave replied, "Did you use my tooth brush? It was wet."

"Yeah" she said, "You said to help myself. I hope you don't have cooties."

"Well you little rascal" Dave answered laughing.

Jim said, "I'm going to check my traps" and he was off again with Slick and Pudd'n right behind him.

"I believe you've got a happy camper there," Molly replied.

"Yeah, this is right up his alley."

"You've done a good job with him. I've never been so yes ma'amed in all my life. He's so sincere and honest. I know you're proud of him. One thing puzzles me. Sometimes he calls you Dad and sometimes he calls you Uncle Dave."

"Well, his mom and dad were killed in a car wreck. His dad was my brother and I was next of kin. I adopted him. I want him to call me Dad but I'm still his uncle. I don't want to rush him. We're both kind of playing it by ear. I'm doing the best I can but I know he's missing a lot by not having a mother. He asks so many questions. And smart! You tell him something one time and he's got it. Hears a song one time on the radio and has it memorized. And imagination! You wouldn't believe the things he comes up with. His mom was really something. She had him reading way before kindergarten. He's quite a little businessman too, makes his own money. He'll never go hungry."

"Well, he worships you. I think you're doing a good job. Those bright eyes and that smile are going to take him a long way."

Jim returned from the creek and said, "You won't believe how many perch I've caught. What time do you want to bait the lines?"

"How about thirty minutes?" Dave answered.

"OK! I'll start getting the bait in the bucket."

"Can I watch?" asked Molly.

"Yes ma'am! Come on."

Molly sat on the creek bank while Jim emptied the first trap. Jim was excited with his catch and said, "Must be thirty!"

Slick was enjoying having his ears rubbed by Molly and Pudd'n was almost at point beside Jim. She had never seen a perch before and was plenty curious. Jim put a perch in his palm for Pudd'n to inspect. Right when Pudd'n took a sniff the perch flounced and Pudd'n literally jumped flat footed three feet backward and let out a "Woof!"

Jim and Molly both got a kick out of it. The perch landed happily back in the creek having just used up one of his nine lives. The next two traps yielded similar results and Jim was excited. "We need seventy-five to bait up with. We have three lines with twenty-five hooks each. I believe you're good luck, I usually don't catch this many."

"What do you do when you don't catch enough?"

"Well, sometimes we bait with Kibbles & Bits and sometimes we use soap."

"Soap?"

"Yes ma'am. We've got some P & G soap that we cut in little cubes. Channels and blues like it but ops won't bite it. Opelousas catfish only bite on live bait."

"You sure know a lot about fishing."

"Yes ma'am. Uncle Dave's a real good teacher. You can come with us in the morning when we run the trotlines. I believe you're going to bring us luck."

"I sure hope so" she replied.

"Do you like my Uncle Dave?"

"Sure do! Like you too! Even ole Slick. Why do you ask?"

"Well, I asked Uncle Dave if he liked you and he said you kind of take his breath away and that you've got class. Says you're spunky too.

"Oh, he did, did he?"

"Yes ma'am. He also said he liked the step in your get along. Sometimes he says things I just can't figure out."

Hearing these tidbits of information from Jim was fun and she watched him as he carried the bait to the boat.

Dave came down and said, "Ready, Bud?"

"Yes sir!"

Molly was just about to ask if she could go with them when Dave asked her if she'd watch the camp and the dogs while they were gone. "I'd ask you to go but the ride will be chilly and I want you to stay warm."

"Yes, doctor" she answered and asked, "How long will you'll be gone?"

"Maybe an hour, max! My cell phone is in the chuck box if you need to make a call. Make yourself at home." He started the motor and they waved goodbye.

Jim hollered back, "We're having pork chops tonight!"

Molly gave him a thumb up with one hand and rubbed her tummy with the other. The dogs started to run after the boat and Molly yelled, "Heel!" Slick put on the brakes and came running back.

"Good dog!" she said and kneeled down and started patting him. As Pudd'n ambled up she said, "You could learn something from Slick, ole girl."

As Jim and Dave pulled up to the first line Jim asked, "Shouldn't take us an hour to bait the lines, should it?"

"No, but when we get through baiting up, I want to take a little run up the creek. Maybe we can find some of the things she lost. She told me her car keys and her camera were in a waterproof pouch. It should be floating."

Dave maneuvered the boat while Jim did the baiting. He bragged on him for the good job he did on catching the bait. Jim asked if it would be OK if they took Molly in the morning when they ran the lines. "She's never done it."

"Good idea! I think she'll get a kick out of it. We'll have to be extra careful that she doesn't get finned."

After baiting they started up the creek and Jim asked, "How far will we go?"

"Don't know for sure. Maybe up to that limb that goes across the creek. Keep a sharp eye."

Dave saw it first but didn't say anything. He wanted Jim to discover it.

"There!" Jim shouted and pointed to something yellow. Dave motored close to the logjam and Jim scooped it up. He opened it up and sure enough, it was Molly's. Her camera and mobile phone all dry and intact but no car keys. A few bends up they found her paddle and a life jacket. They ran another few miles and at last came to the tree she described. They turned around and about half way back they found her soft cooler half submerged. Jim hauled it in and took a look inside. "How about a water logged sandwich?" he asked and held it up for Dave to see.

"No thanks!" he said laughing. "I think we've found about all we're going to. Let's get on back to the camp" and he turned the driving over to Jim.

A couple of bends down Dave motioned for him to slow down and turn around. He thought he saw something. Sure enough the handle of Molly's carry bag was looped on a small limb sticking out of the water. Dave pulled it out of the creek and examined the contents. There were some clothes, two cans of dog food, a can opener, and her dopp kit. "Yep!" he said, "This is what

I was looking for." He opened the dopp kit and took out her toothbrush and stuck it in his shirt pocket. "Head 'er on back, Bud. Mission accomplished."

Back at the camp Molly decided to use Dave's phone and called her best friend to tell her where she was and about the close call she had. She told of waking up in the bedroll with the man and he was praying for her. "Hell!" she said, "He even baptized me. It was probably the sweetest and most tender moment of my life. After he did it, I felt this warm tingling going through my body and I started to warm up."

"Is he a preacher?" her friend asked.

"No! How could he do that?" Molly asked.

"Well, one time I heard a sermon when the preacher said a Christian could baptize someone that wasn't already baptized. Usually it's only done in emergency situations."

"Well, now I've been baptized twice. I don't remember the first one but I'll never forget this last one." She went on to tell her friend how nice he and his nephew were. "Even his dog has manners!"

"Sounds like you're falling for him. How old is he? Is he married? This sounds too good to be true."

"He's maybe thirty or a little older and he's not married far as I can tell."

"Where is he now?"

"They've gone to bait a trotline. Jim caught a bunch of perch for bait. We're having pork chops for supper tonight and in the morning we're going to pick mayhaws after we run the lines."

"Molly, you're making no sense. I've never heard you so happy. What the hell is a mayhaw?"

"Don't know for sure. Jim says they look like little apples. You won't believe how good the jelly is they make. Uh Oh! I hear the boat coming, I've got to go, and I'll call you tomorrow. Take care."

Molly and the dogs went down to the creek to greet the men. Jim did a good job driving the boat and she could see his face was beaming as he eased the boat to the shore.

"Guess what?" Jim asked.

"What?"

"We found your tooth brush!"

"Come on?" she said laughing.

"Yes, Ma'am!" Dave said, "And your paddle, your camera, your cooler, even some dog food and Jim ate your sandwich."

Jim jumped out of the boat and gave her a hug. He was so happy. Dave smiled and handed her the toothbrush and said, "Now you've got your own."

"Thanks!" she said, "I'm indebted to you boys. I never thought I'd see this stuff again. You boys get an A plus."

"Sorry we couldn't find your tent and bed roll. Dad believes they're on the bottom."

"Jim, old bud, what you say we get supper going? I'll start the fire and be in charge of clean up. You be the cook."

"What can I do?" Molly asked.

"Want to be my helper? Jim asked.

"You bet!"

"You like onions and potatoes?"

"Yes!"

"Well, get to slicing" and he handed her two large yellow onions and five Irish potatoes. "We'll make a foil pack."

Molly could tell by the ease with which Jim was working that he had done this many times before. He added salt and pepper and a half stick of butter. "It's important to use heavy duty foil" and he showed her how to fold the foil pack so it wouldn't leak or come apart. When the coals were ready he put the foil pack on the grill.

"Now let's make a salad" and he dug in the cooler and pulled out a tomato, a green onion, a couple of hard boiled eggs and a bag of leaf lettuce.

"This is the prettiest lettuce I've ever seen," she said. "Where did you get it?"

"We raised it. This is Romaine, this is oak leaf, this is Bronze Head, and this is Black Seeded Simpson. It's easy to grow. The more you pick it, the more it wants to grow. It's one of Dad's hobbies."

Molly was impressed with his knowledge and thought, "Wow! He's only nine years old. Wonder how much he'll know when he's twenty one?"

Dave said that all the food preparation was getting the dogs all cranked up so he decided to feed them so they could eat in peace.

Jim moved the foil pack around on the grill several times and finally decided it was time to put on the chops. "We always cook extra because if we don't eat'em all, we can eat'em tomorrow for breakfast or lunch."

The chuck box fascinated Molly. It was so well stocked, so neat, and so well thought out. She examined almost every item and Jim critiqued. Jim showed her the camp logbook of past campouts and the checklist that they used for shopping and planning. "I usually do the checking and dad does the shopping. Sometimes he lets me plan the menus. We always cook bacon. Uncle Dave says its Communism to go camping and not cook bacon. What does Communism mean anyway?"

Molly laughed, "It means your Uncle Dave is full of bull."

She found a clear eight-ounce prescription bottle with a handmade label on it. She picked it up and studied the label. It read "Snake Bite Medicine" and in parenthesis under it was "for bites or sights" There was a picture of a rattlesnake all coiled up that was very scary looking and well-drawn. "What in the world is this?" she asked and took off the cap to take a whiff of the amber contents. "Umm" she said, "Just as I thought."

Jim laughed and said, "That's Uncle Dave's. Sometimes he adds a little to his coffee cup and adds ice and puts in some water. He sips it around the fire. He says it's good for his nerves."

"And what about this bottle?" and she held up a similar bottle with a drawing of an ugly witch riding a broom. The letters W T M were on the label.

"I think it's something called brandy. It's supposed to warm your insides."

"What do these letters stand for?" and she pointed to the W.T.M.

"That stands for "Witches Titty Medicine" he answered smiling. "It's for when it's cold as a witch's titty outside."

"That's not a nice word, Jim."

"What? Titty!"

"Yes, it offends women. You should say bosoms or breasts."

"I like bosoms!"

"OK" said Molly. "Case closed."

"Tonight around the fire after supper Uncle Dave will say, "It's getting a little chilly" and he'll come over here and get his cup and put a teaspoonful of sugar, a little of this (and he showed her a small bottle of vanilla extract) and about this much Witches (he hesitated) Bosom Medicine and some milk. You watch!"

Molly laughed and asked, "What about those chops?"

Jim realized he wasn't paying attention and jumped to the task of basting and turning. After a few more minutes he said, "Get the plates ready." And as he opened the foil pack he said, "Ladies first!"

Dave insisted that Molly sit in his chair. Jim sat on an inverted bucket and Dave sat in Jim's chair. They were all starving and ate like it was their last meal. Molly did lots of bragging on the onions and potatoes and told Jim that she believed the pork chops were the best she had ever eaten.

Jim was loving all this attention and added, "Did you know that they eat pork chops in heaven?"

"No, I didn't know that. I'm sure you learned that from your Uncle."

"Yes Ma'am."

"Your Uncle seems to know a lot about a lot of subjects doesn't he?"

"Yes Ma'am. He sure does."

The two dogs were lying beside each other and eyeing each person as they picked up a chop. Surely someone was going to drop one. And what were they going to do with all those bones? As Dave was gnawing on a bone, all of a sudden out of the blue he sang, "Save the bones for Walker Jones, cause he don't eat no meat."

"Where in the world did you hear that and what in the world does it mean?" Molly asked.

"Jim's mom was from Pine Bluff, Arkansas, and she said it all the time. Don't know what it meant but it stuck and whenever I'm chewing on a bone,

I think about it. I think there was somebody there named Walker Jones but I never got the story" he said as he tossed a bone to Slick.

"Can Pudd'n have a bone?" Jim asked.

"You bet!" and Jim tossed her one. Now both dogs had one. "Life is good!" Dave could hear them thinking.

The meal was pleasant, and the men learned a lot about Molly. Her last name was Goodson and she was a schoolteacher in Greenville, Ohio and was out for the summer. Her dad was a farmer and the closest town to the farm was Bradford. She had read an article about canoeing and decided to give it a try. She had come to Texas because it was warmer. She liked to run and her yellow lab had gotten her name because she was the color of butterscotch pudding. Her grandmother used to say an ole rhyme that went something like, "What's your name? Pudd'n Tane, ask me again and I'll tell you the same." She got the Pudd'n from the rhyme.

Jim asked her point blank, "Are you married?"

"No!" she answered, "Got any ideas?" Jim cooed with an anxiety attack and was off again to play with the dogs.

"Great question!" thought Dave.

"I love the way he coos."

"He's not used to women folk. I believe you've got him a little buffaloed."

Jim returned a little later and was dragging a log and was smiling from ear to ear. "I've got three orders for kindling wood and I believe this log will fill them all."

"What kind of log is it?" she asked.

"It's lighter pine. It's the heart of a pine tree that's been rotting for a long long time and the heart is all that's left. It burns real good and is great for starting fires. It's not good for cooking because it burns real smoky." He chipped off a small sliver and handed it to her to smell.

"Smells like turpentine!"

"That's where turpentine comes from. A few sticks are all you need to start a fire. I sell it for ten dollars a bucketful."

"I'll help you cut it up tomorrow," Dave added.

There was a lull in the conversation and Jim said "You know what time it is?" and he started rubbing his stomach with one hand.

"I'll get the milk," Dave said.

"What in the world are you boys talking about?" Molly asked.

"Ding Dongs!" and Jim started rubbing his belly. "Do you like Ding Dongs?"

"I don't know if I've ever had one. Do you have an extra one?"

"We got a whole box. Dad doesn't let us have junk food unless it's on a camping trip. We always bring Ding Dongs and Lorna Doones. He says it's a tradition."

Dave arrived with the cold milk and added, "Nothing better with cold milk."

The dogs got in line for a handout but Jim said, "Sorry, dogs can't have chocolate."

They all enjoyed the fire and a little later Dave said, "It's getting chilly. I believe the temperature has dropped twenty degrees since the sun went down" and with that statement got up and went to the chuck box and lowered one side. Molly looked at Jim who was smiling and she ka-powed him with her finger like she was holding a pistol.

Molly asked, "Are you into the Witches Medicine?"

"I see you've been snooping around in the chuck box."

"Yes, I have" she replied, "and I saw a snake today if you don't mind."

"Yes ma'am, we aim to please. Water OK?"

"No. Just like yours."

"You got it."

In a few minutes he returned with the brandy milk punches and handed her one.

"This an ole Boy Scout remedy?" she asked grinning as she took a sip.

Jim said, "Dad, show Molly how Slick guards the camp at night."

Dave called Slick over and looked him right in the eye and said, "Slick, I thought I heard a booger out there. Don't you let him get me?"

With this command, Slick seemed to go into a trance. The hair on his back stood up and his chest and shoulders seemed to swell up and double in size. He started making a circle around the camp. Head up, ears perked up, and growling in a deep throaty rolling sound. This was his territory and he dared anyone or thing to come into it.

Right when he started cooling off a little bit Dave said, "I'm serious Slick. Don't you let him get me?"

Slick made another circle or two, woofed a few times and returned to the fire ring.

"Wow!" said Molly. "I'm impressed."

Jim jumped up and gave Slick a hug. "Good dog!" he said.

Molly glanced at Pudd'n who was somewhat cowered down. Slick's new macho personality had thrown her for a curve.

CHAPTER 2

BAM!

I t was getting close to bedtime and Dave said, "Since we only have two
bedrolls, why don't we unzip them and use one on the bottom and one to
cover up with. We'll all sleep with our clothes on and our socks on. It'll be
chilly tonight."

Molly said, "Jim, why don't you and me go in the tent and get everything
ready?"

She told Jim that when she was a little girl sometimes her mom and dad
would let her sleep between them and they called this space the foxhole.
"Sometimes when I was having a bad dream or during a lightning storm, I
would go get in the foxhole."

"I'd like to be in the foxhole tonight," said Jim.

"Good idea!"

Jim let Molly have his pillowcase and she put some clothes in it to make
herself a pillow. He showed her where they always put the flashlight in case
they had to get up during the night, and it was a rule that you always had to
put it back. He told her he was tired and was going to bed after he brushed
his teeth. They all three brushed their teeth together with their own tooth-
brushes and turned in at the same time.

As they all entered the tent Jim said, "Dibs on foxhole!"

They laughed and talked a while and Jim said, "I think this is the best
camping trip I've ever been on."

Molly answered, "Me, too!"

The bedroll plan was working fine and they were all about asleep when
they heard an owl give his "Who who ah who ah" in the distance.

20

Jim said, "Dad, you got to call 'em."

Dave declined but Jim kept nagging him. "Molly's never heard you."

"OK!" he said at last. "I'll try, sounded like he was pretty far off though."

Dave let out his rendition of an owl call that put goose pimples on Molly. She couldn't believe he was doing it with his mouth. He waited awhile and called again. "Waugh, Waugh, Waugh, ah whoo ah." This time the owl answered immediately. He called again and the owl answered but much closer this time and another owl to the east of them also answered. He gave out a single, "whoo ah," and one answered right outside the tent.

"Give 'em the scrambled egg call" Jim whispered.

"What's the scrambled egg call?" she whispered back.

"It's the way they talk to each other when they're close to each other."

Dave gave out a "Waugh, Waugh, Waugh, Waugh, Waugh."

Molly thought it was so unlike an owl's call that it was sure to scare them off but quite the opposite happened. All the owls, maybe three of them started "waugh, waugh, waughing" each other. The sound was unlike anything she ever heard before.

The fly of the tent hadn't been zipped all the way and in slipped Pudd'n. She crawled up in the foxhole between Jim and Molly. She was shaking.

Dave looked through the air vent of the tent that was facing a full moon. There on a dead pine limb was a great horned owl silhouetted with the moon behind him. He whispered for Molly and Jim to come see. While they were all looking, Slick gave out a loud "Woof!" and that was the end of the owls.

"Awesome!" said Jim.

Molly said, "I thought Slick was going to let them boogers get us" and they all had a good laugh. Pudd'n was given her walking papers and they were all asleep in no time.

Molly was first up and snuck out of the tent and made coffee. She stoked the fire and got it going again. As she was just finishing frying the bacon, Jim woke up. Dave was still sawing logs.

Jim gave him a shake and said, "She's up! We let a girl get up before us. Are we a bunch of sissies or not?"

"Yeah, I guess we are." Dave answered.

Jim was out of the tent in no time and ran to Molly and gave her a hug.

"Morning, Sunshine!" she answered and returned his hug.

Slick and Pudd'n ran up for a few pats and some attention. The cool morning was invigorating and the smell of the bacon cooking had the dogs on a high as well.

Dave emerged from the tent and gave a good stretch. Molly saw him and said, "Well, if it isn't the owl whisperer" she said, laughing. "That was one of the most incredible things I've ever witnessed. I thought those hoot owls were coming in the tent, and that owl silhouetted by the moon was one of the prettiest views I've ever seen. I'll never forget that picture. I wish I had a painting of it."

"Yeah, me too. That was pretty. I might try to paint it someday," he said wistfully, as he poured himself a cup of coffee. He took a sip and held his cup up to her. "Not bad! I'm impressed."

She answered him with a "Not my first rodeo, Cowboy."

"When are we going to run the lines?" Jim asked.

"Let's eat breakfast first while Miss Molly earns her keep." Dave got out the eggs and the English muffins and the jar of mayhaw jelly. "Over easy and don't you dare break my yolks."

Molly laughed and said, "I might break your head, now get out of my kitchen."

Jim slipped in her kitchen and poured himself a cup of coffee and added sugar and some milk.

"Don't you know that coffee will stunt your growth?"

Jim said he'd been drinking it for years as he snitched a piece of bacon. "This is just the way we like it. Crisp!" The breakfast was perfect, and Molly got lots of compliments. Dave also said she did well on the bacon, to which Molly responded, "Well, thank you, kind sir. I didn't want to be labeled a Communist."

Dave laughed, refilled their coffee cups and said, "Let's go run those lines."

Jim instructed Molly to sit in the bow of the square-nosed aluminum boat. Dave ran the boat and Jim explained the whole process to Molly. Dave eased the boat up to the down current end of the first line. Jim told Molly to grab the line and hold it a few inches out of the water and to slowly pull the boat to the other end of the line. If they caught a fish he would help her to pull the fish into the boat and if they caught a big one, he would net it. She did as told and grabbed the line and started pulling the boat toward the first hook.

"Do you feel any vibrations?" Jim asked.

"Yes, I do."

They came to the first hook and found nothing. The fourth hook had a channel cat about two pounds. Jim helped her get it in the boat and used an odd shaped tool called a hook-out to get the hook out of the fish's mouth. Next, he took the skinning pliers and cut off the three spiked fins.

"Why did you do that?" Molly asked.

Jim told her how dangerous the spines were and he dropped the fish in a large white plastic bucket. That line yielded seven nice channel cats ranging from two to three pounds. It also caught one red ear turtle, which Jim used the hook-out on and let him go with a flick of the wrist.

"Not bad" said Jim. "I knew you were going to be good luck."

"This is fun! I like trot lining."

The next line was better. It produced four channels about the same size as the others, a nice blue cat about five pounds and an op in the ten to twelve pound class. Jim also released two small stunted looking catfish because he said they weren't good to eat. He said they were yellow cats.

When Molly grabbed the third line she immediately said, "I can really feel one tugging on this line."

On the very first hook was a fish about eight pounds, which Jim hoisted into the boat without a net. The fish went wild in the bottom of the boat. Molly let go of the line and lifted her feet up to the side. "What in the world is that?"

Jim laughed and said, "That's a grinnel. In Louisiana they call 'em shoopiks. They're not good to eat."

"Thank goodness!" she said. "That's the meanest and ugliest fish I ever saw."

Dave added, "They're a prehistoric fish that has never become extinct. They've found fossils of them that are millions of years old that are just the same as they are today. Be careful getting that hook out, Bud. They don't have teeth but they can still bite the dickens out of you."

"Tell her about what that man told you about them. What was his name?"

"Mr. Gordy."

"Yeah, Dad knows this man named Mr. Gordy who says you can take a grinnel like this and wrap him in wet moss and bury him about four inches deep under an old oak tree and cover the hole with leaf mold. If you come back in three days and dig him up, he will have turned into a stump tail water moccasin."

"Come on?" said Molly. "How could that happen?"

"I don't know!" said Jim, "But he says it's true."

Molly said, "I believe your Mr. Gordy is full of prunes."

"Sounds like you already know ole Marvin," laughed Dave.

The third line produced two nice blues and four more channels. Next to the last hook Molly screamed, "Don't you dare let that thing in the boat. Oh my God!" and she moved to the back of the boat.

"Wow!" Jim said, "It's a loggerhead turtle and he's swallowed the hook."

"Hold on a minute" and Dave passed his knife up to Jim. "Just cut the staging close to his mouth and be careful."

Dave went up front to see the turtle and to make sure Jim did it right. "Wow!" he said. "Probably close to thirty pounds. That's the biggest one we've ever caught."

As Jim cut the line he told Molly, "Know what? If a loggerhead bites you, it won't let go until he hears thunder."

"Sounds like another Mr. Gordy story to me."

"No!" Jim answered, "Uncle Dave's grandfather told him that. It's a true story."

Molly looked back at Dave who winked at her and she added, "You're teaching this boy some valuable information. He's a regular walking encyclopedia. Think of all he's going to know by the time he's twenty-one. Wow!"

Dave started the motor and they went back to camp. Molly volunteered to do the dishes. Jim fixed her a wash bucket and then went to help with the fish. In about forty-five minutes Dave had all the fish skinned, gutted, beheaded, and on ice. He said he wanted to clean up a bit before they went mayhaw picking. He got his dopp kit and pulled out his shaving brush and a mug of soap.

Molly watched him lather up and said, "I thought those things were extinct."

"What?"

"Shaving brushes. I think they came over on the Mayflower."

"Well, some things don't always change for the better. This is a badger hair brush. My father gave it to me when I started shaving. No telling how long it will last. When you use a brush, your hands don't get all soapy and mug soap doesn't cost near as much as an aerosol can and it lasts a lot longer than a can. Shaving brushes were good enough for my grandfather, good enough for my dad and good enough for me. Can't beat it! Also economical, and the brush is also good for washing out a kid's mouth when they say a bad word. Right Jim?"

"Yes sir! And that's the truth."

"Well, I didn't mean to get you all riled up" she said.

"You didn't. I just believe that some things don't have to change to be better. Bacon and eggs also came over on the Mayflower and they still go over pretty good."

While Dave was splashing on some aftershave, Molly picked up the bottle and read the label. It was a bottle of Lilac Vegetal. He must have found it in a museum she thought and turned the bottle over and started reading on the back. "Oh my God!" she said excitedly. "Listen to this! Popular throughout the world. First brought to the Americas aboard the Pinta by the Spaniard, Edward Pinaud."

"Funny! Real funny!" he answered.

"Are you all ready to pick some berries?

"Yes sir!"

"Tell you what. Let's feed the dogs first and pack us a lunch." He opened the chuck box and got a jar of peanut butter, three apples, a sleeve of Ritz crackers, and three or four bottles of water. "This will tide us over until supper."

They loaded up and Dave told Slick to stay and guard the camp. Slick seemed to understand. Dave let Jim drive the boat.

On the way there Molly asked if there was anything special she needed to know about mayhaw picking and Dave told her that you have to be careful of snakes because mayhaws grow in swampy areas, which of course is prime snake country. "Be extra careful where you step and where you put your hands."

"Thanks!" she said, "That's just what I wanted to hear."

"We always make a little extra noise and we carry a stick with us just in case." Jim added as he eased the boat to the left and up a little slough about a hundred yards. As they neared the end of the slough a giant bird took off and flew through the woods.

"What in the world was that?" Molly asked.

"That was a Blue Heron." Jim answered.

"This is a spot I found about ten years ago. I've never shown it to anyone but Jim."

"What's the big secret?" she asked.

"A secret mayhaw patch is kind of like owning a gold mine. Only better though because you can't eat gold."

After a short hike they came to the grove of mayhaws. They had hit it perfectly. There had not been a freeze after the blooms had set, and it looked like a bumper crop. Jim picked one off the ground and showed it to Molly. It did indeed look like a tiny red apple.

"Are they good to eat?"

"No." Dave answered, "But they have just enough flavor and the right amount of pectin to make the perfect jelly." He gave a tree a good shake and the tree rained down mayhaws. "Get to picking'."

They broke about noon to take a break and eat their lunch. Molly dug into the peanut butter first and covered her apple with the butter and began gnawing away.

Jim said, "I never saw anybody eat an apple like that."

She told him that she had learned it at a camp she used to go to in Tennessee when she was a teenager. Dave and Jim followed suit and both said, "Not bad" at the same time.

Molly even ate the core and the seeds and when she got through she held up the stem and said, "This is the only part I don't eat" which got a laugh from the guys.

They rested awhile and then shook and picked for another hour. All total they had four five-gallon buckets, each almost full to the brim.

Jim said, "I believe this is the most we ever picked. Don't you think?"

To which Molly responded, "Well I should hope so. This is the first time you've ever had a professional picker with you" which got a laugh from the boys.

All of a sudden there was a strange sound that Molly had never heard before. It sounded like someone was being tortured or maybe giving a distress call. "What in the world was that?" exclaimed Molly.

Jim laughed and said, "That was an Indian hen. Its real name is a pileated wood pecker but some folk's call'em Indian hens." They heard him pecking and it sounded like someone was beating on a tree with a stick.

"I've never seen one." Molly replied.

"Come on! Maybe we can sneak up on him." Jim led her through the woods perhaps forty yards, and they came to a large dead pine tree. They heard him before they saw him. Jim spotted him first and pointed to the top. He motioned for her to come to the base of the tree. "Put your hand on the tree. Next time he pecks you can feel the vibrations." When he pecked again, she could feel them. "Amazing!" she said.

"Pileated are the largest wood peckers in the United States. There used to be one called the Ivory Billed wood pecker that was bigger, but they're extinct now. Uncle Dave thinks he saw one but couldn't make a positive identification. I believe him, though."

They watched the bird a few more minutes and then he flew off. On the way back to the mayhaw area, the brush was heavy and Molly was leading the way. There was a large grapevine blocking the way and she stooped down to go under it. At the low point of her stoop she flushed a bird about three feet from her face. She screamed and said, "What in the world was that?"

Jim was laughing and said, "That was a woodcock."

"Well he almost made me wet my pants."

Jim was still laughing as Dave ran up. "Y'all OK?"

"She just met her first woodcock."

"That's something you never forget. I still remember my first encounter. Almost made me wet my pants" said Dave, which made them all laugh.

They went back to the mayhaw area and Dave said that before they left he wanted to mark a few trees.

Molly asked what that meant and Dave said, "Mayhaw trees are only found in the wild in swampy areas because before their seeds will germinate they have to lay dormant in damp fertile ground for up to two years. If you dig up a small tree and plant it in a sunny spot they will bear fruit. In fact, with a little care and fertilizer they will bear more fruit than in their natural habitat."

They walked around the bottom area looking for small trees and Dave tied a small red ribbon on about ten of them. "We'll come back in the dormant season and dig them up. You've got to mark them when they've got their leaves on to make a positive identification."

Jim said, "You know what? We already have forty-two trees on our farm. Someday we're going to have a mayhaw orchard of our own. They haven't started bearing real good but they're growing real good."

Molly said, "Won't the person that owns this land be mad that you're digging up his trees?"

"Nope." Dave replied.

Molly said, "Well, if I owned the land I would be."

Dave said, "I fell in love with this section of the creek a few years ago and found it was for sale. The price was cheap because there are no roads to it. It borders a national forest. There's about three-quarters of a mile of creek frontage. It's a narrow strip about sixty-two acres in all. Mostly hardwoods and cypress with a few big pines; it's prime deer country. Someday Jim and I might put us up a little deer camp. Probably a poor investment but I wanted to preserve a little spot for nature. It would kill me if all these hardwoods got cut."

It was a good outing. They only saw one snake, a copperhead that Dave slung to kingdom come with his stick.

The dogs were glad to see them return. Dave threw a stick in the water a few times for Slick to retrieve and then made Slick "Stay" and gave Pudd'n a turn.

They got the berries out of the boat and covered them up with a tarp to protect them.

Dave said he was going to take about an hour power nap and retired to the tent. It had warmed up a bit and Jim and Molly sat around the fire, which had just about gone out.

Molly said that the apple and peanut butter was wearing off and asked if she could look in the chuck box for a snack. Jim said, "Sure" and he opened the box for her. She spied a funnel and asked, "Why in the world do you have a funnel?"

Jim said, "Funnel cakes! Want one?"

"Come on!"

"Yes mam, we make'em all the time."

"This I've got to see."

Jim pulled out the camp logbook and turned to the section labeled "recipes" and asked, "You want to be my helper?"

"Sure!"

"OK!" he said, "You be Martha Stewart and I'll be Emeril."

Molly laughed as Jim handed her a mixing bowl and said, "Follow that recipe. I'll get the grease going. We'll be frying fish tonight so we won't be wasting it." He showed her the thermometer and said, "This is a must for cooking funnel cakes. The grease has to be exactly the right temperature, 375 degrees." In a few minutes he said the grease was ready, and he told her to put her finger over the hole in the funnel and he filled it up with the batter. "Now," he said, "Hold it over the grease and move it around like you're drawing a picture." She removed her finger and the batter flowed slowly through the funnel just like it was supposed to. As it hit the hot grease it turned a beautiful golden brown. In a couple of minutes Jim handed her a large fork and told her to turn it over to brown the other side. In a short time it was ready and she placed it on a paper plate covered with a paper towel to let it drain. Jim handed her a box of powdered sugar and she covered the cake with it.

"Bam!" he said which got a laugh out of Molly.

"Want to step it up a notch?" And he handed her a little can of cinnamon.

Together they devoured the cake. Licking her fingers on the last bite she said, "Emeril, I believe that was the best funnel cake I've ever had."

Jim replied, "Thanks Martha! I enjoyed having you on the show today" and they high fived.

Jim slipped in the tent and got something out of his bag. At first she thought it was a ball but when he unrolled it she saw it was a hammock. He tied it between two trees and climbed in. She had never seen someone look so comfortable and peaceful. She decided she had to have it.

"Jim" she said. "I'll give you five dollars to let me have the hammock."

He thought a minute and said, "OK" and he hopped out. "I've got to check my traps and cut some kindling for Mr. Beauchamp."

The hammock was heaven, even better than expected. Her back was sore from the berry picking and the funnel cake was going straight to her eyeballs. Just as she was about to nod off, a small bird lit on a limb just a few feet away. They watched each other for a long time. Finally the bird darted to a hole in the tree that the hammock was tied to. "Has to be her nest", she thought. The bird made umpteen trips back and forth carrying small twigs and bits of grass.

Her curiosity finally got the best of her and she got up and went to the chuck box to borrow Jim's bird book. Finally she zeroed in on it. It was a Carolina Wren. She would show the boys her secret later, but for now, she drifted off. The dogs also decided to catch a few winks and bedded down under a shady tree.

About an hour later Dave emerged from the tent. His little power nap kind of got away from him and lasted close to two hours. The nap did wonders and he felt great. He could hear Jim chopping wood in the distance. He saw Molly in the hammock and judging by its stillness he figured she was asleep. He eased up on her and saw that she was. She looked so peaceful and he wished he could climb in the hammock with her. The thought of how good she felt in the bedroll was still fresh on his mind. Peterson's book on birds was lying across her chest and he thought, "Ole Tory would be pleased. A new birder is born."

God had sure blessed her with good looks. The old saying "beauty is only skin deep" he felt didn't apply here. He felt that she was probably beautiful right down to the core. He decided to capture this moment and went back to the tent and got his camera. After about the third picture Molly opened her eyes and saw him aiming the camera at her and she stuck out her tongue just as the shutter snapped.

"Cute, real cute!" he said.

"And who are you? Steven Spielberg?"

Dave laughed, a little embarrassed at being caught and said, "No, I just wanted to get a picture of you for our camping log book. Jim and I will be talking about this campout for a long time, I'm sure"

"Well I should hope so!" she exclaimed. "Not often that a couple of country bumpkins get to rescue a beautiful damsel in distress."

They both laughed and then she said, "Guess what? There's a Carolina Wren making her nest in this tree. It's the cutest bird. I kept hearing this loud chirping noise and kept looking for a large bird, but it was the wren. Talk about busy. Look! There she goes again."

Dave said, "Yeah, I know what you mean about the little bird with the big voice. We've put up several wren houses but they always prefer the pump house, the tool shed, or a hanging basket. Their nests are architectural wonders."

Jim returned to camp carrying a bucketful of lighter pine he'd just cut and Dave said, "Son, I thought we had an agreement about the hatchet. Nobody's allowed to use the axe or hatchet unless another person is around."

"I know, I'm sorry, Molly was sleeping and I didn't want to wake her."

"OK this time, but I don't want it to happen again."

"Yes sir."

"Look!" she said excitedly and showed Jim the wren nest. "I found her in your bird book. It's a Carolina Wren."

Jim retied the hammock to another tree to make the bird less nervous and Molly asked if she could look at the camp logbook and he fetched the book and handed it to her.

Molly climbed back into the hammock and told Jim to get in with her. Jim critiqued each page. There were pictures of fish caught, birds, flowers, wood spiders, snakes killed, friends that they'd brought camping with them, and even a back view of Jim skinny dipping when he was about six. Each campout was dated; the weather noted and points of interest. Jim loved sharing the book with her. He held back no details and seemed to have a photographic memory. Molly was in stitches most of the time.

"See this man here! Uncle Dave invited him to go camping with us and told him he was in charge of breakfast. You know what he brought?"

"No! What?"

"Turkey bacon!"

"So!"

"You ever had turkey bacon? Yuck! Dad and I couldn't even eat it. Slick liked it though."

"Another form of Communism no doubt," she added laughing.

Dave enjoyed listening to Jim as he went through the book. It made him feel good that he could remember so much and so accurately.

As Jim turned the last page, Molly said, "Guess what? Your Uncle took my picture today and said I would be in the logbook someday. I'd be honored to be in such a fine book."

Molly got out of the hammock and got her camera. "Thanks to you boys I still have my camera. I'd like to take a few pictures of you all to show my folks." She got several including Slick and even one of the wren which she zoomed in on.

Dave asked Jim if he'd had any luck catching bait and Jim answered, "Yes, sir. I've already emptied the traps and have them in the bucket."

"Why don't you take Molly and go bait up. I'll start getting things ready for supper."

Molly was excited and said, "Good, I've never baited a trotline before. It'll be fun. I'll take my camera and get a few more shots to show my folks. My brother is a big fisherman."

Jim motored to the first line and then sat in the bow and sculled the boat like an expert right to the line. Molly handed the perch to Jim one by one and in just a few minutes they had the first line baited. Jim started the motor and they ran to the second line. This line paralleled the bank, which was Dave's favorite way to set lines. Right when Jim was about to bait the first hook a blue bird landed in a small button willow overhanging the creek.

Molly said, "Look! A blue bird."

Jim asked, "How do you feel right now?"

"Good, why do you ask?"

Jim said, "Well, there's something about blue birds that makes anyone who sees one feel good. That's why they call them "the blue bird of happiness." "Know what else?"

Molly loved it when he did this.

"What?" she said knowing that some profound statement was coming. He reminded her of the little boy in the movie, "Jerry McGuire" with his questions like, "Do you know how much the human head weighs?"

"Uncle Dave used to shoot sparrows with his BB gun when he was a little boy. One time at church they sang a song called, "His Eye is On the Sparrow I Know He's Watching Me" and it made him feel so bad he never shot another one." He said that whenever he aimed he felt like God's eyes were on him and he couldn't pull the trigger."

"I think that's commendable."

"What's commendable mean?"

"It means good. I admire him for not shooting them. I hope you won't shoot them either."

"Oh, no, ma'am, all Uncle Dave lets me shoot are starlings, turtles, and snakes. He says we probably shouldn't be shooting snakes because they're supposed to help Mother Nature. We try to shoot just the poisonous ones. Uncle Dave's favorite snake is a dead snake."

"Mine too!" she answered and ask, "Why do you shoot turtles and starlings?"

"We only shoot turtles in our lake because they eat our fish and if you don't thin them out, they'll take over the place. And starlings are no good. They're not even supposed to be in the U.S. They're so lazy they lay their eggs in another bird's nest and the babies get raised and fed by the wrong mamas. We shoot them off our martin house. They'll go into the martin house and eat the baby martins."

"Oh! They are bad. I don't blame you."

After baiting the last line Jim let the extra perch go and they headed back to camp.

Dave had finished cutting the potatoes and was slicing the catfish into small strips when they arrived. Molly asked if she could help and he told her she could make the tartar sauce.

"I'm embarrassed to say I don't know how."

"Well, I'll teach you. We'll use my sister Catherine's recipe. It's the best we've ever had. It's easy to make." He reached in the Igloo cooler and pulled out a sack that contained a lemon, a green onion and a small dill pickle. "Dice 'em all up, squeeze one-half lemon, add some mayo, and a dash of salt and pepper. Works every time, I hope you like fish and potatoes, cause that's all we're having tonight."

"Sounds good to me, I'm starved."

Dave added about an inch of peanut oil to the pot and lit the burner and Molly asked, "Why do you use peanut oil?"

"It has a higher flash point and won't smoke or burn like most of the other vegetable oils. Costs a few cents more but I think it's worth it. It's what all the fast food places use. Last longer and doesn't taint as fast."

Dave asked Jim to feed the dogs "so they won't be sitting in our laps when we eat". He cooked the potatoes first and then started on the fish and said, "We're not very formal around here when it comes to fried fish. When we eat fish we call it grazing. We sit around the cooker and eat it right when it comes out of the grease."

Dave had made a jar of sun tea and Molly fixed each of them a glass of iced tea. After the first batch was ready, Dave said, "Get your plates and help yourselves. I'll get the next batch. You all dig in."

"Delicious!" she said "And your sister's tartar sauce is excellent. You should open a restaurant. The fish is to die for."

Jim added, "They slept in the creek last night. Doesn't get any fresher."

"Believe it or not, I've thought about opening a restaurant someday. Right now I'm into pecans and hay and about ten other projects," Dave said.

"Uncle Dave's an artist" Jim added.

"Come on?" said Molly. "A real artist?"

"You should see him draw!"

Dave said, "Yep! An undiscovered artist. I got a degree in art with a minor in horticulture and took a welding course on the side. I'm certified. Went to New York to become rich and famous and liked to starved to death. After the accident, I adopted Jim and took him back to New York. New York's no place to raise a kid, so I started looking for other options. One of my trade journals advertised a pecan orchard for sale and I bought it. The poor guy who started it ran out of money. I don't think he factored in that you have to wait twelve to fourteen years for the trees to really start bearing good. The trees will be fourteen years old this fall. They were four-year-old grafts when he planted them. If Jim and I have done everything right and the Lord is willing, we should have a bumper crop this fall. The bloom was good and the rain has been just right. The price of pecans has been going up the last few years. We've got our fingers crossed. Last year we harvested 31,000 pounds. This year we should double that."

"Guess how many trees we have?" Jim asked.

Molly thought for a minute and said, "One hundred."

"Higher."

"Two hundred."

"Higher."

"I give up." She said, "How many?"

"Seven hundred and twenty."

"Come on! No way!"

"Yes mam! We've got 180 Mayhans on five acres and 540 Stuarts on fifteen acres. Mayhans have soft-shells and are easy to crack. They're big, too."

"Wow! I'm impressed."

"Know what? Me and Slick are in charge of keeping squirrels out. Last year I got nine and Slick got three. He caught two on the ground and one in the air. You should've seen it. He crunched him."

Molly looked at Slick and said, "Shame on you Slick, poor little squirrels."

Dave said, "You should see what they can do to a pecan orchard. They start cutting the pecans before they are ripe when they're still green. Two or three squirrels can cut every pecan out of a tree and never enjoy a single one. They may be cute, but not if you own a pecan orchard. To me they are just a tree rat, kind of like friendly termites. We don't waste'em though. Jim cleans them and we save them for a friend down the highway."

"You ever cleaned a squirrel?" Jim asked and added, "It's easy."

"No" Molly replied, "and I'm not going to learn."

After supper Jim and Molly did the dishes while Dave dug a hole to bury the fish grease.

Molly asked why he was going to bury the grease and he replied, "To keep the critters away. Sometimes dogs get a craving for grease and make themselves sick."

Dave wiped the pot clean with a couple of paper towels and Molly asked him if he wanted some soap. He replied, "If you soap it, I'll have to kill you. You never soap a cured iron pot."

Molly laughed and said, "I'll have to remember that; you boys are teaching me all kind of good stuff."

Jim brought in several more nice pieces of oak for the fire and said, "Better to have too much wood than not enough."

CHAPTER 3

FOO FOO MAN

A fter cleanup they all moved to the fire because the night chill was moving in. They were full as ticks and the campfire was fun. Conversation came easy and Molly asked Dave to tell her about his ten other irons in the fire other than the pecans and the hay.

Dave told her about his dreams for a full-blown pecan processing operation. A mayhaw orchard, a peach orchard, a blueberry orchard with a new variety of berries called rabbiteye blueberries. He had already planted an acre of them, but they weren't bearing yet. Blackberries, dewberries, iron art, wood carving, someday teaching wood working, learning to play the drums, gardening, painting and someday writing a book. His thoughts were clear, and he completely let his guard down. She felt close to him and she hardly knew him. She would savor the memory of this campfire forever. He told of his dream to have a small vineyard and his own label. He would call it "Spirits for the Spirit."

All of a sudden he realized that he had been rambling for some time and was somewhat embarrassed for hogging the conversation. He paused and said, "Sorry, I didn't mean to talk so much. Can I get you something?"

"Was that a copperhead I saw this morning?" she asked.

"Yes."

"Well then, I'd like a little snake bite medicine or a little WTM."

"No can do. We drank it all last night."

"Well then," knowing that he didn't have any, "I'll have a little Chardonnay, I like a little white wine with my fish."

Dave got up and said, "You're in luck. I just happen to have a bottle" and he went to the cooler and pulled a bottle of Chardonnay out from under a bag of ice. He opened the bottle and poured each of them a glass and said as he handed her a glass, "Your wishes are my command."

Jim said that he wanted some which got a "Hello!" out of Molly.

Dave poured him about an inch in a small Styrofoam cup and told Molly, "He needs to learn how to handle himself at a young age so he won't go wild like so many kids do nowadays. Kids in foreign countries learn to drink at an early age and it's no big deal. He only does this on camping trips and when I'm with him."

Molly bit her lip as Jim took his first sip. Maybe he was right. If he could handle alcohol at a young age, hopefully he would not go wild his first time out with the guys. Dave was doing such a good job raising him; it would be hard to argue. Any parent would die to have a son like Jim. Bright eyed, loving, caring, smart, full of life and humble.

Her thoughts were broken when Jim asked, "Know what they make beer out of?"

"What?"

"Horse piss."

Molly said, "Jim, that's another one of those words that's not nice and women don't like to hear. Who taught you that?"

"Uncle Dave and I believe him. I tasted it one time and it was terrible."

Molly glanced at Dave who was smiling and said, "Well, I sure didn't know that. I for sure won't be drinking any beer."

Jim finished his wine about that time and threw his cup in the trash bag. Molly made a mental note, "No big deal."

While they were enjoying the fire and the wine, Molly asked Jim if he would take her picture next to Dave. She wanted to remember this special time forever. She adjusted the settings on the camera and positioned Jim on the other side of the fire. She pulled her chair closer to Dave and Jim took the picture. She got him to take one more just in case.

"Another thing I've thought about" Dave said as he refilled their glasses "is if we ever get the vineyard going and have our own label is to put on the label "End Your Day with a Chardonnay" and have a picture of a campfire on the label."

"I like it!" she said. "Very clever!"

Another thought popped into her head. Maybe the silhouette of Dave and Molly could be next to the picture of the campfire on the label. Who knows? The magic and the chemistry seemed to be working.

"This is really good wine! What's it called?"

Dave handed her the empty bottle, which had the cork back in. She studied the label a while and said, "I'll have to remember this one."

Dave said, "I like it. It's affordable but definitely a cut above a lot of other brands. Champagnes and red wines give me a headache for some reason. Even after just one glass. A good Chardonnay however is hard to beat. Makes me want to philosophize."

As Molly was holding the bottle, an idea popped into her head and she kind of slipped into a daydream and she let her mind race.

After a couple of minutes of no conversation Dave asked her, "Are you OK?"

"Yes!" she said "I was thinking" and she got up holding the bottle. All eyes were on her. She walked over to Dave and said, "Rub on the bottle!" which he did and then she walked over to Jim and said, "Rub on the bottle!" After Jim had rubbed on it she knelt down beside Slick and said, "Rub on the bottle" and she picked his paw up and rubbed it on the bottle. She held the bottle out in front of her for them to see and she took the cork out and made a pop sound with her finger in her mouth. "See this bottle! Well, I'm a Genie and I just came out of this bottle. I'm going to grant you boys' three wishes for saving my life. One wish to your dog who saw me and sounded the alarm. One wish to Jim who pulled me ashore and is Slick's master and one wish to the hoot owl man who gave me first aid and baptized me." She paused to let them think a little bit and then she said, "I'm going to let your dog go first." "Slick" she said. "What's your wish?"

Without hesitation, Slick who was lying on the left side of Pudd'n lifted his right paw and placed it across Pudd'ns' neck. Everyone started laughing. The scene could not have been acted out any better. Lassie would have been impressed.

Molly said, "Slick, I think I'm beginning to see how you got your name." and then she asked Jim, "What's your wish?"

"Can I wish for anything?"

"Well, anything in reason; can't wish for a million dollars because I'm just a school teacher."

"How long do I have to make up my mind?"

"Five minutes."

Jim was excited and said he'd be back in a few minutes. "I've got to think." He ran to the boat and laid down one of the seats and looked at the stars. He prayed, "Dear Lord, help me to make a good wish." He closed his eyes and in seconds a wish popped into his head. He ran back to camp and said he was ready.

"Wow!" said Molly, "That was fast. What's your wish?"

"Well" he said, "Uncle Dave's been wanting me to have a nanny. He thinks I need to learn a lot of things that he's not teaching me. I want you to be my nanny."

"For how long?"

"Forever."

"I couldn't be your nanny forever. My school starts back in about sixty days."

"Well then, I want you to be my nanny for sixty days. You promised me one wish and that's my wish."

Molly pleasantly thought "what a great trap to be in. Show me your parlor said the spider to the fly. God, I love this kid." She turned to Dave and said, "Sixty days is OK with me. I know it would make Slick happy. What about you?"

Dave said, "Jackie would probably kill me."

"Who is Jackie?" Molly asked.

"His girlfriend, her name is Jacquelyn but he calls her Jackie."

Molly looked at Dave with eyes rolling and asked, "Well, who wears the panties? You or your girlfriend."

Dave was silently thinking and kind of went numb. Jim walked over to where his Uncle was seated. He placed both hands on his shoulders. His back was to Molly. "Dad!" he said in a low voice, "Just think! Sixty days with Molly. Are we going to have a good time? Think of all the fun we'll have. You've been wanting me to have a nanny. She's already taught me two words not to say. I think God sent her to us."

Dave looked into his eyes. He knew everything he said was true. Jim's thoughts were so clear. "What a great wish," he thought. "Sixty days of Molly. Wow!"

"OK bud! You've got yourself a nanny."

Jim gave him a hug that almost broke his neck and said, "Thanks Clancy."

He ran to Molly and gave her a hug. She hugged him back and he cooed. The dogs knew something good had just happened and the moment was contagious. They were up jumping and playing and running around in circles like Labradors like to do.

"I guess that means it's a GO?"

"Yes ma'am!"

Molly looked at Dave and said, "I've never been a nanny before; I hope I can measure up."

"We'll pay you of course."

"No pay!" she said, "Just room and board. It's a small payback for saving my life, which brings us to you. What's your wish?"

"That Jackie won't kill me."

"Can't help you there big boy! Wish again."

Dave bent down and put his face in his hands and tried to think. This must be what a panic attack feels like. He wanted to wish something meaningful, maybe something clever, maybe something like "Will you marry me?" Why was this so hard?

"One more minute" said Molly who was enjoying his predicament but at the same time didn't like the pressure she had put on him. Jim's wish was so fine that he didn't have to make one.

While Dave was thinking, Jim turned on the radio and tuned in the Louisiana Hayride. The DJ said, "And here's an oldie by Bob Wills, "If Once Again You Were Just Mine."

Dave stood up and looked at Molly and said, "Dance with me" and he took her hand. The song was perfect and the mood was perfect.

Molly said, "I'm confused. Is dancing with you your wish?"

"Yes!"

"Seems like you could have made a better wish than that!"

"Actually, I wanted to hold you again and dancing with you seemed a quick fix. My real wish is that you will dance with me once a day for sixty days."

His wish seemed to please her and she moved in a little closer and said, "Your wish is granted."

They were a perfect fit. "Have I died and gone to heaven?" he thought. "How could anyone feel this good?" They were cheek to cheek when the song ended.

The station announced that the next song would be "All of Me." And Molly said, "One more dance."

"Nope!" said Dave, "Don't want to use up one of my dances now."

"This one's on the house."

"Deal!" he said and he took her in his arms. "Hot damn!" he thought, "Sixty days of Molly."

"You feel good, for a nanny."

"No talking." she said. She could tell she was in control and moved in closer to let him know how good he felt. Had their belt buckles sparked there would have been a fire for sure. As the song ended he thought, "Thank God!" and he commented that he didn't know if he could last fifty-nine more dances with her. Molly laughed and didn't tell him that she was a little weak in the knees also.

Dave went to the tent and got a towel and a change of clothes and then went to the chuck box and got a bar of soap.

"Where are you going? She asked.

"For a swim and a bath."

"The waters freezing!"

"Good! That's what I need."

Molly smiled and a little thought raced through her head, "Miss Jackie! You have a problem and it starts with "M"."

Jim returned from the woods with the dogs and asked, "Where's Uncle Dave?"

"Gone swimming!"

"No way! He hates cold water."

"Well, that's where he is. He went down to the sand bar."

"Guess what? We got a fish on the line."

"How do you know?"

"Well, I tied a little turkey bell on the limb that the trotline was tied to and the bell is ringing."

"Come on!" she said.

"Yes ma'am! I'll show you in a minute."

"I saw you and Uncle Dave dancing. Did he make his wish?

"Yes!"

"What was it?"

"Well, he wants me to dance with him once a day for sixty days, so after today he's got fifty-nine dances coming."

"Cool!" said Jim, "I didn't know he could dance."

Molly giggled and said, "Oh, he can dance, believe me, he can dance."

"Maybe you can teach me to dance when we get home."

"I'd love to," she said.

Dave returned from the creek and looked refreshed. In fact, he looked real handsome, she thought. Dave suggested they all turn in and they all thought it was a good idea. They passed the toothpaste and Molly made a trip to the blue potty. When she returned she said, "Slick! I thought I heard a booger out there." This time Slick and Pudd'n both bristled up and started making a tough man circle around the camp. There was a lot of low growling with a few good woofs thrown in. When they returned Molly said, "Good dogs!" and gave each of them a hug and said, "And Pudd'n, I'm really proud of your new trick."

Jim was first to enter the tent and yelled, "Foxhole!"

"Thank God!" thought Dave. The thought of lying next to her sent a shiver down his spine.

Molly entered next and piled in next to Jim.

"I liked your wish," she said. "Are we going to have fun or not?"

"Yes ma'am!" he said, "You're going to love our farm."

"I can't wait to see it. Do you think Jackie is going to kill your Uncle Dave?"

"Yes ma'am."

"Do you think she'll kill me?"

"Yes ma'am."

"Will you help me stay alive?"

"Yes ma'am."

"I want to be a good nanny but I'm going to need your help."

"I'll help you."

Dave was last to enter the tent. The smell of Ivory soap, his Speed Stick, and his aftershave overpowered them. Jim said, "Smells like a French whore house!"

Molly said, "Where did you learn that?"

"Uncle Dave, he says it all the time."

"Well that's another word you can't say. OK?"

"Yes ma'am! What is a whore anyway?"

"You'll have to ask Mr. Foo Foo here, but I don't want to hear that anymore. OK?"

"Yes ma'am. I won't."

"We may have to get your uncle's shaving brush and wash his mouth out if he keeps teaching you those bad words."

"That would be fun" Jim answered and added, "It's his fault, he's teaching me bad stuff."

"Well," she said. "We're going on a sixty day crash course starting right now. Mr. Potty Mouth will have to watch his P's and Q's."

Dave chuckled to himself inside. He loved her wit and her spirit. He knew Jim's wish was going to be good for all of them.

Molly asked questions about their house and Jim told her there were only two bedrooms. A large bedroom upstairs with four beds which was his and a bedroom downstairs which was his dad's. Jim said she could share his bedroom but it was decided that Molly could have Jim's room to herself and Jim would have a daybed in Dave's bedroom. Jim told Molly that she was going to love his room. He said, "My room is long with windows at each end and a cool breeze all the time. There are big shade trees outside and you'll hear the birds' right outside your window. We call it the Martin Room."

"Why is that?" she asked.

He explained, "There's a Martin house close to the window and you can hear them chirping and singing. They sound real pretty. They come in March and leave in July. You ought to see them fight the sparrows. They take'em right down to the ground. And when they teach their young to fly, other Martins come from other homes and help them learn. They fly all the way to South America for the winter. They can eat up to 2,000 mosquitoes a day."

"Come on?"

"Yes ma'am. Tell her what you did when you were a little boy."

"Well Jim, I'm not very proud of that story. No need to tell it again."

"Yeah you do," said Molly, "I want to hear."

Reluctantly Dave told his story, "When I was about ten years old I used to have a BB gun. My dad always had two Martin houses and when the Martins were resting they would sit on some power lines next to the houses. Funny thing about Martins is that they're not afraid of humans and if you shoot at them they won't fly off. The power lines were pretty high and my BB gun didn't have much power but finally I got one. I knew I shouldn't have done it and that if dad found out I would be in big trouble. The flowerbed next to the

Martin house had been lined with pieces of concrete from an old driveway that had been torn up. I pulled one up and dug a hole under it and put the bird in the hole and put the top back on. The next day I got another one and put him in the hole. My mom saw me shooting at the Martins and said that if she ever saw me doing it again she was going to tell dad. I knew it was time to stop. Three or four months later my dad was pulling St. Augustine grass that was growing between the rocks into the flower beds and he pulled back the rock I had buried the Martins under. Guess what?"

"They turned into water moccasins!" said Molly.

Jim died laughing and Dave said, "Cute, real cute!"

"No" he said, "The Martins were still there. They were like preserved. My dad picked them up and called over and asked me if I knew anything about this and I confessed. My dad had tears in his eyes. He took me in the garage and took off his belt and gave me the licking of my life. That was the last licking I ever got. Since then, I've grown to like the Martins like my dad and I try to help them by building Martin houses."

Jim said, "He builds them and gives them to people. One time he made one for a man named Martin. Now he has a Martin Martin house."

Dave continued, "One weekend I was home from college and it was February the twenty-eighth. Dad needed some help getting the Martin houses back up and as we were raising the house, the Martins started swarming around the house. It was like they were hiding in the trees waiting for us. Three minutes after we got it up the birds were on it chirping away. That was the earliest I ever saw them arrive. Usually they come in March. The year my dad died, they didn't come in March. We all figured something bad had happened to them and there was this weather thing called El Nino that was doing all sorts of crazy things to the weather. Dad's funeral was on April seventh and when we came home to mom's house from the cemetery the Martins were on the house. I pointed them out to mom and she said it made her feel good. She said that the Martins were his friends and they knew it. She said that one time dad told her that the Martins coming each year was one of his barometers that everything's going to be OK that year."

"Well, I can't wait to see them and sleep in the Martin Room."

Dave started talking about breaking camp in the morning after breakfast and said, "I think we'll tow your canoe to the boat ramp. When our boat is on the trailer we'll put your boat on top of ours and then drive to the ramp where you put in. You can follow us back to the farm. Jim can ride with you."

Molly said, "I'm afraid I've got some bad news. I've been through all my stuff and I can't find my car keys. I think I must have had them in my pull-over along with my sun glasses and a tube of sunblock."

Dave thought a minute and said, "We'll go check on your car and get the license and motor numbers. I know someone in town that will be able to help us. Is your key one of those that has a chip for the ignition?"

"I don't believe so. It's a Jeep Cherokee. It has a beeper to unlock the door but the ignition key looks like a regular key."

"That's good!" said Dave. "I'm a member of AAA. We'll call them in the morning and get a game plan. I know they can help us."

There was a terrifying noise outside the tent that put goose pimples on everyone. Probably even the dogs.

"What in the world was that?" she asked. "It sounded like a baby screaming."

"That was a screech owl." Dave said, "You wouldn't believe how small they are to make such a big noise."

"Well, please don't call them up. I'll have bad dreams all night."

Things got real quiet and she thought she heard Dave give out a little snore. Jim was also real quiet and she heard him make a little sigh right before he dropped off. A sound like all's right with the world. The tree frogs that had been making so much noise suddenly stopped like someone had pulled a "No More Croaking" switch. All of the air vent flaps to the tent were open and there was a nippy breeze blowing through the tent. This is going to be some good sleeping weather she thought as she pulled the bedroll blanket closer to her face. It was amazing how quiet it had become. She thought she heard the tinkling of a little bell. I must be having a dream she thought and then she remembered Jim saying that he had tied a little bell to a trotline. She smiled and thought, "He did have a fish!" She felt good and warm all over. Her last thought before she closed her eyes was "Fifty-nine more dances with the Foo Foo Man. Hot Dog!"

When she finally woke up she saw that the boys were already up and at'em. She spruced up and went outside. Dave saw her coming and poured her a cup of coffee.

"Early bird got the worm I see!" and she thanked him for the coffee. She noticed that he had already shaved. She patted the dogs who were glad to see her and gave Slick a handshake. Jim gave her a hug.

"Well, what's the nanny to do today?"

"You could help me cut up some fruit. That's about all we've got left; three bananas, two oranges and an apple. Coffee and milk."

"Sounds good to me, after all that fish last night, I'm really not that hungry. Gosh that was good fish."

Jim said, "While you're doing the fruit, I'll start folding up the bedrolls and taking down the tent."

Dave, who had been hauling things closer to the boat, came back to the chuck box for another cup of coffee. As he was pouring Molly asked him; "Are we going to dance in the morning or at night time?"

"Hey!" he said, "I'm sorry about that. The rest of the dances are called off."

"No way!" she chuckled, "Genies don't take back wishes. Maybe we can fast dance or tango."

"Maybe I'll break a leg."

After breakfast Dave and Jim went to pick up the trotlines and she said she would stay and do a little KP while they were gone.

Jim asked, "What's KP?"

"Kitchen Police!" she answered.

Picking up the lines was a snap. They had used clip on stages, which they hung on the inside of a five-gallon mud bucket. Dave had cut a wooden circle about a half-inch thick and bolted it to the inside of the bucket near the top. He had drilled seventy-five holes in the wood, one for each hook. The lines were wrapped around small boards that had a "V" cut on the ends. The

ROY M. PHILP, JR.

trotline weights were placed in the bottom of the bucket and the lid was snapped on. It was neat. No tangles, nothing to blow out of the boat and no hooks exposed to foul up anything or snag a kid or pet. He was proud of his invention and wondered if it was marketable. He decided probably not to because there weren't many cat fishermen out there and if anyone saw it, they could easily make one of their own.

The lines only produced nine fish but they were chunky. One blue, seven channels, and a nice op about seven pounds.

Out of the blue, Jim says, "Don't you just love her? I like the way she says, "Come on!" all the time. She said she would teach me how to dance. What does a nanny do?"

"Well, lots of things. Maybe she could take you to baseball practice. You said you wanted to learn to play the piano. Maybe this summer would be a good time to start and she could take you to lessons. Since she's a teacher, maybe she can find your weak spots and tutor you a little. Maybe she can help out a little around the house with the cooking or the laundry. Maybe she'd like to cut hay or run the baler. Maybe she'd like to work in the garden. I've been putting off getting a computer for too long. Maybe she knows how to set one up. We've got plenty to keep her busy. Main thing we have to do is to make her feel at home and have a good time. Who knows, maybe at the end of sixty days if she still likes us we'll offer her a full time job. Don't tell her that last part that's just a shot in the dark. OK?"

"And remember Dad, you got to watch your P's and Q's."

Dave laughed and said, "You're right!"

Jim asked, "What is a P and Q anyway?"

"You know, I really don't know. We'll have to ask somebody."

Molly was sitting on the bank playing with the dogs when they returned. "How many?" she asked.

"Only nine; I told dad we should have brought you because you were our good luck."

"What was that ringing the bell?"

"An op about fifteen pounds."

"Closer to eight" Dave interrupted

"I believe Jim's going to be a good story teller someday," she said laughing. "His Uncle Daveisms alone are going to take him a long way."

Dave cleaned the fish and iced them down with the others and commented, "I believe we've got some powerful fish here."

The canoe was lashed to the side of the boat and loaded with most of the light gear. Jim poured water over the coals and pitched a ring of dirt over the ashes. Molly went with Jim to retrieve the potty seat and on the way back Jim stopped by a small tree and asked Molly if she knew what kind it was.

"No!" she said, "I don't believe I know this one."

Jim said, "Yes you do! You just don't recognize it." He dug it up and shook the sandy loam off and held it up to her and said, "Smell the roots."

She did and immediately said, "Oh my God! It's a root beer tree."

Jim said, "It's a sassafras tree. Root beer smells like sassafras. Sassafras trees have five different kinds of leaves" and he showed them to her. "This one I call the "bear claw" and this one is the right foot and this one is the left foot. I think they used to make tea out of the roots. Know what they use the leaves for?"

"What?" she asked.

"Have you heard of "File' Gumbo", well File' is ground up sassafras leaves. You let them dry and then grind them into a powder."

"Jim, you amaze me. I feel I'm going to be a lot smarter when my sixty days are up."

Jim replanted the tree and they all gave the campsite a last look over for litter. Dave was satisfied that they were leaving it in good shape and they got in the boat after Molly said goodbye to her new friend, the Carolina Wren. Dave said he would do the driving on the way back.

A colorful bird seemed to be leading them on the way back. When they would get too close he would fly about fifty yards down the creek and wait for them to catch up. Molly was fascinated by its behavior and asked what kind it was.

Dave said, "That's a Kingfisher. They like to sit on limbs overhanging water and dive for fish. They're real pretty birds. I wish we'd brought the binoculars. I'd like for you to see him up close"

"Bound to be a female, she's so pretty." She said laughing.

Dave was pleased with her interest in birds and wanted to tell her that the males of most species of birds were the prettiest but decided against it. "You're right, bound to be a female Kingfisher, probably from Ohio!"

Molly smiled at him. He had a quick sense of humor and he made her happy.

The trip to the boat launch took longer because they were going slowly. Most of the gear was loaded into the bed of the pickup and Molly's canoe was tied on top of the boat. Slick was put in his dog box and Pudd'n got in the backseat along with the bedrolls. Jim hollered, "Shotgun on the way back."

On the way to get her car, Molly commented, "Don't see many stick shifts nowadays. Figures the Mayflower Man would have one."

He loved her wit. She was getting under his skin. Visions of sugarplums danced in his head.

Jim said, "Yeah! This is a real cowboy truck. It's the kind of truck I'm going to have someday."

"Why's that?" she asked.

"Well, you see, it's got no hump in the middle like those fancy trucks."

"So?"

"Well, if you ever get a girlfriend, she can slide over next to you and you can put your arm around her."

"Come on?" she said laughing, "No doubt where you learned that! Is this where Jackie sits?"

"No!" he said, "She hates this truck. She hates about everything except Uncle Dave. She doesn't like dogs. She doesn't like to fish or camp. She thinks my chickens are nasty and she says she's allergic to pecans."

"OK Bud. That's enough." Dave interrupted.

"Well, it's true! Know what else?"

"What?"

"She has a cat!"

Molly wanted to laugh so much she was about to cry but she bit her tongue. She said, "I'll bet she doesn't eat bacon either?"

"You're right!" he said, "She's a vegitory or something like that."

"Adios Miss Jackie" she thought, "You cat loving Communist."

Dave could tell she had enjoyed all this new information that Jim had given her. He could almost hear the wheels turning in her head. Everything he'd said was pretty much the truth.

A few more miles down the road Jim asked her if she wanted to play "Crow" 'till they got to her car.

"Don't believe I've ever played "Crow" before. How does it go?"

"Well" he said, "Every time you see a crow you play like you shoot it. Who gets the most wins the game. Dad and me play it all the time. I always win because I've got the best eyes."

"Ok! I'll play. What kind of gun are you shooting?"

"I'm shooting a double barreled twelve gauge."

"Well, I'm shooting a Model 1100 with the plug out."

"Can't shoot with the plug out, It's against the law."

"Yes, you can. When duck and goose season is closed, you can."

Jim said, "Wow! Where'd you learn so much about guns?"

"My dad and brother are both big hunters. They've taken me with them a few times."

As they came to a pasture Jim looked to the right and there were about a dozen crows on the ground holding a powwow of some kind.

"Bam, bam" he said, "I got two!"

Molly play aimed and said, "Bam, bam, bam, bam, bam, I got five."

Dave laughed and said, "I believe you've got your hands full, Pard."

A little further down the road a bird swooped across the highway and Molly reflexed a shot. "Bam" she said and blew make believe smoke off her barrel.

Jim said, "Minus one! That was a buzzard. It's minus one anytime you shoot anything but a crow."

By the time they got to the park turnoff Jim was ahead seven to five due to the fact that Molly had shot three broadtail grackles and a chicken hawk by mistake. Jim was the winner and said, "You're good. You just have to learn your birds better."

"Maybe you and the hoot owl man will give the nanny a fifty-nine day crash course in bird watching. I've already learned a couple of new ones."

"Yes ma'am, we will!"

As they turned into the parking area for the boat launch there were three vehicles with boat trailers but they did not see a Jeep Cherokee. "My car's gone!" she said excitedly. "I parked it right by that light post because I thought it would be the safest spot."

They all got out of the truck not knowing exactly what to say or do.

"Maybe you parked at another ramp further up the creek." Dave suggested.

"No! This is the one, I'm positive." She walked over to the edge of the parking lot and picked up something out of the bushes. "Look!" she said, "This is my canoe rack. It's been stolen. I just made the last payment two months ago. Look! Here's my license plate."

Sure enough, she was holding up an Ohio license plate. Dave thought a few minutes and said, "Let's go report it to the police. Lots of times they find people's cars in just a few days. Let's cross our fingers."

There was a long silence in the truck and Molly started crying. Dave and Jim didn't know what to say or do; girl's crying was new to them. Jim was in the middle and reached over and took her hand. After a few minutes she gained back most of her composure and said, "I feel like my life is falling apart. A couple of months ago I met this cute guy and he came over a few times to the apartment. We had some laughs and he met my roommate. I had to go out of town for a week but halfway through the seminar it got canceled and I came home a day early. When I went into the apartment I found my roommate in the arms of my cute guy. My roommate and I had it out and I kicked her out. The apartments' in my name and now I have to pay all the rent until I can find a new roommate. She took half my stuff with her. Even took my TV and left me with a phone bill that is out of sight. Now my car is gone. I'm wiped out. It's hard enough to make it on a teacher's pay."

She started tearing up again and Jim said, "It's OK. You're a genie, and you know us."

Molly answered by saying, "Well, at least I'll have room and board for sixty days."

Jim said, "Did you know I have a chicken named Molly?"

"Come on!"

"Yes ma'am. Dad named her after a song. He says that if he ever gets married and they have a little girl he's going to call her Molly." And he started singing, "Just Molly and me and the baby make three, we're happy in my blue heaven. Something like that. You ever hear that song?"

"Yes!" she said feeling much better now. "I'm looking forward to meeting your Molly."

"Damn!" thought Dave. "The kid is so smooth. It's like he says everything I want to say or what I'm thinking but he says it before I can get the words to come out."

Dave thought a while and then said, "There's not much we can do today since it's Sunday but we'll go to the police station and report it and give them the plates. Maybe they can get some prints off the plates. We'll call your insurance company tomorrow and see about getting you a car to rent. Some insurance policies provide for that." He looked at Molly and said, "It's gonna be OK, you're a genie and you know us." He rubbed Jim's head and while he was rubbing it he winked at her.

The wink went straight to her heart. It had been a long time since someone had winked at her. She felt like she was seventeen again. "Wow!" she thought. "What a rush! What in the world is happening to me? Maybe he just had something in his eye. No, it was a wink."

The police station was about empty when they arrived. The dispatcher gave Molly some forms to fill out and while she was doing so, Patrolman "Chip" Johnson walked in. Dave knew Chip and introduced him to Molly. He wanted to know all about it and Dave and Molly filled him in on all the details. Chip told them that there had been three cars stolen from the same ramp in the last two months, and it was giving the county a black eye. The department had installed a surveillance camera about a week ago and they might have a film of the theft. He would go over in the morning and pick up the film. He was pleased to get the plates and put them in a plastic bag. "These plates might help tie the knot if we catch them." He said he would keep them posted and if they'd come back to the station tomorrow, they'd have the report all typed up for the insurance company. "I gotta feeling we're going to catch these guys. Hopefully we'll get your car back too."

Chip walked with them to the truck and said, "Saw your boat, figured that was you. Did you have any luck?"

"Yeah, Buddy" Dave answered, "Caught us a mess of catfish and one scrawny little nanny. Have you got a cooler? I'll give you some. We got plenty."

Chip had a small soft cooler in his patrol car that he used for his lunch, and Dave put in three nice cats.

"Man, this will be perfect. The wife's mom and dad are visiting and we'll fry'em up tonight." Dave added one more fish for good measure and a little ice. "And already cleaned" Chip said, "I'll be a hero."

When Dave got back in the truck Molly said, "Were you bribing him with catfish?"

Dave chuckled and said, "Well, maybe a little. But it was a legal bribe. They were powerful fish I gave him."

Molly was a little puzzled by his answer but didn't say anything.

Jim asked, "What's a bribe?"

"Well" said Molly, "It's when you try to get someone to do something for you by giving them something or giving them back a favor if they'll do something you ask. Like saying to a crying baby, I'll give you this piece of candy if you'll stop crying."

CHAPTER 4

THE SALT OF THE EARTH

When they got to the Reverend Perkins house Jim saw them working in their garden and said, "There they are," and he bolted from the truck and ran to see them. "Hello Mrs. Perkins" and he gave her a hug. "Guess what? I got a nanny!"

"Your Uncle bought you a goat you say?" the reverend said.

"Noooo," he laughed, "I got a two legged nanny. Her name is Molly. You know what else?"

"What?"

"She's got a dog named Pudd'n. Come see her. She's real pretty."

The Perkins ambled over to the boat and Dave introduced Molly to Mary and Bob Perkins.

"And this is Pudd'n" Jim added.

Pudd'n was glad to meet them and the Perkins gave her some attention and a few pats.

Mary said, "Matthew tells me you're going to be his nanny. Is that right?"

"Yes!" she said, "For two months. I'm confused. Did you just call Jim, Matthew?"

Jim said, "Matthew is my real name but Uncle Dave calls me Jim. Have you ever seen "The Man from the Snowy River?" It's the best movie ever made. There's a man in the movie named Jim that Uncle Dave says I remind him of. That's why he calls me Jim and sometime I call him Clancy because he's cool like Clancy. There's a girl in the movie named Jessica. She's real cool too."

Bob said, "We missed you in church this morning."

"Yeah" Dave said, "Jim and I went AWOL. We had us a sunrise service on the creek. The catfish were calling and we wanted to do a mayhaw check. We had us a good luck charm," he said looking at Molly. "Fish bit real good and got a few mayhaws to boot, thought you might like some fish."

"Man, you know it. Let me go get a pan to put them in."

"Bring a bucket too. I want to give Mary some mayhaws."

"Man, you sure do know how to please." he said as he went to get the pans.

Mary was ecstatic about the mayhaws and took Molly inside to show her the house. A good-looking girl going to be living at Dave's farm would be big news in their little town. She wasn't really a gossiper but they loved Dave and Matthew and they were members of their church and she wanted to have the facts straight.

When they left, Molly and Mary were best friends and Mary had put a big stamp of approval on her nannyship. Mary gave Molly an invitation to come back for a visit. They left in good spirits with a tin full of freshly baked chocolate chip cookies and a sack of tomatoes, for which preacher Bob was somewhat famous.

"I liked them," said Molly.

"Good friends!" said Dave.

"Good cookies!" said Jim.

"Powerful fish," Dave added and Jim asked Molly, "Were you trying to bribe me when you told me you'd give me five dollars for the hammock?"

"Well kind of, No!" she said, "That was a business proposition. I had to have that hammock. I was so tired. And I forgot to pay you" she added as she reached for her purse, somewhat embarrassed.

"I told you he was a good little businessman," Dave said jokingly but at the same time hoping that Jim wouldn't accept the money.

Molly handed the money to Jim and Jim said, "No!" he said, "I won't take it"

"Why not? We made a deal."

"I didn't know you were a genie when you asked. Its bad luck to take money from a genie."

"Well thank you, Sir Jim. Your true colors are showing. Chivalry is going to take you a long way." And she put her arm around him and gave him a hug.

Jim cooed and wondered what chivalry meant but he didn't ask. He liked the hug. Jim passed the cookies again and said, "Mrs. Perkins makes about the best chocolate chip cookies in the world."

Molly said, "These are good but you've never tasted mine. I know Mrs. Tucker's secret recipe. I'd put it up against anybody's."

"Will you make us some?"

"Sure!" she said, "But I'll have to blindfold you when I make them."

"Why's that?" Jim asked.

"Well, I promised Mrs. Tucker that I wouldn't show the recipe to anyone. They're so good that I've thought about opening a cookie business on the side."

"Talk talk talk," Dave replied.

"I'm serious," she said.

"Well, Jim and I will be guinea pigs if you want to whip up a bunch. We're cookie connoisseurs."

"You're on!" she snapped back.

A few miles down the road Dave put on his blinker and took a right and Molly asked, "Is this the road to your farm?"

"No." Dave answered. "We're going to stop at the Neels. They're an older couple I met at the nursery a few years ago. They've both got green thumbs and have taught me a lot about plants. I usually stop when I've got fish. Herschel used to love to fish but he has a bad heart and can't lift much or launch a boat."

"They're cool." Jim butted in. "They've got Beagle dogs. One's named Scooter and one's named Belle. Did you know that Beagles can't bark?"

"No! I didn't know that. Why can't they bark?"

"They're hounds. They howl. They make good rabbit and fox dogs. They go ooooooh."

"Well Matthew, I mean Jim, you amaze me."

The Neels house was in the middle of about ten acres, which had never been timbered except for some thinning that Herschel had done when he was much younger. The trees on the drive in were magnificent. Jim spotted a doe on the way in. The only cleared part was about a two-acre plot in the middle where the house was. There was a small garden, some fruit trees, and several beautiful flowerbeds. There were three large Sycamore trees close to the house. One of which Herschel claimed was the largest Sycamore in Texas and if one saw it they wouldn't doubt it.

Mrs. Neel was working in one of her flowerbeds when they drove up and Herschel was pruning one of his prize camellias. Company was a treat for the Neels because they didn't get out much anymore. Her eyesight was failing and he got winded easily. Two or three trips to town each month was about all they got out. They watched TV on Sunday for their church service. They both came over to the truck and Dave made introductions. Jim gave each of them a hug. Dave asked if it would be OK to let the dogs out for a little run and some water.

"Fine" said Herschel, "They can't hurt a thing."

The Beagles were also happy with the company and took the big dogs off on a tour of the property. They had already marked it pretty well but the two Labs found a few places they'd missed and laid claim to them.

"Thought you all might like some catfish and some mayhaws." Dave said.

"Lordy, yes!" said Fannie, "We ran out of mayhaw a couple of months ago and we haven't had any fresh fish since the last ones you brought us." She took Molly with her to see the house and to get a pan for the fish. Herschel got a bucket from the shed and Dave poured in a couple of gallons of berries.

"Whoa!" he said, "That's too many. That'll keep her busy the rest of the day. Man, I can't thank you enough. We've had an eye out for someone selling berries but haven't seen anyone yet. I figured maybe a late freeze had got the blooms."

Fannie gave Molly a tour of the garden and she called Dave over and said, "Last time you were here you went on about how good the Ginger Lilies smelled, so I dug some up and I've got you a start. These five pots are yours. Plant them in a shady spot with a little cow manure and they'll do just fine. Fact is, the more you ignore them the better they seem to do. And this here is a Gardenia. Herschel grafted it and it's from good stock. The blossoms don't last that long when you pick them, but they can sure make a room smell good."

"Thanks" said Dave, "I've been looking at the nurseries for the Ginger Lilies, but they don't seem to carry them. These are real treasures," and he asked Molly if she'd ever smelled one. She didn't think she had and Mrs. Neel said, "They cut real good."

Herschel asked Dave to come to the shed with him. He had something to show him. Belle, the female Beagle, had slipped back into a pen he had put up and was nursing four of the cutest puppies you'd ever seen.

"Lord have mercy, if that ain't a sight?" Dave chuckled.

"I meant to separate them when she came in heat but I was too late as you can see. I was going to ask Matthew if he wanted one but I didn't want to without your permission. They'll be nine weeks old tomorrow and it's time to wean them and give 'em their shots. Got papers on the mom and dad, they're good pups. I started them on Puppy Chow last week but they still like the tit the best."

Dave said, "Thanks for asking. Knowing Matthew he'd want them all but we got our hands full right now with our dog and Molly's dog."

"Well, I've got to find them a good home."

"I think I might know someone that would want one. Is there a male in the bunch?"

"Yep, I've got one left!" Herschel said.

"I'll take him. I believe this is going to make a young man real happy, and I can promise you he'll be well taken care of."

The rest of the group came over to the shed and there were more oohs and ahhs made over the puppies. Dave told Matthew that Mr. Neel had given them one and he was going to offer it to the Phelan boy.

Herschel asked Dave for a jump on his car. They hadn't driven it enough and the battery was down. Dave cleaned the terminals and gave him a jump. His car fired right up and Dave suggested he let it run about ten minutes.

Dave said they had better be going and told Jim to go get the male puppy. Molly went with him and watched him as he examined each puppy.

"What are you looking for?" she asked.

"The one with a weenie." Molly bit her lip to keep from laughing.

They bid the Neels goodbye and left with Jim holding the puppy in his lap.

"That was fun!" Molly said and added, "Mrs. Neel thinks you hung the moon. She says you remind her of Herschel when he was a young buck."

"I'm real excited about the ginger plants. They're a real treasure. You'll have to come back in the fall and take a whiff."

Molly had a wild thought, "I bet I see the first bloom," and she answered him, "Yeah, I might just do that! Maybe over the Thanksgiving holidays."

Their next stop was the grocery store and Dave asked Molly if she would stay and watch the dogs while he and Jim did a little shopping. They returned a short time later with a gallon of milk, two pounds of bacon, a loaf of bread, a sack of Puppy Chow, eight cases of Mason jelly jars, sixteen packages of Sure Gel, two twenty-five pound sacks of sugar and a sack of ice to put on the fish. He put everything in the boat and they were off again. He also brought each of them a bottle of water.

Molly said, "Thanks, I didn't know I was so thirsty."

Their next stop was at the Beauchamp's so Jim could deliver some kindling wood. Matthew knocked on the door and Frank came outside and walked over to the boat. His son Brad was right behind him.

"Been fishing?" he asked.

"Yes sir!" Jim said, "We caught some catfish."

Dave said, "Get a pan and we'll give you some if you've got room."

"Hot dog!" he said "Haven't had any catfish in a month of Sundays. I'll go get a pan."

He hurried to the house and returned with a large pan and Dave put in four nice cats. Dave offered him some mayhaws but Frank declined saying that his wife wasn't a jelly maker. Frank paid Matthew for the wood and he thanked him.

Frank said, "I probably won't need anymore 'till the fall. I'll call you when I do."

As they were getting ready to drive off, Frank's wife, Theresa, came out of the house carrying a loaf of still hot homemade bread and handed it through the window to Dave and said, "You are so kind. You bring us ten dollars' worth of wood and give us twenty dollars' worth of fish. I always feel like we owe you when you leave."

Dave said, "You don't owe me anything. It's me that owes you. You've taught my boy responsibility and how to earn money. You've been a repeat customer and make him feel important. God gave us the fish for free and we had the fun of catching them and a good camping weekend. We're just sharing some of God's bounty with you all. If this bread tastes one half as good as it smells, it's us that's going to owe you. You made it with your own hands and that makes it special."

"Thanks!" she said, "You always brighten our day."

Dave said, "Say, I was watching young Brad with the puppy back there. He's about the right age for one. I know someone who has three more from the same litter that he's trying to find a good home for. They're females so you might want to have her spayed down the line."

"How much is he asking?"

"They're free. He just wants them to have a good home. He's got papers on the mom and dad. They're shorthaired so they won't shed and they're small so they won't eat a lot. You could probably get all three, sell two of them and make a little money on the side. He wouldn't care. If you're interested let me know and I'll tell Herschel. Matthew and I will take you to the Neels and Brad can pick out the one he wants; nothing better than a first puppy."

"Thanks!" she said, "I'll talk it over with Frank and we'll get back to you."

As they drove off, Molly said, "That was nice! They help Jim, you help them, and they help the Neels."

"Yep!" Dave answered, "That's the way it works. The fish are working."

Molly said, "Doesn't this bread smell good? Should we try it now?"

Dave said, "Let's wait 'till tonight. How about apple, cheese, bread, and a little white wine?"

"And a campfire!" Jim added.

"Deal!" said Dave.

A few miles further down the road and they were in farm country and Molly asked, "How much further, Daddy?"

Dave laughed and said, "I want to give some of these fish to the Phelans and I want to try and make a business deal with Shelley."

"Know what?" said Jim. "They got no TV and no shoes."

"Come on?" Molly answered.

"Know what else? They don't know where babies come from."

"OK Bud. That's enough."

"Well, you said it."

"Well, I shouldn't have. We won't say that anymore. OK?"

"Yes sir."

Dave said, "Let me give you a little history of this family. John is an only child and both of his parents passed away while he was in high school. John inherited the farm and all the work that goes with it. He had dyslexia and was having trouble in school and dropped out to run the farm and take care of the livestock. He's probably the hardest worker I've ever known. He married his high school sweetheart about eight years ago and they have four children, three girls and a boy. They're the most polite, well mannered, and best-looking kids I've ever seen. They look like kids off a Minnesota farm. They're the picture of health. I'd adopt them if I could. That's how fine I think they are. They've got land and cattle but very little money. They'll never go hungry because they work so hard. They're always strapped for cash. I try to do little things for them when I can. John helps me with my hay and I've been helping him with his cows and fencing. Shelley's a great cook and jelly maker. I'm going to offer her two dollars for each jar of jelly she makes. We'll supply the supplies and she'll provide the labor. I believe Jim can sell the jelly to his egg customers and make a little extra. Two of their girls will be in school this year so I know they'll need a little extra this fall. Jim's right about the shoes. They go barefooted most of the time. When the kids get older I'm sure she'll get a part time job but right now she's got her hands full. You'll like them. They're the salt of the earth."

"Know what else? If you drive in Mr. Phelan's truck in the pasture, his cows come up to the truck and stick their heads in the window and want you to pat'em on the head."

"Come on?"

"You just wait!"

When they pulled up to the house, Shelley and the kids were sitting on the front porch. Shelley was sitting in a porch swing working on a quilt. The kids swarmed Dave like ticks on a dog. Dave reached in his top pocket and pulled out a peppermint stick for each. They were thrilled. Dave was sure it was their first piece of candy since his last visit and that was a month ago. They all gave him a hug and he introduced Molly to the group.

"Shelley, this is Molly. She's going to be with us for a couple of months."

Jim said, "She's my nanny and she's a genie, too! Know what else? She's got a dog named Pudd'n."

"Hold on a minute, Bud," and he continued with the introductions. "This is Morgan, this is Caroline who's a little shy, this is Isabel, and this young man is Jackson."

Morgan had taken one of Molly's hands and Isabel the other. They were both claiming her. Any friend of Dave's was their friend, also. Molly had seen this reaction many times as a schoolteacher. The kids were starving for attention. Everything Dave had said about the kids was true. They were the picture of health and they were all barefooted. Shelley was also very pretty. She had the kind of complexion that women dream of. She had beautiful auburn hair, an infectious smile, dimples, a twinkle in her eye, no makeup, a natural beauty. A thought popped into her head that Dave would adopt the mother also.

Molly admired the quilt. "It seems to have every color in the rainbow," she said. "My grandmother used to make them. She made one for each of the grandchildren. She was about half through with mine and she had a little stroke and couldn't sew anymore. I never got mine. I've wanted one ever since."

Shelley told her she had learned it from her mother and she sold them for a little mad money.

"How much do you sell them for?"

"Well this one is a queen and I think I can get ninety dollars for it. I know that sounds like a lot but it takes so much time. I've probably got close to eighty hours in it already."

"Is this one sold?"

"Not yet."

"I'd love to have it."

"Really?"

"Yes. I'm serious."

"Sold! I should have it finished by next week."

She glanced at Dave and he winked at her, which completely disarmed her again.

Dave ran his jelly idea at Shelley. Shelley did a quick little calculation in her head. Seventy-two jars at two dollars per jar equals $144 for maybe one day's work.

"Deal!" she said smiling. She already knew where the money would be going.

Dave brought the mayhaws and the other supplies to the front porch and Shelley said, "I'll cook the berries tomorrow and get the juice. It will keep. Then I'll start on the jelly the next day. Do you want me to label them?"

"If you don't mind."

"What do you want me to put on the label?"

He thought a minute and said, "Mayhaw Jelly in large letters and the date under it and in smaller letters, "Jelly by Shelley."

"I like that!" she said. "You always make me feel good."

"Where's John?"

"He's at the barn working on his tractor or maybe petting his cows," she said laughing.

"I need to ask him something. I'll be back shortly."

The kids were on the other side of the house swinging on a tire swing. Jim was the center of attention and loving it. Dave went to the truck and got the puppy and the sack of dog food and headed to the barn. When he got to the barn John was just cleaning up from greasing his tractor. Dave had always admired John's work ethic. Every tool was in working order and had its place. John could take anything apart, fix it, and put it back together. He had helped Dave with repairs on several occasions. John was glad to see him and they shook hands.

"What'cha got there?" and Dave showed him the puppy.

"This is one of Herschel's pups. This was the only male. He was trying to get rid of them and I took one thinking young Jackson might want one."

"He'd love it! I've been meaning to get him one but can't seem to find the time."

"Well, this one is nine weeks old and Herschel has just started him on Puppy Chow. Probably after this bag he'll be ready for table scraps. They make good rabbit dogs so maybe he can scare some of those bunnies out of Shelley's garden."

John was excited. "Let's go give it to him now."

Dave said, "We're just about to leave. Why don't you wait 'till we leave and then give it to him? A first puppy ought to come from a boy's dad, it kind of bonds 'em."

"Thanks Dave. You're a true friend. I'll be a hero. He's had his lip stuck out lately, says I like the girls more than I do him. Has the pup got a name?"

"Well, if you didn't want him I was going to call him Rudi Kazuti. Maybe Jackson will want to name him himself."

"No!" said John, "The kids will love that name. Rudi Kazuti it is!"

"Let's go back to the house; I want you to meet Molly."

John put Rudi in a large tub with a little bowl of water and they started back to the house with Dave telling him what they'd hauled out of the creek and how it happened that she was going to be Matthew's nanny for a couple of months.

Back at the house Molly enjoyed visiting with Shelley. She seemed to be the perfect mom. Her mannerisms were quiet and natural. She made all the kid's clothes but they didn't look homemade at all. Molly saw several catalogs lying around. Gap, Osh Kosh, and Target and she bet that was where she got her ideas. Shelley loved talking about Dave and said, "Next to John, he's about the nicest man I know. I could eat him with a spoon. He invents things just to keep us afloat. He comes over with articles about ranching and shows them to John. John does everything he says. He showed him an article about rotating pastures and cross fencing, then he comes over and helps John build the fences. Our ranch is now fenced like a sliced pie. The cows stay in one slice for a few days and then he opens a gate and they go into another slice for a few days. No more overgrazing. The cows love it and are putting on good weight. The center of the pie is where they get their water. He calls the center the hub and there's a gate to each slice of the pie. He hays them in the hub during the winter. It's solved the problem of overgrazing. One slice is for the bulls and seven are for the cows. He's got John keeping books on each cow and if they don't have a calf when they're supposed to he sells her. Thank God! He hates selling them. Each cow has a number on her ear. We've got sixty-two cows right now and two bulls. John's goal is to have ninety cows and three bulls. Someday we hope to put in a lake like Dave's but smaller."

"I didn't know Dave had a lake."

"Oh honey! You're in for a treat. He's got one of the prettiest lakes you've ever seen. You should latch on to him. That man is going to make some girl live happily ever after.

Talk about imagination! He has more ideas than a dog has fleas. Jelly by Shelley, now that's clever. I love it."

Dave and John arrived at the house just as Shelley was serving lemonade to the kids. Dave introduced Molly to John and John said, "Pleased to meet you. You're as pretty as Dave said you were. Any friend of Dave's is a friend of mine."

Molly glanced at Dave who was kind of blushing.

"Dave tells me you're a school teacher."

"Yes!" she said, "And I hear you're running a state of the art cattle ranch, happy cows and two real happy bulls."

He laughed and said, "Matter of fact, them bulls is real happy." He instantly liked Molly and her wit. "You'll have to come back sometime and I'll show them to you."

"I'd like that" she said. "Jim's been telling me how friendly they are."

He laughed and said, "Yeah, they're pretty much spoiled."

Dave asked John to come out to the boat because he wanted to give him some fish before they left. He gave him the rest of the fish except for three.

"This will make Shelley happy. Just yesterday she told me she was tired of beef. She wants me to trade in a calf or two for some pigs. Hell!" he said, "I'm a rancher, not a pig farmer."

Dave laughed and said, "Why don't you trade in a nice young steer for three or four already butchered pigs?"

"Maybe that's what I'll do. I've been craving some pork chops myself."

They said their good-byes to the Phelans and there were lots of hugs. Shelley said she would call when the quilt was ready. She was going to start on the jelly tomorrow.

As they were about to drive off, Caroline appeared from around the corner of the house with a handful of flowers she had just picked. She reached up and handed them to Molly and said, "It was nice to meet you. These are for you."

Molly said, "Why thank you, Caroline! No one has given me flowers in a long time. They're beautiful. I'll put them in a vase right when we get home."

As they drove off Dave could see John and Jackson from his side mirror heading to the barn. "Wish I was a fly on the wall to witness the happiness," he thought.

"That was fun!" said Molly. "I'm so glad you boys saved my life."

Jim asked, "Where's the puppy?"

"I took him to the barn."

"I thought we were going to give it to him."

Dave answered him saying, "John doesn't give his kids many presents. I wanted him to give it to Jackson."

"And why did you give him all our fish?"

"I saved enough for a good fish fry. We can catch fish anytime we want to. The Phelans needed those fish. Those were powerful fish."

Molly said, "I've heard you mention several times that these are powerful fish or that the fish are working. What do you mean by it?"

Dave said, "Ever since I heard the story about how Jesus fed the masses with a few fish and a couple of loaves of bread, I've been intrigued by the story. I really don't know what I'm trying to say but to me the fish are kind of like magic. For example, we gave the Perkins a few fish and what happened? They gave us cookies and tomatoes. What else happened at the Perkins?"

"Mrs. Perkins asked me to church and also to sing in the choir."

"And they gave us iced tea." Jim added.

"And Molly made new friends. And I guarantee you the next time we see them they'll be glad to see us. They'll be talking about the fish and how the jelly came out and we'll be talking about how good the cookies and the tomatoes were. To me, it's magic. Maybe when Jesus brought out the fish and the bread it was all he had and the people saw it and started sharing what they had stashed away. I don't know why, but it seems that the more fish I give away the more good things happen to me and the better I feel. The Neels gave us ginger plants and a gardenia bush. What else?"

"And a puppy" said Jim, "And we got homemade bread."

"And I got flowers!" said Molly.

And Dave said, "If we had taken all those fish home, we wouldn't have had all that fun. We made friends, we gave away a puppy, maybe two, we made business deals, we jump started a car, Molly bought a quilt which helped the Phelans, and we got lots of hugs. I guarantee you the next time we see all those folks they won't be talking about the weather. They'll be talking about the puppy, or the fish, or how their jelly came out. And we'll be talking about how good the cookies were and how's the garden growing. They'll be thinking of ways to pay us back and we'll be thinking of ways to pay them back. And all we were doing was sharing some of God's bounty. Several years ago I caught a cooler full of speckled trout and flounder. I filleted them and froze them. Guess what? The freezer went out and I lost them all. To dishonor all of those beautiful fish was a wakeup call for me. Fresh fish are meant to be shared, not hoarded and allowed to become freezer burned. That will never happen to me again."

Molly thought, here she was in a truck with a beautiful sensitive man that wouldn't dishonor a fish. She imagined she felt a little like Cinderella when the prince slipped on her slipper. She had always been fascinated by coincidences and how different circumstances can make things happen or not happen. She hated snakes but had the snake not dropped in her canoe would she be here right now? Had Slick been sleeping would she be in this truck right now? What if Jim hadn't made his wish? Her mind was racing with what ifs. What was his house like? How much farther? What does a nanny do? What about my car? What about me being almost broke? And I need some clothes! She started making a list in her head of things she needed to do. She needed to charge her phone and to call home. What was she thinking about with the canoe? "I'm lucky to be alive."

CHAPTER 5

MONEY! MONEY!

U p ahead she could see some cars stopped on the side of the highway. Several people were outside their cars standing by the fence looking out towards the field on the right. "Do you think there's been a wreck?" she asked.

"No!" said Jim, "They're looking at the Indians."

Molly looked to the right and out on to the field. "Oh my God!" she said. "Look! Stop the truck." They got out of the truck for a better look. Out in the field were six Indians on horses. The sun was at their backs and they were silhouetted. They appeared close but at the same time far off. The breeze was moving the grass and they appeared to be slightly moving also. The details of the braves were unbelievable. Feathers were on their spears and appeared to be blowing in the breeze. Their posture was proud and perfect. Two of the horses were sideways and the others were facing the highway. The braves had one or two feathers on their heads and one had a headdress with buffalo horns. One of the horses appeared to be trying to grab a bite of grass. One of the braves carried a shield and another had a lance with a crook on the top with feathers on it.

Molly said, "Oh they're so beautiful. Who did them?"

"Clancy!" Jim said. "People stop and look at them all the time."

Molly looked at Dave and said, "You made these?"

"Yes ma'am."

"Well someday you're going straight to heaven. They are awesome. They take your breath away. I can't tell how far away they are."

Dave thought a second and wanted to say, "You take my breath away," but answered. "They're fourteen feet high. The brave with the tallest spear makes him about twenty feet tall. They're about one hundred and ten yards away."

"I just love them." She said.

"Well thanks; I've always had a soft spot for Indians. They're some of my real heroes and besides, I needed someone to guard my hayfield."

"This is your farm?"

"Yes ma'am."

"Oh Dave, it's beautiful!"

"Thanks, let's go to the house."

The Indians were on a gentle hilltop that dropped off and you couldn't see the view behind them. Back on the highway, the hill dipped and there was a beautiful view of the farm. She could see the house on another little hill several hundred yards away. The road to the house was lined with Crepe Myrtle trees all the way from the highway to the house. The trees were in bloom and the sight was incredible. They turned on to the road to the house and Molly thought "these trees aren't supposed to be here, these are city trees." She asked, "Are these crepe myrtles?"

"Yes ma'am."

"Did you plant them?"

"Yes ma'am! One time I went through Kentucky and I saw several farms that had pink dogwoods lining the roads to the farmhouses. I decided to try it someday if I got a chance. When I looked into it, the dogwoods were expensive. They are slow growers, and the bloom doesn't last very long. Crepe myrtles have always been one of my favorite trees, especially when they're not pruned and allowed to grow big. Hopefully they'll make a canopy over the road someday. The blooms last for months and they're not much trouble. The leaves do a color change or two. A lot more bang for the bucks."

The drive to the house was breathtaking. She felt like she was inside of a pink cloud. There was a fence around the house that had been painted white. There was a cluster of large pines in the yard as well as a few maples, a tremendous bald cypress, three large pecan trees and a large catalpa tree. There were several large hydrangea bushes. Some were blooming pink, but most were blue. They stopped in front of the house and let the dogs out. Slick and Pudd'n took off. Slick was anxious to show Pudd'n around.

Dave told Jim, "We'll unload in a little bit. I want to show Molly around and where her room is."

Molly was excited. The house was ten times prettier than she thought it would be. It was oozing with personality. With a little landscaping it would be a shoo-in for a feature story in "Country Living Magazine." The yard seemed alive with birds. She saw several feeders in use. The house was two stories and had a tin roof. There was a continuous covered porch that connected the east and west sides to the front porch. She could see several wooden swings and as they approached the house she said, "I can't wait to sit in one of those swings. Did you make them?" she asked, already knowing that he did.

"Yep! He said, "I'm a sucker for a sunrise and in the morning I have coffee on the east porch and in the evening, I have a glass of wine on the west porch to watch the sunset. Winter time, we sit on the front porch to because it's protected from the north wind."

There were three windows on each side of the front door. The first room to the right was the den, which had wood floors and a fireplace with a deer head over the mantle. The fireplace was on the east side of the room and there were double windows on each side. There were two couches, one, which faced the fireplace, and one, which faced a large armoire that hid the TV and a music center. The floor in front of the couches and the fireplace was covered with a large crocheted rug that would surely win any crocheted rug contest if it were entered. On the middle of this rug was a genuine bearskin rug with the head and all.

"My God!" she said, "Where did you get the bear rug?"

Dave laughed and said, "A friend of mine got it in Canada a few years ago and when he put it in his house his wife thought it was the ugliest thing she had ever seen and wouldn't let him keep it. I'm kind of babysitting it for him. He says if he ever remarries, he might want it back."

"Know what?" Jim said. "Slick won't get on it. He looks at it and kind of growls"

Dave said, "It's strange, he's never seen a bear but he knows to be careful and has respect for it. It'll be interesting to see if Pudd'n has the same reaction."

Molly laughed and said, "Knowing Pudd'n she'll probably lick it on the face." She spotted the piano and asked, "Who plays?"

Jim said, "I do! Want to hear?"

"Yes!"

"It's a player piano! Dad wanted me to hear all these old songs that they used to sing when he was growing up. He loaded "Bad Bad Leroy Brown" and then lifted the top of the piano seat and raised a small hinged bar that made the piano seat slant down a couple of inches. "This keeps you from sliding off the stool." He said as he sat down and put his feet on the pedals. "You can sit by me and help me sing."

She sat down and Jim started pumping. The sound was magical. Jim pointed to where the words were on the roll as it came up and the three of them sang the song together. Molly had a great voice and Jim was excited she was singing with him. The song finished and Jim started looking for another one to play and Dave said, "Let's show Molly around first. There will be time for the piano later."

There was a super set of drums next to the piano and Molly asked, "Who plays the drums?"

"I'm kind of in the learning stage." Dave answered.

On the opposite side of the entrance hall was another large room that Dave called his studio and office room. It had windows on the south and west walls. There was a large roll top desk, three drafting tables, and several easels with drawings and paintings in progress. She stopped to admire the original drawings of the Indians he had made of iron.

"Seems like I've seen these guys before" she said. "This is good but the ones in the hayfield seemed to be alive. I'm impressed! Your paintings are really good."

"So good I liked to starved to death." Dave answered.

"Know what?" said Jim. "A man drove up one day and tried to buy our Indians for 10,000 dollars."

"Are you serious?"

"Yes ma'am! But Dad wouldn't sell 'em. He told him they were part of his soul."

Dave said, "I've got his name and number, though. I don't believe he's got money problems. He's called a couple of times and upped his offer. I told him I'd start on them this winter after the harvest."

"This is my table" Jim said, "Dad's teaching me how to use the T square and how to draw things to scale. This is my 45 and this is my 60 angle."

"Maybe you can teach your nanny how to draw."

"OK, that'll be fun. And see this desk right here. Someday we're going to get a computer and this is where it will go."

"I can't believe you don't have a computer!"

"Well, that's my fault. I've been dragging my feet because I don't know how to set one up and I'm too embarrassed to tell anyone. Do you know anything about setting one up?"

"Enough to set one up and teach a couple of Bozos like you two to run it."

"Well, that'll be your first official job. Order us a computer and a printer and maybe some kind of small business software. I want to be able to invoice and keep records."

"Deal!" she answered. She knew she could do this task. Instantly she felt more confident of herself. She had a mission.

"What's my budget?"

"Under a thousand."

"Great! That will get you a Cadillac system with six months of AOL thrown in for free. You'll get Windows, Word and the Encyclopedia Britannica thrown in to boot. Oh, Jim, you're going to love it. It will really help you in school."

Outside the study was a hall that ended with a door to the west porch. There was a small bathroom at the end of the hall and a small closet next to it under the stairway. There was a row of coat hooks of the study side of the hall and there seemed to be a hat for every occasion on the hooks, and also rain gear and a few umbrellas. The hall ended at the entrance hall with the stairs to the second story. There was another hall separating the den from Dave's bedroom. This hall ended with a door to the east porch. Jim continued the tour he was conducting and took Molly into Dave's bedroom. "And this is Dad's room."

Molly and Dave followed him in and Molly turned to Dave and scolded him with her finger. "Bad boy" she said, "You didn't make your bed."

"And this is his bathroom."

There was a towel on the floor and she scolded him again. "Messy! Messy!" she said.

"And that's his closet! Come on" he said, "I'll show you my room, "and he led her to the stairs.

She was dying to see the inside of Dave's closet. All she had seen him in so far was blue jeans, a white shirt, and boots. She would be nosey another time.

At the top of the stairs to the right was the bathroom. Nice mirrors, good lighting and a super shower. She could tell Jim was proud as he showed it to her.

"Nice!" she said, "And no towels on the floor." She gave him a rub on the head and he cooed.

The upstairs was a single room probably twenty by forty feet but appeared to be much larger because there were four dormer windows and each dormer space had a single bed in it with a couple of feet of space on each side of the bed. "Right now all of these beds are mine but when I have brothers and sisters, we'll all share."

Molly raised her eyebrows at Dave who was enjoying Jim's tour.

"Well, someday we hope." He said, smiling.

There were two ceiling fans. Dave said, "Sometimes I wish this was my room. When you open opposite windows you get cross ventilation and it seems like there is always a good breeze. It's got a tin roof and when it rains it makes for good sleeping. And when it gets too hot up here, I've put a sprinkler hose on the ridge of the roof and hooked it to the well. The water spray will drop the temp so fast you wouldn't believe it."

"Where in the world did you come up with that idea?"

"From my granddad, He had a house on a farm with a tin roof and one summer we all went to visit him. It got so hot one night nobody could sleep and all the babies were crying. I can still hear my grandmother saying, "Albert, you have to do something. These babies are burning up." He got out of bed and got an ice pick and went outside. He punched holes in a garden hose and got up on the roof and laid it on the pitch of the roof and turned it on. It was like air-conditioning. Didn't cost much and worked like a charm. Ours works the same way. If you get hot up here you can try it. All you have to do is turn this handle here."

"I can't wait to try it out."

Jim showed Molly his closet, which was in the northeast corner of the room. "You can hang your stuff in here and these two drawers are empty if you want to use them."

"Thanks! Don't have much stuff to hang or put in the drawers right now though." She asked, "So this is the Martin room?"

"Yes ma'am!" and he led her to the east window and showed her the Martin house. "The babies are still in the house so some of the Martins stay around all day. In the morning they sing real pretty. This is the bed I'm using right now. The breeze is mostly from the east and I like to see the sun when it comes up. We've got down comforters so it doesn't matter how cold it gets. The colder the better is what Dad always says. You take this bed."

"Well thanks, Jim; I'll take good care of it."

"Come on" he said, "You got to see our kitchen. We got rainbows in the kitchen."

"Come on!"

Sure enough there were rainbow reflections everywhere. The sun was coming in the west window where several prisms of various shapes and sizes had been hung. The effect was dazzling. Molly gave one of the prisms a little touch and reflections started dancing all around the room.

"Awesome!" she said, "I love it!"

Dave showed her the pantry, which was hidden under the stairway. It was stocked and well thought out. The kitchen was all electric except for the stovetop, which was gas. A combination light ceiling fan hung from the ceiling. The washer and dryer were in a neat little room of their own next to the back door. There was an island in the shape of an L that had a tile top that matched the other counter tops. The floor was a beautiful Spanish tile and was spotless. She noticed a small locked box on the island labeled "Cuss Box". It had a slot in it like a piggy bank and she asked, "What's this?"

Jim answered saying, "Dad thought we were saying too many bad words so he made that box. If you say a bad word, you have to write your name on one of these little stickers." He opened a drawer and showed her the stickers and continued, "You stick the sticker on a quarter and drop it in the box. The F word cost a dollar and the Lord's name in vain costs you five dollars. It's the honor system. If you say a bad word you have to put the money in even if nobody hears you. We open it in January to see who wins. I've won the last two years."

"And this was your idea?" she said looking at Dave.

"Yeah, but I'm getting better."

"Do you want to play the game with us?" Jim asked.

"Sure! But I can only play for a couple of months."

Jim gave her a high five and Molly asked, "Is D A M N a curse word?"

"Yes ma'am! It's a twenty-five cent word."

"Well, each of you boys owes the box a dollar."

"How do you figure?" Dave asked.

"Well, a while ago when we sang "Bad Bad Leroy Brown," I believe there were four choruses to that song, meanest man in the whole D A M N town. Am I right?"

Each of the boys went and got four quarters, put their autographs on them and dropped them in the box.

"You said them, too." Jim said.

"But I didn't know about the box then." and asked, "What happens to the money?"

Jim answered, "The person with the cleanest mouth gets to keep the money and the loser has to wash all the dishes for the month of January."

Molly laughed and said, "Well, get to cussing boys. I need the money and I hate washing dishes. I'll be listening like a hoot owl for your bad words."

There was a round kitchen table five feet in diameter that was supported by a single pedestal about fifteen inches in diameter that had four very graceful feet attached.

"I love this table! My grandmother had a table very similar to this. This brings back memories."

"Matter of fact" said Dave "This was my grandmother's table, solid maple."

There were six chairs around the table. There was no clutter in the kitchen. Everything had a place of its own. There was even a small broom closet, which housed the garbage can.

Jim said, "We have a dishwasher but since there's just the two of us we usually do the dishes by hand. We take turns."

"Maybe when you get those brothers and sisters you'll start using it more."

Dave added, "We have our own well. The water is sweet. We use the disposal some but most of the wet garbage we add to the compost pile. Some of it Jim feeds to his chickens and we put those scraps in this little pail. Slick takes care of most of the bones. Extra bread, apple cores and such we open the kitchen window and feed to the birds."

Dave opened the window and put out a scoop of sunflower seeds on the platform feeder. Ten seconds after he closed the window there was a Cardinal on the feeder.

"Money, money!" Molly said excitedly.

"Why'd you say that?" Jim asked.

"My Aunt Sue used to say that when she saw a red bird. She says that if you say, 'Money, Money' it's supposed to bring you good luck financially. My whole family says it now. Dad swears it works. Lots of times people call him big orders right after he sees one."

Jim pulled a list out of a drawer and showed it to her. It was a list of birds that had visited the kitchen feeder. There were twenty-six names on the list.

"Know what? One time a Baltimore oriole lit and ate on an orange for two days. But that only happened one time. He never came back. Another time there was a dove on the feeder and a hawk nailed him!"

"Come on!"

"Yes ma'am, I was washing dishes and there was a big flash of wings and he had him. I ran outside and the hawk was on the ground standing on him. I yelled at him and he flew off carrying the dove. There were feathers everywhere. Dad saw him."

"I see a crow visited your feeder. Did you shoot him with your double barreled 12 gauge?"

"No! But dad got after him with a slingshot. We don't like crows because sometimes they try to get the baby Martins out of the house and they rob our pecans. Dad hunts them with a shotgun, but they're so smart they know when you have a gun and they won't let you get close enough to shoot. We just scare them off mostly."

Molly turned to Dave and said, "I just love your home. It's warm and has a lot of personality. Who designed it?"

"You're looking at him."

"You seem to have thought of everything!"

"There are still a lot of little things that could be done to make it more of a home. Pictures, lamps, end tables, things like that. And plants! My mom used to have some of the prettiest houseplants. We need some of those."

"Why don't you get Jackie to help you?"

"Well, Jackie's idea of decorating is 18th century cherry wood, crystal chandeliers, Persian rugs, and very expensive stuff. That's not what I'm looking for out here. I'm trying to get back to basics and kind of live off the land. I'll probably never be rich but will do OK. Make enough money that I can buy wine with corks in the bottles rather than screw on tops. Maybe I'll marry rich." He said smiling.

"Not with your looks! You pig!" she said laughing.

On the east wall of the kitchen was a large map of the world. She commented, "I believe that's the largest map I've ever seen. Where in the world did you get it?"

"I ordered it from a map company. Its five by nine feet and it's mounted on plywood. We have a lot of fun with it; one of my better ideas, if I do say so."

"Want to play a game of WORLD?" Jim asked.

"What's WORLD?"

Jim went to the map and picked up three darts that were on a little shelf at the top.

"We play this all the time. I'm pretty good. Closest to the target wins. First game will be a practice game. You go first."

"What's the target?

"Snowy River Country."

"Where's that?"

"Australia."

Molly threw. "Thunk!"

"You hit India" Jim said.

Dave threw next.

"New Zealand!" said Jim.

"I'm impressed" said Molly. "You seem to know your geography pretty well."

"You wouldn't believe it!" Dave answered, "He never forgets where he hits. We play almost every day."

Jim threw, "Bingo, a direct hit."

"Nice shot, Bud, but that was a practice round."

"I like this game! Let's play again."

"What's your target?" Jim asked.

"Texas!"

They all hit the target and Jim said, "No winner. It's a tie."

"I'll pick the target this time" said Dave. "Loser washes dishes tonight. Target is Easter Island."

"Where is it?" she asked.

"You can't shoot 'till you know where the target is. You have to look it up. That's the rule" and he showed her the "World Atlas" on the table.

Molly looked it up and read, "A small island off the coast of Chile approximately 2,100 miles in the Pacific." She went to the map and pinpointed the target and said, "OK, I'm ready!"

"It's the island where they found all those giant stone statues." Jim added.

"Thanks for the history lesson, Professor Jim."

Jim and Molly both threw and each was about five inches off target. Dave was the clear winner. Jim grabbed a piece of string that was hanging from the map and did a measurement to determine the loser.

"Beat you by a half inch."

Molly looked at Dave who was holding up the big L loser sign, which he made with his thumb and forefinger on his forehead. He was grinning.

"Why you stinker!" she said. "This is war! Let's play again Mr. Smarty Pants."

"Later!" he said. "We got a few chores to do before it gets dark. Jim, you need to tend your chickens and while you're doing that I'll put up the boat and the camping gear. Maybe Molly can put the fish in the icebox and take the perishables out of the Igloo. Then we'll all get cleaned up and have a campfire."

"Sounds like a plan!" Molly answered.

Dave left the kitchen to drive the boat around to the garage. Molly asked Jim if it would be OK to start a load of wash because everything she had needed washing.

"Sure!" he answered and he showed her where everything was and the soap they used.

"Do you think your uncle might have a robe I might wear while my duds are washing?"

"Yes ma'am" and he led her to Dave's closet.

The closet was a large walk-in and on a bar were about thirty white shirts on hangers and at least fifteen or so pair of Wrangler jeans. On the floor were five pairs of boots in a neat row. There was little else hanging. She saw a black suit and a blue sports coat and maybe a couple pair of slacks.

She asked in astonishment, "Is this all he wears?"

"Just about!" he answered, "White shirts, Wranglers, and Red Wings."

"What's a Red Wing?"

"Boots! See this pair here, these are his dress blacks; these are his dress browns; these are his ruff outs; these are his working boots; and these are his insulated hunting boots. This pair here is eleven years old. You can't wear'em out. They're the best! Winter time he wears these old chamois shirts and this old blue sweater Red gave him."

"Who's Red?"

"One of his old fishing buddies."

She spotted a white terry cloth robe and borrowed it along with the blue sweater. When she got back to the kitchen, she saw that the coolers had been brought inside. She put the perishables in the icebox and put the fish in a large zip lock bag in the freezer. Next she took a wonderful hot soaking bath. She couldn't find any shampoo and washed her hair with a bar of Ivory soap as a last resort. "What the heck!" she thought. "At least I'll smell good."

After the bath, she went downstairs to check on the laundry. The boys were in the kitchen. She was wearing his monogrammed robe and her hair was wet.

Dave commented, "Nice doo!"

Molly answered, "I believe it's what you call my "wet rat" look! I borrowed your robe, hope you don't mind."

"I don't, but it might tick Jackie off. She gave it to me."

"Well, thanks, Jackie. You have good taste!"

"Say Jim, I couldn't find any shampoo in your bathroom. Where do you hide it?"

Jim answered, "We don't buy shampoo, we use Ivory for everything."

"Cavemen, that's what you all are! Genies have to have shampoo. Pudd'n too!"

Dave broke in; "We normally do wash on Tuesdays."

Molly answered, "Well, all my Victoria Secrets, which by the way are no secrets to you Bozos, needed a little cleaning. No chance you guys would have a hair dryer?"

Dave wagged his head no and Molly said, "Stupid question! Don't know why I asked!"

She asked Jim for a pen and a piece of paper, which he got for her. She wrote, SHORT LIST and on it she wrote,

1. Shampoo
2. Conditioner
3. Hair dryer

"If you boys need to add anything to the list please do. I'd like to go to town sometime tomorrow if you're going."

"We need orange juice!" said Jim.

Molly put down # 4. Orange Juice

Dave and Jim couldn't take their eyes off Molly. New things were happening. Washing on Sunday, a short list, shampoo! What next?

"I can feel you boys gawking at me. You all better get cleaned up or I'm going to eat the whole loaf of bread all by myself."

The boys started for the showers and as they left the room she said, "Chop, Chop!"

Back in Dave's room, Jim asked, "What's Chop, Chop?"

"I think it means get a move on it in Chinese."

Jim showered first and after he dried off he said, "Guess what? All my clothes are upstairs."

"Well, go get some. She won't mind but knock before you go in."

Jim was back in a jiffy with an armload of clothes. "Guess what! We got a system. Whenever I go upstairs, I'm supposed to knock first and then say, "Permission to come on deck ma'am," and if it's OK she says, permission granted."

After he finished dressing, he went outside and started hooking Slick up to the travois. Dave was just a few steps behind him and started loading a medium sized cooler. A bottle of Hawaiian punch for Jim and a couple of bottles of Chardonnay for the big folks. He added ice, a sleeve of Ritz crackers, a hunk of baby Swiss cheese, a few bunches of green grapes, a couple of apples, a small tub of butter, a knife, napkins, paper plates and the loaf of homemade bread.

Molly came outside just as Jim was strapping the cooler to the travois and she asked, "What's this?"

"I'm training Slick to be like an Indian work dog. This is a travois. He's going to pull the cooler to the campfire for us."

"I'm impressed, Slick. You are a dog of many talents" and she knelt down and gave him a few pats on the head.

Molly had on her warm-up pants, a white cotton tee, and a case of the Ivory frizzes on her head. Dave suggested she get a jacket because it was a little cooler with a breeze coming off the lake. She went upstairs and returned wearing the blue sweater.

Dave said, "Hey, I've got a sweater that looks just like that one."

"Finders keepers! I'm sure old Red won't mind," and she gave him a flirty grin.

CHAPTER 6

ONE LUMP PLEASE

The campfire area was near the lake, which was about five hundred yards from the house. The sun had just set but there was still enough light to see the path, which zigzagged, through the hay field. The path had been recently mowed.

"I like the path! This would have been hard walking in the field."

Dave said, "Every week or two we ride the mower to the lake and back, same way from the house to the highway. I usually walk to the highway each morning to get the paper but sometimes I ride the mower and cut the grass down around the Crepe Myrtles. A few trips each month is all it takes. I'm trying to keep the upkeep of this place to a minimum but it still mounts up. Jim's turning out to be good help and John helps me when he can. When the hay's ready, we work like Trojans, cutting and bailing, stacking and delivering. Fall we're busy with the pecans and wintertime we sit around like chipmunks hoping we've put enough acorns in the bank to keep us going 'till next year."

Jim led the way with Slick heeling and pulling the travois. Jim kept encouraging him by saying, "Good dog, Slick! Good dog!" Slick was enjoying the attention and the work was no problem for him. Pudd'n walked beside him and also seemed to be nudging him on.

Molly enjoyed the walk and the view of the lake was thrilling. The north side and the east side of the lake had trees right down to the shoreline. There was a small grove of trees to the left of them on the west bank. As they approached the lake a few Mallards took off and headed to the south end, as did a large white Heron. The lake was alive with noises. Bass were striking, minnows jumping, frogs croaking, and a few birds flew by that made a sound that sounded like it should be coming from a jungle.

"What in the world was that?" she asked.

Dave laughed and said, "Wood Ducks!"

"I thought ducks quacked."

"Not Wood Ducks, they squeal."

The campfire area was on the west side of the lake and close to the grove of trees and about 100 feet from the water's edge. The path led them to a covered wagon.

Molly said, "What in the world, a covered wagon!"

Jim said, "It's a prairie schooner. It's the kind of wagon the pioneers used on the Oregon Trail. Uncle Dave built it. Want to see it?"

"You bet!" she answered.

Jim unhitched the harness from Slick and said, "Good Dog" one more time. He climbed up on the wagon and said, "Come on up!"

Molly and Dave both climbed up and Jim turned on a battery-powered lantern that was hanging from one of the bows.

"Awesome!" said Molly.

"I got the plans from a historical society and built it pretty much to scale except that I did a little innovation on the back and made a chuck box. The original Conestoga Wagons were watertight because they had to ford rivers, but this one isn't. I found the wheels and axles in Oklahoma and got an awning company to make the canvas cover. The braces for the canvas were the hardest part. I made them out of willow."

"We've slept in it before!" Jim added.

"What's this?" she asked "This doesn't look too authentic" pointing to a small icebox.

Dave laughed and said, "No, it doesn't. It's run on propane. We keep a few things out here because we cook out pretty much."

"Why is it locked?"

"Well, one time a coon learned how to open it so we started locking it."

"Want to see inside?" Jim asked.

"Sure!" and Jim dialed the combination and opened the icebox.

Molly looked inside and saw a couple six packs of beer, a bottle of wine and also catsup, mayo, mustard, peanut butter, bacon, butter, jelly, and a few other odds and ends.

"I thought you didn't drink beer."

"Well, I keep it around because sometimes the guys loading hay like to have a cold one at the end of the day. I keep it mostly for John. He likes it and Shelley won't let him drink in front of the kids."

"Know what? We got a club. It's called the Chuck Wagon Club and only members of the club get to know the combination to the icebox."

"How does one get to be a member of the Chuck Wagon Club?" she asked.

"You have to get nischeated!" "What's that word? Dad"

"Initiated," Dave answered.

"Yeah, you have to be initiated."

"How do you do that?"

"You have to spend the night at the campfire all by yourself. You only get two matches. Do you want to join?"

"Sure!"

"When?" Jim asked.

"Let me think about it a few days. OK if Pudd'n stays with me?"

"Sure! She'll help keep the coyotes away."

"Come on! You're just trying to scare me."

Dave made a howling sound like a wolf and she said, "You guys don't scare me one bit."

"You have to sleep on the ground!"

There were two fifty-five gallon plastic drums in the rear of the wagon and Molly asked what was in the drums. Jim lifted the lids and showed her. "We keep the bedrolls and polypads in one and boat cushions and lifejackets in the other, also bathing suits and some raingear."

They got out of the wagon and Jim showed her the side storage boxes which contained tools, ropes, bug spray, a set of horseshoes and washers for pitching.

"Pretty neat, boys," and she asked the question, "Is Jackie a member of the club?"

"Are you kidding? She's afraid of her own shadow," Jim said as he opened the chuck box to show her. The contents of the box were hidden by a ply board cover about two feet high and four feet long. The lid was hinged on the bottom and held open by a small brass chain on each end. It provided a perfect workspace and was just the right height. The way the lip was constructed, even a blowing rain could not get inside the chuck box. It too was locked with a combination lock, which Jim said was the same combination as the icebox. He unlocked the lid and showed her the inside of the box. There was a set of old timey canisters with rubber seals and wire tops. She could see flour, sugar, cornmeal and coffee. The box didn't have as many items as the camping box but she could see it was well thought out and most of the essentials were there. There was a gas stove that was connected to the same propane bottle that ran the icebox. She spotted a small box that had X-ACTO printed on one end and she asked, "What's this?"

"That's my carving knives and my cork box. Me and Dad make our own corks." And he opened the box and showed her its contents. There were several pieces of wood, each about an inch in diameter and six inches long. "These are cypress roots. They're real light and they float real good. They're easy to carve. We cut off the barbs on hooks and stick the eyes in each end for the line to go through. Then we paint them so they won't get water logged." Molly noticed that there were several bottles of nail polish that they used for painting. She picked one up and said, "Oh my God! Who made this one?" and she held up a cork about five inches in length of a very voluptuous woman.

Jim laughed and said, "Dad carved that one. He calls it his Dolly Parton cork. You get it?"

"Yeah, I get it!"

"He's not through painting it though. He has to get some yellow paint for the hair."

Molly admired his workmanship. He had painted her pleasing personalities pink and he had put a tiny dot of red on their points.

"What about this tall skinny cork?"

"That's what dad calls his Lyle Lovett cork. It's for white perch. Know what? Dad wonders how anybody that ugly can sing so pretty. He has all his CD's. He says he would sing for free if he could sing like that."

"When are you going to get that fire going?" Dave asked and said, "Chop Chop!"

Jim grabbed the matches that were kept in a glass jar in the chuck box and started gathering wood. The fire pit was a circle about three feet across and one foot high. Dave had made it out of flagstone and mortared it together. There was an iron pipe on the outside of the pit that had a grill that could be swung over the pit for grilling a steak or it could be swung to the outside when not needed.

"I like your pit. I guess you made it?"

"Yes ma'am, kind of out of necessity. Can't be too careful about grass fires if you're a hay farmer"

"Good point!"

There were four Adirondack chairs around the fire pit that were real works of art. "I guess you made these chairs too?"

"Yes ma'am."

"You're kind of a jack of all trades. Is there anything you can't do?"

"Lots of things."

"Shelley said you'd make a good catch. She's probably right if it weren't for your looks."

"Yeah!" he replied, "I was thinking the same thing about you." And they both laughed.

She enjoyed watching Jim start the fire. One match was all he needed. It was against the rules to use charcoal lighter fluid. He had it crackling in no time and added some larger pieces from a nearby woodpile.

"Nice fire, Jim!"

"Thanks," he said and added, "If you become a member of our club you can start your own campfire whenever you want, but you have to know the rules."

"What are the rules?"

"Well, you can't start a fire if the wind is too high and when you leave the campfire, you have to be sure it's out. We keep this bucket by the fire to get water from the lake."

"Good rule!" she said.

They all sat down to watch the fire and Molly said, "Since I have to wash the dishes tonight, I'd like to be pampered and waited on."

Jim jumped up and said, "Yes ma'am" and bowed and asked, "What can we do for your highness?"

"I'd like food and drink. Chop Chop!"

"Yes ma'am!" and he jumped up and went to the cooler. Dave also got up and took a bottle of wine from the cooler and went to the chuck box to open it. Molly watched him and made a note of where the wine opener was. Always nice to know where the wine opener is. Dave got two wineglasses from the cooler and poured each of them a glass.

Molly held her glass up and said, "I'd like to make a toast. A toast to the men who saved my life, a toast to the powerful fish and a toast to a perfect campfire." and they clinked glasses.

Shortly after, Jim passed cheese and crackers and grapes.

"Thank you, Sir Jim. I will report to your master what good work you do!"

Jim and Dave were both in kind of awe. This was the first girl at their chuck wagon campfire other than Jackie, and this one was unpredictable. They didn't know what to say or do. Molly could feel them staring at her and said, "It wasn't so nice of you boys taking advantage of a damsel in the game of World. I want you to know that it won't happen again. Next time we play I plan to beat the pants off you bumpkins."

She held her glass high in the air and said, "Long live the Queen!"

Dave followed suit and held his glass up and said, "Long live the Queen!"

Jim not knowing exactly what to do but wanting to be a player held up his Hawaiian Punch and said, "Long live the Queen!"

They all had a laugh and Molly said; "Now I'd like the Royal Bread!"

Dave got the bread and the tub of butter. He got a knife and was just about to cut the bread when Molly said, "This is like the bread on picnics in foreign movies. You can't cut it. You have to tear it."

Dave tore off a chunk and passed it to Molly and another to Jim. The boys had never had so much fun eating bread. Molly too!

Dave had been right about it cooling down at night and she said, "Thanks for telling me to bring the sweater. It feels good."

"Yeah!" he said, "I didn't want you to get hypothermia again and have to throw you back in the bedroll."

"Yeah, me either! No need to get baptized a third time," she laughed.

"How about some dessert?" Jim proposed.

"What have you got in mind?" Molly asked.

"Baked apples! You core'em, put in Red-Hots, and fill the hole with brown sugar. Then you wrap them in tin foil and put them in the fire. We do it all the time."

"That sounds good but I'm too full right now. Will you give me a rain check?"

"What's a rain check?"

"It means another time."

"OK!"

"Me, too, Bud, Let's do it another night. The bread filled me up."

"Tell me about your lake. I couldn't see it real well because it got dark so fast. I thought I saw fish striking."

"You did!" Jim answered, "We've got bass, brim, white perch, goggle eyes, and catfish. We put bass in about five years ago and they're starting to get big. I'll take you fishing tomorrow if you want to."

"I like to fish but I don't have very good luck. Dad always said I made too much noise in the boat."

"Well, you will here. There's a fish behind every bush. We catch and release unless we're going to have a fish fry."

"You're on!" she said.

Dave added, "I'm really proud of the lake. It was the perfect spot. The highway needed dirt and I needed a dam. We donated the dirt and they built my dam and rocked my road. It was a win win deal for everybody. The county was happy, the state was happy and we're happy. They got a jillion yards of dirt, and we got a jillion dollar road and a two jillion dollar lake. Would you believe we had an offer to buy the lake plus fifty acres for more than we paid for the whole farm?"

"Would you sell?"

"No way, I've fallen in love with the place. This is the one thing in my life that I know God is pleased with. You won't believe how many waterfowl visit us during the winter. One morning I came down to the lake about dawn. I walked through those trees right there and when I got to the lake there were about forty Canadian Geese on the lake."

"Come on?"

"They looked like 747's on the water. I couldn't believe how big they were."

"Did you shoot them?"

"There was a time in my life when I would have, but when they land on your very own lake something came over me, and I gave up hunting ducks and geese. Nowadays waterfowl need friends and I've decided to be one. You know, if you shoot them they fly off and you don't see them anymore. But if you don't shoot them, they stick around and you get to enjoy them for a long time. Those Canadas stayed with us about three weeks. I swear when those geese swam by me that morning one looked over at me and said, "Nice job on the lake."

Dave said, "Sorry, I didn't mean to ramble on so long."

Molly said, "I enjoyed hearing about the geese. You know I kind of got a similar feeling when that Carolina Wren lit on the hammock. I felt a bond between us."

"That's it! That's the feeling I got, definitely a bond with the geese. They've come back for the last three years. I don't know if they are the same geese but I think they are."

"They've got to be!" she replied.

"I kind of think they are too. They act like they own the place."

"The offer for the land has really started me thinking. We could probably make a better living developing land with small lakes than hay farming. Two or three home run land deals would be nice. I can feel the town moving this way and property values are bound to go up. Hay farming is hard work. Last year we sold close to eleven hundred bales and that was a lot of work. Cut, bale, stack, haul, unload, fertilize, and pray for rain to make it grow, pray for dry weather to harvest it, and pray for cold weather so the ranchers will need more of it. It wouldn't be hard to talk me out of the hay business. Helps pay the bills though, and we'll do whatever we have to do to keep the place together. Believe it or not I kind of get a high off seeing the bales in the field. The work is rewarding and it's only for a few months each year. Do you know how to drive a tractor?"

"No, but I'm willing."

"Good! Dave answered, "Because Jim and I usually work our genies. We don't let them sit around and drink wine all day."

"All work and no play make Jack a dull boy!" she added.

Dave suggested they turn in for the night and they all agreed. While Jim was hooking Slick up to the harness he said, "Maybe I could teach Pudd'n to be an Indian work dog too."

Molly answered him saying, "You Indian braves are all alike. Make the women do all the work."

Molly did a little KP and loaded the cooler onto the travois. Dave put out the fire and they started to the house. "Do you think we'll cut hay tomorrow?" she asked.

"Nope!" Dave answered, "It's supposed to rain and the humidity and the dew point will be too high for a few days. We'll work around the house, make jelly, pay bills, go to town, and maybe you could go to Mrs. Perkins and borrow her computer to order ours. We'll just play it by ear."

When they got back to the house, Dave got an extra dog box he had and put it on the front porch next to Slick's for Pudd'n and said, "The dogs always sleep outside."

Molly said, "I don't know if Pudd'n will sleep in that thing."

Dave answered saying, "I don't know why they like these boxes but they do. A friend of mine, Jack Ormand, put me on to them. He says he thinks it gives them a feeling of security. They know they're protected on three sides and they like that feeling. He has three yellow Labs and they love them. You'd have to witness it to believe it." He put an old blanket in the box and called Pudd'n. She got inside the box with very little coaxing and lay down. It was kind of like magic. Dave told Slick to kennel up, and Slick got in his box and lay down. The dogs were pooped. Their full day of play and the retrieves in the lake that Jim had them do had taken its toll.

"Well I'll be!" said Molly, "I've seen it all now. You're a dog whisperer too!" and they went inside and turned off the front porch light.

When they got in the kitchen she said, "Where are all the dishes I'm supposed to wash?" Dave reached in the cooler and pulled out the two wine glassed they had used and handed them too her. They all had a good laugh and Molly said, "Sometimes losing is not so bad!

"How about another game of World, loser washes dishes after breakfast." She asked.

"I'll play!" said Jim. "What's the target?"

"Baton Rouge! I used to have a sorority sister from there."

"Where's that?"

"Look it up!" she said and Jim went to the atlas and in a few seconds said, "Found it! It's in Louisiana." He went to the map and quickly found the target. "Baton Rouge means red stick in French."

"I knew that!" she said, "It's also where the tigers live."

"What kind of tigers?" he asked, "We don't have tigers in the U.S."

"The L.S.U. Tigers!"

Jim went first and hit Mississippi. Dave dropped one in the Gulf of Mexico close to the Louisiana shoreline and Molly hit Shreveport. Dave was the clear winner. Jim and Molly agreed to have a shoot off for doing the dishes.

Molly asked, "What's the target?"

"France!"

Jim said, "I'll go first, I know that target." As he was aiming, he kind of did a little dance and sang "All the girls in France wear tissue paper pants" and he fired.

Molly went over to the map to see where he had hit but really she went to verify the target. "Nice shot!" she said, "I believe you hit the Eiffel Tower. I kind of believe I'm going to be doing the dishes in the morning." She fired and drowned in the Atlantic.

"I didn't know the girls in France wore tissue paper pants!" she said.

"That's what Uncle Dave says."

"Well, I'm sure he would know!" she said looking at him. "He seems to be an authority on about everything." And she added, "You know, I don't think I'm going to be tutoring Jim much on geography. He's light years ahead of his class in this subject. This map was really a good idea. It makes learning fun. By the way, what time do we get up around here?"

Jim answered, "Early! Don't worry about setting an alarm. You'll know. Dad always gets up first and makes coffee and cooks the bacon."

"Good! I'll have my coffee in bed, one lump please."

Jim and Dave looked at each other with a surprised look on their faces and Dave said, "Dream on, maybe a lump on your head!"

Molly gave them one of her best flirt looks and started up the stairs. "I'll see you yo yo's in the morning."

She was asleep almost as soon as she hit the sheets. She was awakened about two in the morning by the sound of rolling thunder in the northeast. There was a drop in the temperature and the breeze coming through the window was chilly. All she had to keep warm was a sheet and she pulled it up around her neck but she was still cold. She knew she should get up and scrounge around for a blanket but she couldn't seem to make herself do it.

The thunder also woke up Dave and his mind raced about several things at the same time. Were the windows in the truck up? Had he closed the shop doors? Looked like the weatherman was right, they would get rain. Wonder how Molly is? He lay there thinking and finally his kidneys won and he had to get up. His comforter had hidden the fact that it had gotten much cooler and he couldn't wait to get back in the warm bed. He glanced at Jim to make sure he was covered up good and he was. He started thinking of Molly again and wondered it she was warm enough. It dawned on him that Jim was using the comforter off his own bed from upstairs and that Molly probably had only a sheet.

He went to the closet and got a comforter and went upstairs. When he got to the top of the stairs the door was closed and he paused. Should he knock or should he say, "Permission to come on deck." He decided she was bound to be sleeping and he opened the door and went in. She was sleeping lightly and thought she heard the door open and then a creak in the floor. She decided to play like she was sleeping. Dave spread the comforter over her and said softly, "Thought you might be needing this" and left.

The magic of the down comforter started to work immediately and she warmed up quickly. She tried to remember the last time someone had tucked her in. She couldn't. There was another roll of thunder that was much closer and soon the rain started. The sound of it on the tin roof was very relaxing and she drifted off. About sunrise the rain had stopped and she started to hear the Martins singing their little tunes just as Jim said she would. The peace of the morning was broken by a loud chant from the kitchen. "The sun is up, the sun is up, the birds that sing are on the wing, the sun is up!"

Dave had left her door open and the words carried up the stairs loud and clear. She thought, that must be what Jim was talking about when he said I'd know when it was time to get up. Surly this was a joke. It was much too early to get up. She was eager to appear raring to go so she decided to get up. She was just about to slide out of the bed when there was a knock at her doorway.

"Who is it?"

"Permission to come on deck?"

"Permission granted."

Pudd'n entered first wagging her tail and ran to Molly. Jim was right behind her carrying a small tray with a cup of coffee and a small vase of flowers.

"Dad said to tell you this is one lump."

"How sweet! Say, how'd Pudd'n get in? I thought you didn't let dogs in the house."

"Oh, that's just at night. We always let Slick in, in the morning for a piece of bacon."

"I heard your Martins this morning. You were right. They do sing real pretty and thanks for the flowers. I love being spoiled. Let me get dressed and I'll be down in a minute."

"Yes ma'am!" and he and Pudd'n went downstairs.

She thought about wearing the robe downstairs but decided against it and quickly put on her jogging outfit. She thought, "I've got to get to town today and buy some new duds. I've got to get a new look. They've seen everything I have at least three times. Maybe he'll let me borrow his truck today."

When she got downstairs she saw that Dave had cooked bacon, toasted biscuits, and set three places at the table. He was browning some chopped potatoes in a skillet and the smell was to die for.

"Thanks for the coffee in bed and the flowers. I was just joking about the 'in bed' part."

"We aim to please around here. Us Shepherds always take care of our flock."

"Well, thanks!"

"How'd you sleep?"

"Like a baby! And guess what?"

"What?" Jim asked.

"Last night a little gremlin snuck into my room and covered me up with a nice down comforter." And she looked at Jim.

"Wasn't me!" Jim said.

Molly looked at Dave who turned his palms up and shrugged his shoulder like, "I don't know either."

She smiled and said, "Well, whoever it was. Thank you! I think I was about to go into hypothermia again. I've never slept so well. Say, what was all this business I heard about 'The sun is up. The sun is up!'"

Jim laughed and said, "That's our alarm clock. Dad says it every morning."

"Where in the world did you hear that?"

Dave said, "Back in my high school days I used to go duck hunting with a friend whose family owned a duck camp. The camp was first class and would sleep about seventeen or eighteen. The Ohmstedes used it mostly to entertain customers and sometimes if they had an opening Buddy would ask me to go. Sometimes they would be short a family member and they would ask me to be a guide. It was a blast. Dr. Stuart Weir was a close friend of theirs and an avid duck hunter. They asked him to go almost every time. He looked kind of like a leprechaun. He had gray hair and always seemed to have a little smirk on his face. You couldn't help but like him. He was a hoot. The Ohmstedes always took a cook with them named Jerry who was always the first one up in the morning. He would make coffee first and then start on breakfast. Jerry would always wake up Dr. Weir first. Dr. Weir would get dressed, pour himself a cup of coffee and come into the bunkroom and sing, 'The sun is up! The sun is up! The birds that sing are on the wing. The sun is up!'"

"First time I ever heard it I could have killed him. Almost everyone else felt the same way, especially the ones who drank too much and stayed up till two in the morning playing poker. Later it became funny and I looked forward to hearing him. He did it every morning."

"Sounds like a colorful character."

"That he was. He was a crack shot also. Most of the hunters thought the prize duck was the greenhead and next was probably the pintail drake and any one shooting the female of the species was considered a bad guy and got made fun of. Dr. Weir would only shoot green wing teal and he would only shoot the drakes. The limit back then was ten but he would only shoot five. People would ask him why he didn't shoot the limit and he'd say he didn't want to be a hog. He was probably the first person I'd met really concerned about conservation. He was an inspiration to me. He passed on a recipe for cooking teal that is the best duck recipe I've ever tasted. It was so simple I thought he was joking until I tried it. He would take five handpicked teal and stuff them with apple and onion. He would salt and pepper them and place

THE HOOT OWL MAN

them in a pot on top of the stove. He'd pour in orange juice to the top of the birds and cook them on low heat for exactly two hours with a top on the pot."

"Orange juice? Come on!"

"Yep! I swear, and the orange juice would turn to brown gravy and you'd serve the duck on a bed of rice. They were so tender that the meat just fell off the carcass. I've tried it and it works. People who don't even like duck will ask for a second helping. How do you like your eggs, Queen Molly?"

"Over medium."

"Gotcha!"

She watched Dave ladle a small amount of butter into a small skillet like they use at a Waffle House. "I'm impressed!" she said, "You're a regular little ole short order cook."

Jim said, "Dads a nut about his eggs. Everything else can be served warm but the eggs have to be served hot."

"How about you, Bud?" Dave asked.

"Scrambled, scattered, smothered."

"Got it." And he poured Molly's eggs on a plate and handed it to her. "Everything else is on the table; go ahead and start."

The breakfast was delicious. The eggs were perfect. Was she really here? Was this really happening to her? Dreamboat man, perfect son, perfect home, perfect lake, clean air. She pinched herself. It hurt! This was real.

Molly gathered the dishes when they were all through because it was her time to wash. They didn't know it but if everything went according to her secret little plan they would never have to wash dishes again. When she was through, she poured herself another cup of coffee and joined Dave on the east porch. The sun was touching some low clouds over the trees across the lake and the view was spectacular.

"Isn't the sunrise pretty?" she said.

"I ordered that for you. I wanted your first morning to be special."

"Well it was! Coffee in bed, flowers, perfect eggs, Martins singing to me, gorgeous sunrise, sitting on a porch swing drinking coffee not a bad way to start the day!"

Then she asked, "What's our plan for today?"

"Well, I was thinking we might make a round of jelly before we get all hot and sweaty. Then we'll plant the plants Mrs. Neel gave us. Then maybe we'll go to town and fill your short list or if you want to you can take the truck yourself."

"Would you mind? I'd love to shop a little. I'll take Jim with me to show me around."

"Deal! What you say we start on the jelly?"

"I've never made jelly before. You'll have to show me how."

Dave went through the whole process with her but making sure she did most of the work. They boiled the jars and lids, measured the sugar and set everything up in the order they would be using it. They cooked the mayhaws and strained the juice through some cheesecloth. Next they put the juice in a copper kettle that Dave was quite proud of. He said that the pot came from France and that the copper helped the fruit juices and the pectin do magical things to produce a better jelly. They added Sure Jell and brought it to a rolling boil while stirring constantly with a wooden spoon. Molly added the sugar and brought it back to a rolling boil for one minute. Dave removed the pot from the stovetop and let Molly fill the jars. After all the jars were filled, he had her invert them for five minutes and then stand them right side up again. Dave said, "Listen for a clicking sound from the jars. If they click, that means we did everything right."

"Does it always gel?" she asked.

"Most of the time by the next morning, but sometimes it may take a couple of weeks. Sometimes if you try to double a recipe it doesn't gel. That's happened to me a couple of times. We used undiluted juice so we shouldn't have any trouble."

A few of the jars clicked and Molly said, "This is fun!"

She saw the set of little labels that came with the jars and asked, "What do you want on the labels?" and she wished her name were Shelley.

Dave thought a minute and then took one of the circular labels and wrote MAYHAW JELLY in capital letters with the date under it. Around the curve of the circle he wrote, "by Molly by golly."

"Something like that!" he said.

"I love it!" she said, "I've got to send my mom and my grandma a jar. They won't believe it."

"Well, these are all yours. You picked them and you made the jelly. Jim and I would like a couple of 'by Mollys' to remember you by."

"Thanks!" she said and she felt a secret bond with Shelley as she remembered her saying to him, "You always make me feel so good."

They cleaned up the kitchen and Molly was on a jelly high. How could making jelly make you feel so good? Surely she was losing her mind. Maybe it had something to do with the instructor.

Next they planted the ginger plants and the gardenia bush. Molly was eager to help and got right in up to her elbows. Dave commented, "It seems like you know what you're doing."

"Well, my mom is a Master Gardener and I was around it so much that some of it probably rubbed off on me."

An idea clicked in Dave's head and he commented, "I've always wanted a bunch of plants on the porch and some vines growing on the post. Plants that aren't too much trouble and vines that were evergreens. Do you think that's something you might like to tackle?"

"What's my budget?"

"Cheap!"

"That's right up my alley. I'd like to try it."

"There's one vine I've been looking for called Bignonia that's an evergreen but I haven't been able to find it. My grandmother used to have it growing on her back porch. It had lavender flowers in the spring."

Molly had a plan now. Get them computerized and green up the place. She started thinking about some of the things she had observed and helped her mother do over the years. Why hadn't she been more observant?

When they finished with the planting she asked Dave for a short lesson in driving the pickup because it had been a long time since she had driven a stick shift. By the time they got to the highway she had it pretty much down pat and only ground the gears one time. They went a few miles on the highway and he gave her a lesson of starting on an incline because this move required a little extra finesse. She did fine and he was satisfied. He adjusted the side mirrors for her and moved the seat up a little.

When they got back to the house Dave started on some of his chores and Molly told Jim, "I think I'll go for a run."

"Can I go with you?" he asked.

Molly told him that she usually ran a long distance that would be too far for him but he was welcome to come if he promised to turn back when he got tired.

"Can I bring the dogs?"

"Sure, but we don't want them to get too tired so when you turn back they can go back with you. Deal?"

"Deal!"

Molly changed into her running outfit and came to the front porch and started doing a few warm-up exercises. Dave appeared and asked, "What's up?"

"Jim and I are going to take a little jog before we go to town. Want to join us?"

"No way! I'm allergic to running."

Molly laughed and said, "No pain, no gain."

Jim came out wearing gym shorts and called the dogs. Molly went inside to get a couple of bottles of water.

"Isn't she pretty?" Jim said.

"Yea buddy."

"I think she has pretty legs. Don't you?"

Dave was surprised by his sudden interest in girl's legs and answered him saying, "Yeah buddy! Like a racehorse! Good sticks! Just between you and me I'd say she's put together like a fine Swiss watch."

Jim was thinking about the Swiss watch part when Molly appeared with the water. "What are you two lugs talking about?"

"Sticks! Dave answered, "I was telling Jim that the wind had blown down a bunch of sticks in the orchard and we'd have to pick them up." He winked at Jim and the joggers were off.

Dave didn't know what to do. Her sticks had kind of unnerved him. He thought about a cold shower or maybe a dip in the lake. He settled for a glass of ice tea and a book on the porch.

Jim was back in about 45 minutes pretty much pooped. The dogs looked worse and went straight to the water bowl.

"Where's your partner, bud?"

"Still running, she runs five or ten miles! I quit after two. That was all I could go. She wasn't even breathing hard. Man, she knows all about running. She said she would teach me. Maybe I could be on the track team someday. Know what else? Pudd'n is in better shape than Slick. Slick and I ran out of gas about the same time. Pudd'n was still going strong. Did you know that man can run further than dogs? It has to do with the way they sweat. Dogs sweat through their tongues and get too hot. Man can even outrun wolves."

"I'll have to think on that one" and he went to get Jim something to drink. He was glad he hadn't gone with them. He probably couldn't have even gone the two miles.

They both sat staring at the road waiting for her return. About forty-five minutes later she showed up smiling and breathing easily. Her sweaty outfit showed that she had had a good workout.

"That was fun!" she said, "Running up the hill to the Indians almost did me in."

Dave said, "You ought to be ashamed of yourself!"

"Why?"

"You ran my little bunny's battery down. He's re-energizing right now, said you could outrun a pack of wolves."

"No I didn't!" Jim interrupted.

"Just kidding, he said you were a good runner." And he gave Jim a rub on the head and asked, "How about a glass of ice tea, one lump?"

"That would be nice! Thanks! Lemon if you have it."

She felt good. She had new status, a distance runner she was no longer a sissy girl. She had a secret hope that they would all be running together someday. "Everyone has different talents," she thought. She could easily outrun Dave but she knew he was strong as an ox and could do a thousand things she couldn't. She wondered if Jackie was a runner.

The cool down on the porch was perfect. Jim and the dogs came back to life. Molly suggested to Jim that they get cleaned up before they went to town.

Dave said, "I'll fix lunch."

"No bacon!" she snapped back.

He laughed and said, "No bacon!"

After showering and sprucing up she returned to the kitchen. Dave had cut up some fruit and was serving it up with pita bread and peanut butter.

While they were eating Dave suggested that they do the grocery shopping on the way back. He got the short list and added several things he knew they needed.

"Whatever you think we need get it, I've got a growing boy here," and he handed her his credit card.

"Well thank you kind Sir! I've always wanted to have fun with someone else's credit card. What's the max? How much fun can I have?"

"The computer and the groceries will just about do it in. Maybe enough left to get Jim a good pair of running shoes. He told me you said they were the most important thing about running, might as well start him out right."

CHAPTER 7

COUP DE GRACE

A s they drove, Jim critiqued her about everything. They decided to go to the Perkins first to order the computer. Mr. Perkins was at the church, but Mrs. Perkins was at home and delighted to let Molly use their computer.

She ordered a Gateway computer with even more features than she had on her own. A small business package, TurboTax, six months of AOL for free with the modem thrown in, and a Hewlett Packard combination printer, fax, scanner, and copier, the works, eight hundred, seventy-two dollars turnkey job. It was all in stock and would be shipped UPS within the next three days. Should arrive next Monday or Tuesday at the latest; freight was included in the price. Hewlett Packard would send a fifty-dollar rebate when they received the proof of purchase. She decided to blow the rest of her computer budget on the plant project.

As they were about to leave, she told Mrs. Perkins about Dave giving her the job of getting a bunch of plants going for his porch. Mrs. Perkins wanted to help and donated a giant plant of aloe vera that had out grown its pot and needed to be divided. She showed Molly how to divide it and told her how hardy they were and that they could take almost any weather except a hard freeze. She also told her of the plant's medicinal value and showed her how to apply the juice to a wound or burn. She gave her a beautiful hanging basket of an airplane plant, which she said she might want to divide to make several more hanging baskets or she could snip off the little airplanes that hung down. They would sprout if placed in dirt. She also gave Molly several wire hanging baskets that she wasn't using. She suggested that she buy a bag of sphagnum moss to line the baskets with before adding the potting soil. "You'll like these airplane plants. They're easy to grow. They do like water."

Molly thanked her and they were off to stop number two, which was the Neels. The Neels were glad to see them and Molly offered to drive Mrs. Neel to town to do some grocery shopping and to help charge the car up. She was thrilled with the offer and off they went in her car. Jim stayed with Mr. Neel to play with the puppies.

On the way Molly told Mrs. Neel how excited she was that Dave had given her the job of getting some plants for the porch and some evergreen vines for the porch. She described the porches to her and told her that the front porch faced south and the other porches were on the east and west sides.

"Sounds like you're going to need a lot of plants."

"Yes ma'am. After I saw what a green thumb you had I decided to ask you for some ideas."

"Honey!" she said, "You've asked the right person. After sixty years of gardening, I know what grows and doesn't grow in this part of Texas. When we get back to the house, I'll get you some starts of things that will make you feel like you're the Jolly Green Giant. How are you fixed for flower pots?"

"Zero, I'll have to buy a bunch."

"No you won't. Out behind the shed, I've got stacks of them from over the years. All sizes even got saucers to go under them. You're welcome to all you want and the price is right. I suggest you start with some Confederate Jasmine vines up the post. It's an evergreen that's easy to grow and the blooms smell nice."

They drove in silence a few miles. Molly could almost hear her thinking. She knew she had asked the right person.

On the way back from the grocery store they passed a nursery and Mrs. Neel suggested they stop. Fannie was familiar with where everything was and took Molly on a tour. Molly pulled a cart and whatever she suggested she put on the cart. The cart was full in no time and Molly told the owner that she would stop back by with the truck and pick everything up and probably get some more things that she just had to have.

When they got back Fannie showed her the flowerpots and told Herschel and Jim to load a bunch of them in the truck. "Get most of the large ones" she told them, "Can't ever have too many pots."

She got a shovel and took Molly with her to the flowerbeds. She had her dig up several large clumps of Asparagus Ferns. "This fern does well in pots or hanging baskets. They stay green all year. All you have to do is act like you're going to water it and it perks up." She had her dig some large clumps of Aspidistras and showed her how to divide them and prune back the bad leaves. "No flowers on these but nice to look at and the leaves are good in arrangements." She gave her some clumps of Maidenhair Fern and said, "This fern is hard to grow but once you get a stand, you'll be proud. It's great for arrangements and nice to look at. I pour a little blue on it once in a while which seems to make it happy." She dug up several types of begonias of different varieties and wrapped them in newspapers. She showed her how to pinch off the tops and said, "Just stick 'um in the dirt and get out of their way." She got starts of Leatherleaf Fern, Sego palms, and a vine called Yellow Jasmine that she said was not an evergreen but nice to have around because it was one of the first flowers to bloom in the spring and would make you feel good. She also got starts of Plumbago, Butterfly bush, Humming bird plant, Mexican Heather, and a few large clumps of liriope that she said look nice in pots.

Molly asked her if she had ever heard of a vine called Bignonia and Fannie led her to a trellis and pointed one out to her. "This in one of my most prized possessions. This one is probably close to forty years old." Molly told her of Dave's desire to have one but he hadn't been able to find one. Fannie scrounged around and found a few maverick shoots and had Molly dig them up.

"Oh thank you! He's going to be so pleased."

She had Molly dig up some nandina bushes and told her they were evergreens and they bloom and have red berries which the birds love, the leaves change colors and all you have to do is talk to them once in a while and they'll do fine. She suggested some hibiscus plants for the east and west porches because they love the sun. "They're good for color and they bloom all summer."

She showed her how to snip off the tops of impatiens and stick them in the ground. "Freeze will get them but they will come back next year. They like shade and water. You like that young man don't you?"

"Yes ma'am, I really do."

"Well, I can tell. It shows. You want to please. I'll be pulling for you."

"Thanks, I think he's committed but I'm not sure how much."

"Well," she said. "You seem to have put a twinkle in his eye. Herschel said he thinks Dave has an extra step is his get along whatever that means. I think this will be enough to get you started. You're welcome to more later if you need more."

"Wow!" She said, "I know he will be pleased, especially since they came out of your yard. He's really proud of the butterfly ginger plants you gave him. We planted them this morning and he invited me to come back in the fall to smell the blooms. I might just take him up on it."

They wheeled her garden cart back to the truck and loaded the plants. Mrs. Neel noticed that the boys hadn't loaded any saucers and she got them to put about fifty in the truck.

"These saucers are really important. They keep ants from coming through the hole in the bottom of the pot, they protect the porch and you won't have to water so often.

They thanked the Neels and were off to the nursery. She added several showstoppers that she just had to have and Dave's credit card didn't blink. They covered the plants with a tarp so they wouldn't get windblown.

Next stop was a Target where she got a hair dryer, a couple of outfits, a pair of pajamas, some slippers and a few pairs of unmentionables.

An Academy store was next where she got a couple of more running outfits and some fun clothes which she hoped would make her more interesting to Mr. Dave. She took care in choosing them. She was conservative on the top half of the outfits but didn't care if she let a little leg show. She knew the look she was going for, tasteful but a little sassy. She had caught Dave staring at her several times and she liked it. She loved the stalk of this new romance. She had never felt this way before. She needed a new "war" drobe because this was war. She wondered what the word wardrobe meant and made a mental note to look it up.

She helped Jim pick out a good pair of running shoes and a few pairs of good running socks to wick away moisture. She used her card on her stuff and Dave's on the shoes.

Last stop was the grocery store and she let Jim do most of the shopping because he knew what they liked. She tried to get him to settle for a different brand of bacon that looked healthier but he said his dad would skin him alive if he didn't buy this brand. She pulled a few of her favorites she thought she would try on them. She also got some chocolate chips because she wanted to try her secret recipe on the doubting Thomases. She found shampoo, conditioner, lipstick, a ladies razor, and several other girlie things to make her irresistible. She hoped!

The store had a very nice cosmetic section and she decided to browse it looking for secret ammunition. She laughed to herself and wondered if they had a perfume that smelled like ginger lilies. That would probably put the coup de grace on him. She decided to pull out all the stops and bought a small bottle of Chanel No.5 perfume. She had never used it before but remembered that one time her dad told her if she ever wanted to drive a man crazy to use it. He said that her mom had used it on him and two months later they were engaged. Why not, and thought "funny coincidence that I've got two months left on my genie contract."

She paid for these purchases with Dave's card and wondered if he would check the receipt. She thought, "wonder what his reaction would be if he sees the perfume on the bill. Pheromones to help "do him in" paid for with his own money. It would be kind of like shooting yourself in the foot with your own gun. This is funny!" She thought. Maybe this is an oxymoron. She wasn't quite sure of the meaning of oxymoron and decided to look this word up as well. Maybe they would all laugh about it someday in each other's arms.

They loaded the truck and were off. On the way home, Jim said, "I forgot something."

"What?"

"Some stamps and stationery, I ran out."

"Do you want to turn around?"

"Naw, I'll get them next time we go in. I might have a few left."

"Are you going to write a letter?"

"No, I need to write a thank you note. Dad and I always try to write a note or two on Tuesday nights."

"That's nice. Who are you going to write to?"

"Not sure yet, Dad and I usually talk it over. Dad will probably write to Mrs. Neel for the plants and I'll probably write Mrs. Perkins for the cookies."

"Your Uncle Dave is teaching you some good manners. Good manners never go out of style."

"Yes ma'am! He says notes make people feel better and we should write them whenever we can. Know what? He says that a good letter is one of the most powerful things in the world. Do you believe that?"

"Probably so, your uncle is a pretty smart man. He's probably right."

"Dad says when you write a thank you note you're counting your blessings."

"Wow," thought Molly, "nine years old and writing thank you notes." What great values this gentle man was teaching him. It dawned on her that she was behind in her letter writing. She needed some stationery of her own and she slowed down and did a U turn on the highway. "We'll go back. It won't take long."

She thought to herself, "I have a few blessings to count also." They would all write together.

When they got home there was a note in the kitchen from Dave. He was in the orchard doing some spraying and would be back about dark. She liked the way they wrote notes to each other. Dave had hung a bulletin board in the kitchen that was half cork and half the kind you write on with erasable markers. They were both in the habit of checking it when they came to the kitchen. Jim was good about writing down important numbers for Dave's business. Jim said they were on the buddy system. "You always have to know where your buddy is," he had told her. "It's important when you live on a farm."

Dave had gotten in the habit of carrying his cell phone for business reasons and also for safety. He told Molly he wished she would take her phone with her when she ran on the highway for safety reasons. She told him she would think about it and thanked him for his concern but she thought it would be in the way. He had said, "Well if you won't carry a phone would you at least carry a spray can of mace." She agreed and said laughing, "I might spray you if you get too frisky!"

After a glass of iced tea she told Jim, "I'd love you forever if you'll help me with the plants. I'd really like to get some potted before your uncle gets back."

He said he would and she drove the truck around by the carport under a big shade tree.

Jim got a couple of sawhorses and made a makeshift table for her to work on. They unloaded the pots and saucers and the twenty bags of potting soil. Jim ran the hose around to her and got her some rubber gloves, a bucket, and a brush. She scrubbed each of the pots and saucers with a strong Clorox solution and when she rinsed them off; they came back to life and looked like new.

Mrs. Neel had given her several broken pots for covering the holes and she told Jim to get a hammer and break them in small pieces. He did it and she added a few to the bottom of the pots. Jim got a wheelbarrow and poured in several bags of potting soil, which made it easier for her to fill the pots. After each plant was potted, she watered them and added sphagnum moss to the top of the pots to prevent the potting soil from splattering and for a more professional look. After they were watered the plants seemed to perk up immediately.

"You do good work!" she said, "You work chop, chop!"

Jim never knew that work could be such fun. He went to the shop and came back with a four-wheeled cart that had large rubber tires and could be easily pulled across the grass. Together they loaded several plants on the cart and Molly told him what a great idea the cart was.

Dave walked up just as they were finishing the east porch.

"I like! Good job!" he said.

"Your wishes are my command. If you don't like the way they're arranged, we can move them."

"No!" he said, "They're perfect! They make the porch come to life. I couldn't be more pleased."

"Well, we're only one third through; we'll do the other porches tomorrow."

"You sure we can afford anymore?"

Jim said, "Dad, you won't believe all the plants we got. All for free, even the flowerpots!"

"Come on!"

"Yep!" Molly said, "Those fish are still working. Mrs. Perkins and Mrs. Neel are sharing their bounty now. Come see. I've got a surprise for you," and she led Dave to the truck. "Mrs. Neel sent you these two vines, one for each side of the front porch. Bignonias, just like you ordered."

"No kidding!"

"Yep!" and she said, "Let's plant these now and then call it a day? You dig the hole and I'll plant."

They planted one on each side of the porch and tied their tails up on the porch poles. Jim watered them in and Molly added some bark to protect them.

When they finished Dave said, "How about we all get cleaned up and cook some dogs. I'm hungry as a horse."

Jim said, "Hot ziggity diggity dog."

The dogs, who had been supervising this whole operation, were getting excited and started to jump around. Molly wondered if they were excited about the word "hot dog" or was it the way Jim said, "Hot ziggity!"

She couldn't wait to use her new shampoo and hair dryer. She would have a new look tonight, Smoke and mirrors. She'd even try some of her Marilyn Monroe red lipstick on them. They hadn't seen her with lipstick yet. She'd lay off the Chanel for tonight and save it for a rainy day, might use a touch of eye shadow to accent the positive. She heard the thud of darts and knew they must be playing a game of World. Normally she wasn't so conscious about the way she looked. The fact that she hadn't looked much different than when she fell in the creek four days ago was what was bothering her. She wanted to look her best since she was in the race.

She made her way downstairs just as Dave was about to throw. Jim saw her first and said, "Oooh La La!"

She had on new sandals, red toenails, khaki shorts, a white cotton tee and a long sleeved blue denim shirt worn out and unbuttoned with the cuffs rolled up a couple of turns. She smiled at Jim and said, "Thanks for the Ooh La" and added, "You look mighty handsome yourself."

She could feel Dave staring at her and she looked up quickly and caught him. He just kept on looking.

"Do you have a staring license?"

He snapped to and said, "You look nice."

She paused a few seconds and asked, "Do you mean it?"

"I mean it. Times ten."

"Scouts Honor?"

"Scouts Honor!"

"Well you don't look so bad yourself, times six."

Dave loved the way she made everything exciting and started staring again.

"How about those dogs boys?" and she made a howl like a beagle and said, "I'll cook the dogs!"

"Think you can handle that?" Dave said smiling.

"Yes Mr. Smarty Pants, times two," and asked, "How many should I cook?"

Jim looked at the package and counted ten hot dogs. "Cook'em all, two for you, two for me, two for dad, two for Slick and two for Pudd'n."

She dropped them in the pot. Pudd'n was about to get her first Oscar. An Oscar Meyer that is.

Molly was in charge of the dogs and chili. Jim grated cheese and got out mayo, mustard and relish. Dave chopped up a white onion real fine and made ice tea for everyone. Jim got out some Fritos and made the statement, "You have to have Fritos with dogs."

"I know," perked Molly, "its communism if you don't." She looked at Dave for his reaction and he gave her a thumb up and smiled and she stuck out her tongue at him.

Dave got out another pot and put about one-half inch of water in it and put it on a burner on high. He placed a colander on top of the pot and put in six buns and covered them with tin foil. He saw Molly looking at him with a puzzled look and said, "We like our buns soft and hot."

Talk came easy at the dinner table and everyone was in a good mood. She couldn't believe she ate two whole hot dogs by herself. Maybe the hot buns made the difference, maybe the company, maybe the hard work and as she ate the last Frito she said, "Best hot dogs I ever ate! Damn, I'm a good cook." She realized the second she said it but it was too late.

"That'll be a quarter!" Jim and Dave both said at the same time.

She got her purse and dropped her signatured quarter in the cuss box. She was mad at herself for slipping up. She looked at Dave who was smiling as he shook his finger at her. "Bad girl!" he said.

Molly did the dishes and the boys retired to the den to catch the news and the weather. The weatherman predicted rain the next day so the hay cutting was put on hold.

The next morning and after another lumberjack breakfast, Dave left the house to cut grass along the fence lines. He said he would probably work till dark thirty and would probably finish at the pecan orchard unless the rain forced him in. He packed an apple, a couple of granola bars and a gallon of water. Molly made a note to get him a little cooler and pack him better lunches or at least something to keep his water cold.

Molly and Jim finished the planting project and when they had gotten cleaned up Jim asked her if she would like to watch a movie.

"Well, you know how your dad is about TV. Do you think he'll mind?"

"No ma'am! He lets me watch movies from his collection when he's not here. During the winter and rainy weather we like to watch movies."

Jim opened a cabinet and she could see maybe a hundred plus movies in his collection.

Jim said, "These are the best movies ever made. Dad says they're classics. What's a classic, anyway?"

She started to answer but had a flash thought. Jim was accustomed and at ease with using the "World Atlas," maybe she could get him using the dictionary in the same way. She knew he was eager to learn, and she needed to start practicing being a teaching nanny. "I forgot." She said, "Have you got a dictionary? Let's look it up."

Jim went to the study and returned with one. Jim found the word and read, "It means highest quality of rank, having recognized and permanent value, having enduring interest and appeal."

"Thanks for looking it up. I had forgotten."

She inspected the collection and was impressed. They were indeed classics. A quick inventory and she recognized most of them, The Music Man, The Sound of Music, My Fair Lady, Old Yeller, Cool Hand Luke, and The Yearling. He had numbered them, No. 1 was Lonesome Dove, No. 2 was The Man from Snowy River, No. 3 was Shane, No. 4 was Dances with Wolves, No. 5 was Sleepless in Seattle, and she commented, "Well, I don't know about your uncle's classification system, but these are definitely classics." She thought, "I've got to hand it to him. He has a great collection. Good wholesome family oriented movies, probably not a curse word in the whole bunch." Whoops, she thought, "there goes that theory. Here's Gone with the Wind which has the first curse word ever used in a movie."

"Let's watch The Man from Snowy River," Jim suggested.

Somehow she had missed this one and said, "Sounds good to me!" and suggested they make some popcorn before they started it.

"Yes ma'am!" Jim answered as he was loading the movie.

Molly went to the pantry where she remembered seeing the Boy Scout popcorn canister. Same brand her brother used to push. She opened the can expecting to find some microwave pouches but the corn was loose. "You don't have the microwave kind?"

"No ma'am, we don't have a microwave. Dad says it's a form of communism whatever that means."

"It means your dad's full of prunes!"

"Really?"

"Really!"

Jim got a pot, covered the bottom with just the right amount of oil and added the corn. He put on the top and turned the burner to one less than high and said, "I like to shake it after the first kernel pops. Secret to good corn is to take it off the burner a little early before it has a chance to burn."

Molly fixed each of them a big glass of Hawaiian Punch while he popped the corn. She was fascinated at the ease he showed in the kitchen. Here she was almost twenty-seven and was still having trouble cooking eggs. No microwave, heaven forbid! How would she survive?

They watched the movie and Jim was on a high. He filled her in as they went. He had memorized almost every word of all the characters in the movie.

"How many times have you seen this?"

"A bunch!" he said.

He liked Clancy and said that his Uncle Dave reminded him of Clancy. She could actually see resemblance in the personalities and mannerisms of Clancy to Dave. Jim liked the campfire scene when Clancy snuck up on Spur and Jim. He liked the piano scene when Jessica wasn't playing well and then started playing beautifully after Jim brought them tea. He loved the part when Jim chased the brumbies down the mountain and then finally rounded them up single-handedly and drove them back to the ranch. The movie was thrilling and she could see why Matthew liked being called Jim. What nine-year-old boy wouldn't?

"Great movie Jim!" she said as it ended and she hi-fived him. "Before I saw the movie I was torn between calling you by your real name or calling you Jim. After seeing the movie, you are definitely a "Jim". From now on, you're Jim and your uncle is Clancy."

She got up from the couch and walked to the piano and sat down. From memory she played "Fur Elise," which she had learned a long time ago when she took piano lessons from Mrs. Hines. Jim's eyes got as big as saucers. Half way through the piece he took off and ran out the front door. He ran to a large bell, which was mounted on a post by the front gate and started ringing the bell. He rang it over and over. She went outside to see what the matter was. She had been told that the bell was an emergency bell.

Dave was working in the pecan orchard when he heard the bell. His heart sank and he shut off the mower and put the tractor in fourth gear and ran wide open all the way to the house. The tractor had never been that fast before. He couldn't see smoke and as he got closer he could see Molly and Jim standing by the bell. They're both alive he thought. He was instantly relieved to see them. He stopped the tractor and shut off the engine. "What's the matter?" he said looking at both of them.

Jim said, "She's Jess, Dad! She's Jess! You're not going to believe it."

Dave glanced at Molly who was smiling and gave him an I don't know gesture.

Dave's emotion went from a fear that something was wrong mood to a contained anger mood and said, "Bud! You know that the bell is for emergencies only. Why did you ring it? I want an explanation and it better be good. I almost burned the tractor up getting here.

"Come inside!" he said and grabbed Molly's hand and led her to the piano. "Play it again!"

She played the song again. Perhaps even sweeter this time since Mr. Dave was listening.

"See! She's Jess, Dad! From now on we'll call her Jess."

"Ok Bud, Jess it is."

"I'm glad you're both OK," and he gave them each a rub on the head.

Molly had a flashback and thought; thanks Mom for making me take piano lessons and thanks Mrs. Hines for making me learn that piece. Her new status as Jess made all the years of lessons and practice worthwhile. She was their new hero and she loved it.

Later that night as they were about to finish supper Molly asked, "How about a game of World to see who washes dishes?"

Jim jumped up and grabbed the darts. "What's the target?"

"The Aleutian Islands," Molly answered.

Jim went to the atlas and Dave asked, "How in the world did you pick that?"

"A friend of mine's dad, Albert Adams, was stationed there in World War II. Mr. Adams was a diver in the Navy and used to tell us stories about the war. He knew all kinds of knots and used to show us how to tie them. I've forgot all except one. He said it was important and might save a life someday."

"Would you teach it to me?" Jim asked.

"You bet! But you have to have two ropes to do it."

Jim found the Aleutians in the book and said, "They're a long chain of islands running almost all the way from Alaska to Russia, almost always foggy and almost no trees." He went to the map and found the target. He went first and hit Russia. "Darn!" he said.

Dave hit Alaska, which was closer, and Molly actually hit one of the tiny islands called Rat Island. Jim did the measuring and said, "I lost."

Molly handed him the bottle of soap and said, "You de Man!"

Dave and Molly retired to the east porch and made small talk. They talked mostly about the new plants, and he bragged on her a lot.

Jim appeared shortly and suggested they do their letter writing now. Molly asked if she could join them and they all went to the study.

Dave said he wanted to write Mrs. Neel to thank her for the plants and the flower pots and Jim said he wanted to write Mrs. Perkins and thank her for the cookies.

Molly said, "Those are the same two people I wanted to write. Do you think we should both write them?"

Dave said he would mention how much Molly appreciated Mrs. Neel helping her and that she wanted to invite her out to see the plants when she got through with the project.

"Sounds good to me, I would like to invite her out."

Jim said that he would tell Mrs. Perkins that Molly said "thank you for the plants" in his letter.

Her field was narrowing. She thought a few minutes and asked herself, "What blessings do I have to count?" Instantly a thought popped into her head. Bingo! Got it!

She wrote a note to Caroline thanking her for the flowers she had given her. She told her how good they made her feel and that she had placed them in a vase beside her bed. She enclosed two barrettes in the letter that she had planned to give her the next time she saw her. She taped four pieces of Doublemint gum to the letter and told Caroline that one was for her and for her and the others for her sisters and brother. She wrote beside each piece of gum," For Morgan, For Jackson, and For Isabel if her mother says she can have it and For You," with a smiley face beside it. She asked Dave for the Phelan's address and he got his address book.

"Who'd you write?"

"Caroline, for the flowers."

"That's nice. Probably be the first letter she's ever got."

She also wrote a note to Theresa thanking her for the bread. She told her how the three of them devoured the whole loaf around the campfire. She left out the part about the two bottles of wine they drank. She hoped she would teach her how to make the exact same recipe someday. She invited her and her son, Brad, to the farm if they ever needed an outing. She told her that there were plenty of fun things for the boys to do and maybe they could visit or make bread. She had talked it over with Dave and he said to bring Frank, too. The men could fish and they'd have a fish fry or cook some burgers. And she told Theresa be sure to bring swimsuits. Molly asked for the Beauchamp's address, which Dave found for her. She read the letter out loud to see if her invitation was OK with him.

"Nice!" he said, "That's a good idea. I've been wanting to take Frank and his boy fishing and if you learn how to make that bread, I'll give you a raise."

Molly smiled as she licked the envelope and said, "You're on!"

Jim finished his letter and addressed the envelope. She asked Jim if she could read it before he sealed it. "I'm not trying to be nosey, but your dad said he wanted me to look for any weak spots you might have and maybe I could help if I saw any before school started."

Jim handed her the letter and she asked if she could read it out loud. He nodded and she read:

Dear Mrs. Perkins,

Thanks for the cookies. They were real good. When we got home Molly showed us a new trick. Put 2 scoops of Blue Bell vanila in a glass. Put in 2 chocolat chip cookies and fill up the glass half way with milk. Mix them all together and you have chocolat chip cookie ice cream. It's real good. You should try it. We haven't eaten the tomatoes yet. I helped Molly plant some of the plants you gave us today. They look real nice. Molly was real glad to get them. • *Dad too. I told dad about the lo vera plant in case we get burned. I showed him how to use it. He says that is good to know. We had hot dogs last night. We will see you Sunday. I hope Molly will come with us. I don't think she has a dress. Did you know that Molly can play the piano? She plays real pretty.*

Your friend,

Jim

When she finished she looked at Dave who had a very proud look on his face and she said, "Excellent Jim. A very, very nice note! Your handwriting is very neat and your thoughts are clear. She will like this note and it will make her feel good. Let's check a few words in the dictionary."

Jim did and he added an A and an E to lo vera and added an E to chocolat and put another L in vanila. They put stamps on the letters and Dave said he would take them to the post office in the morning.

Molly made a mental note to buy a dress before Sunday.

Jim said he had one more letter to write and Dave asked, "Who?"

"Mr. Neel."

"Why are you going to write him?"

Jim said, "Just a minute" and he made a dash for the truck and returned with a pocketknife, which was in a box and wrapped, in an oil skin paper. "Mr. Neel gave this to me. He said a man named Mr. Birdwell gave him two of them a long time ago and he wanted me to have one of them. It's made from Sheffield steel and came from England. He said it's not as pretty as some knives but the blades are made of carbon steel and hold an edge real good. He said it's a collector's item and might be worth some money someday."

Then Jim showed them a fishing lure Mr. Neel had given him. It was in the original box and was in mint condition. It was a Pumpkinseed Spook. "Son!" he said, "This is a real treasure. I've been reading in some of the fishing magazines that people are paying fortunes for these old plugs. Finding one in this condition is rare."

"Well, you should see his tackle box. He made it himself. He's got seven more Pumpkinseeds, all different colors. He's probably got a hundred plugs in it. Most of them are in boxes. He's got Pico Perch, Dalton Specials, Devil's Horses, and one called a Lucky 13. It has glass eyes and is big around as a broom stick and about this long" and held his hands about six inches apart. "Know what? He's got a plug in his box called a MudBug. He says it was outlawed in Texas about thirty years ago and that fisherman were supposed to destroy them. He kept three of them though and he told me not to tell anyone he had them."

"Why were fishermen supposed to destroy them?" Molly asked.

"Caught too many fish! He said that one year on Lake Rayburn fishermen caught so many fish on MudBugs that the water level went down two inches."

Dave started laughing and Jim asked, "What's so funny?"

"I believe old Herschel's been pulling your leg. In your letter ask him to come fishing. Tell him to bring that 'outlawed plug' of his. Tell him I'd like to see it."

"Know what else? He's afraid to throw the Lucky 13 again because only big bass hit it and it might give him a heart attack."

Dave started laughing again and said, "Tell him to bring that one too. Tell him I know CPR."

Dave left the room laughing and Molly stayed with Jim to help him with his note and while he was writing she also wrote another note herself. She wrote a note to Jim thanking him for his part in saving her life and rescuing her and Pudd'n from the creek. She knew he would probably show it to Dave so she said some nice things about him. She thanked him for being so nice to her and making her feel at home and for letting her have the Martin room. She signed the letter much love, Molly and Pudd'n. She drew a paw print under Pudd'n and drew a smiley face with a few curls under her own. She got the farm address from one of Dave's business cards. She would sneak it in the mailbox when they went to town. When they were through, she went out to the porch and found Dave sipping on a drink.

"Snake bite medicine?" she asked.

"Martini! Would you like one?"

"Maybe a glass of wine, kind sir."

"You got it" and he went to the kitchen.

When he returned he thanked her for helping Jim with his writing and for getting him to use the dictionary. She said, "If that young man keeps that same drive and desire to please he might be President of the United States someday. I'm serious!"

Jim appeared from around the side of the house carrying two ropes and asked, "Would you show me that knot that Mr. Adams taught you?"

"You bet!"

There was a picnic table under the sycamore tree and she said, "Let's do it over by the table." They followed her over and she took one end of the rope and threw it over a large branch about fifteen feet up. Next she pulled the table near the rope and got up on the table. She had Jim pull the rope so the end of it was dangling about a foot or two out of her reach. "Now here's the way Mr. Adams told the story and why it's a good knot to know. You and your men are returning from a mission and you approach the ship that's supposed to pick you up. They throw you a line from off the deck but it's not long enough." She pointed to the dangling rope and said, "That's the line they threw you. Now this table is your boat and you and your men need to grab that line and climb to safety. The seas are rough and the waves are taking you up and down but won't take you quite high enough to grab the line and attach another line to it. What do you do?"

"Stand on somebody's shoulder" Jim answered.

"Might work but the seas are rough and you have a thirty pound pack on your back. Here's what Mr. Adams showed us." She tied a quick loop in the line and held the rope in one hand and the end of the rope in the other. She crouched on the table and said, "The waves are taking us higher" and she started standing up. When she was fully extended she jumped up and off the table. When the hanging rope went inside of the loop she jerked the rope she was holding in opposite directions and went to the ground still holding the rope which was now attached to the other line.

"Cool!" Jim said.

"No way will that hold" was Dave's comment.

"Oh, we have a doubting Thomas in the group" as she made a little harness and tied it around her bottom. "Pull me up" she said.

Dave pulled her about ten feet up and the knot held. "Well, I'll be damned."

"That'll be a quarter" Jim and Molly said at the same time.

She taught the knot to Jim and he tried it a couple of times. It worked each time. Dave still couldn't believe it and said he would have bet money that the knot would not have held.

"I'll have to remember that the next time I need a little spending money," Molly replied.

Jim insisted that his dad try the knot and it worked again.

While they were playing with the rope Molly slipped back into the house and gathered what she thought she'd need for her "Chuck Wagon Initiation Campout." She got her doppkit, PJ's, pillow, insect spray, matches, and a jacket in case it got chilly. She made a sashay through the kitchen and got an apple, a sleeve of Ritz crackers and the partial bottle of Chardonnay. She packed all her goodies except the pillow in a small backpack and went outside to bid the boys bon voyage. She also put on a touch of Chanel.

Dave and Jim gawked as she approached. Why was she carrying a pillow? They wondered.

"Thought I'd join the chuck wagon club tonight; got to have a pillow."

Jim said, "We'll go down with you and start you a fire."

"Nope! I'm doing this by myself. I've got matches. I would like to borrow a flashlight."

"Yes ma'am!" and he took off to get the flashlight.

"I took a bottle of your wine, hope that's OK?"

"Sure you don't want company?"

"Normally I would, but not on initiation night. I'm taking Pudd'n. We'll do fine."

Jim returned with a 3-cell flashlight that was as heavy as a brick. He showed her how it would spot if the head were twisted.

"Nice light!" she said, "And if a bogeyman gets after me, I'll hit him over the head with it."

"You smell good." Jim said.

"Thanks!" she said, "I think I read one time that wolves don't like perfume."

"Is that my perfume you're wearing?" Dave asked.

"What do you mean?" she asked.

"Well, I looked at the grocery receipt and it said I'd bought some perfume."

She looked at him with one of those Bambi-eyed hand-in-the-cookie-jar looks and he winked at her.

"Sorry about that."

"No problem, we like our genies smelling good. What's it called?"

"Coup de grace!" she said laughing, "I'll see you boys when the sun is up. Come on Pudd'n."

Jim said, "Remember, you have to sleep on the ground."

"Gotcha!" she said and gave him a thumb up.

She stopped about thirty yards down the path and hollered to the boys, "Call Slick, this is a girl thing. No boys allowed."

The boys sat on the porch and watched her hike to the lake. "Wish I was there." Jim said and Dave answered him with a "Me too, Bud, me too."

CHAPTER 8

WELL, THANK YOU, FORREST

Molly had her fire going in no time, a handful of pine needles, three pieces of lighter pine and a teepee of small sticks. She would add larger pieces when it got going good. She climbed up into the wagon and opened the barrel with the sleeping gear. She got out a bedroll and a polypad and pitched them to the ground. She made her bed near the fire and fluffed her pillow. This is going to be fun, she thought. It would be more fun with the boys but she was going to make the best of it. She pulled a chair closer to the fire. There were no bugs and the stars seemed extra bright. She poured herself a glass of wine and toasted the great outdoors and said, "Thank you Lord for making that snake get in my canoe and thank you for not letting him bite me."

She ate her apple and shared her crackers with Pudd'n. Wine had never tasted better. She laughed a little at Dave's slogan, "End your day with a Chardonnay" and the more she thought about it the more she liked it. With her resources depleted and the fire almost out she decided it was time for bed. She brushed her teeth and wished she had brought a bottle of water to rinse with. There was no moon and when the fire went out, it got dark in a hurry. Pudd'n curled up next to her and she gave her a few pats. The night sounds seemed to get louder and she swore she heard every frog on the lake. And what were those splashes? Don't fish go to bed at night? Maybe they were alligators.

Just as she was about to close her eyes she heard a scream from the woods on the other side of the lake. She looked at Pudd'n who had raised her head and was looking in the direction from which the sound came. She finally concluded it must have been a bobcat. A little later she heard Pudd'n make a growling noise and saw that she was standing and the hair on her back was bristled up. "What do you see?" she asked and Pudd'n barked. Molly shined the light and chewing on her apple core was a raccoon. It's OK, it's only a coon. The coon, not wanting to have a confrontation with the dog, got the heck out of there.

Molly couldn't seem to get back in the sleep mode and finally decided it was because she had to potty. She put her shoes on and grabbed the flashlight. Come on Pudd'n, I need an escort to the outhouse. Half way there an armadillo crossed their path which scared Pudd'n more than it did her. She finished her business and got back in the bedroll feeling much relieved. Just when she thought nothing else could possibly happen, she heard it and a chill went through her. A coyote howled to the north of her. A minute later there was an answer from the other side of the lake. They wouldn't stop. It was also Pudd'ns first time to hear a coyote and though she had never seen one, she was shook. Pudd'n started for the house and Molly shouted at her. "Pudd'n, don't you dare leave me" and she came back knowing that she had done wrong. The howls put goosebumps on her and she could swear they were getting closer. She shined the flashlight on the field but couldn't see anything. She remembered the spot feature and gave it a twist. She couldn't tell how far away they were but maybe a hundred yards out there were five sets of green eyes. "That does it" she said, "We're sleeping in the wagon." She pitched her sleeping gear up in the wagon and tried to lift Pudd'n but she was too heavy and the first step was too high. In desperation she pulled the chairs over and made a make shift ladder and got Pudd'n inside the wagon. She passed out from exhaustion and the last thing she remembered saying was "Pudd'n, don't you let them boogers get me."

Dave was up before the sunrise and slipped out of the room trying not to wake Jim. He quietly made coffee and filled a thermos. He was anxious to check on Molly. He had thought about her all night. He loved her spirit and he kept comparing her to Jackie. Would Jackie have wanted to join the wagon gang? No way! He left Jim a note where he was and started down the path. He told Slick to "Stay" which he did.

Dawn was breaking as he got to the wagon. He thought her dog would have given him a greeting but Pudd'n was nowhere in sight. There was no sleeping bag and no Molly. At the front of the wagon were three of the Adirondack chairs. Two of them were facing each other and the third was on top of them with the back of the chair resting on the wagon. He climbed up to take a peek. Pudd'n was up and excited to see him. She let out a woof. Dave gave her a pat and said, "Where's your other half?"

Molly threw back the bedroll and sat up. She'd been caught! This wasn't going according to her plan. She had hoped to be up and perky when the boys came down to check on her. She had planned to have the fire going.

"How'd you sleep?"

"Terrible! The wolves almost got me. They started howling and wouldn't stop."

"Those were coyotes." He said laughing.

"They were coming to get me! I could see their eyes."

"Come on!"

"I put the light on spot and shined it in the field. I could see five sets of green eyes."

"Those were deer."

"Well, I didn't know what they were. They could have been the Hounds of Baskerville for all I know. They liked to scared me and Pudd'n to death."

"How about a cup of coffee to settle your nerves?"

"Coffee in bed again. Yes, I'd love some."

He helped Pudd'n out of the wagon and fetched the coffee. He climbed back up and handed her a cup. "One lump" he said.

She laughed and asked, "Is Jim with you?"

"No."

"Would you help me in a little white lie?"

"Maybe, what's the lie?"

"Well, I was supposed to sleep outside and I didn't."

"Your secret is good with me."

"I want it to look like I slept by the fire" and she handed him the bedroll and pad.

He put them by the fire and rearranged the chairs. When he went back to the wagon she pitched him the pillow and asked him to hand up her backpack, she wanted to change.

When he returned, she was standing on the seat of the wagon barefoot and in her shorty PJ's which didn't leave much to the imagination. He handed it up to her and she said, "Why don't you be a good Boy Scout and start me a fire. I meant to have one going before Jim came down."

The first rays of sun were streaking from behind the trees across the lake and hit Molly's hair from behind. The edges of her hair lit up like they were ablaze. What a picture! He thought. Where's my camera when I need it? Maybe he'd ask her to pose and he'd try to duplicate the picture someday. He just kept staring.

"The fire!" she said, "Chop chop!" snapping him out of his daydream.

He got the fire going and she joined him. They were working on their second cup of coffee when they saw Jim and Slick running toward them. He arrived out of breath and said, "Why didn't you wake me up?"

"Well" he lied, "I made a bunch of racket but you didn't stir. I made coffee and saw smoke from Molly's fire so I decided to bring her a cup of coffee. I've just been here a few minutes." "Another white lie" he thought. "Funny how one white lie begets another white lie. She was sitting here waiting for the sunrise when I came."

"How was it? Were you scared?" Jim asked.

Molly answered, "At first the frogs kept me up but finally they quit. Then there was a scream from across the lake. I don't know what it was."

"Probably a bobcat" Jim added.

"Then there was a raccoon that ate my apple core that made Pudd'n's hairs stand straight up. Then there was an armadillo that almost ran us down when I went to the potty. Then the coyotes started and Pudd'n got so scared that she tried to run to the house. I threatened her with her life and she stayed with me. I shined the light on the field and I saw their eyes. There were five sets of green eyes."

"No way!" Jim said excitedly.

"Your dad said they were deer."

"He's right. Coyotes' eyes glow red in the dark."

"All I know is that if I ever spend the night out here again, I'm going to have a gun."

Jim went over and gave her a hug. "Why didn't you get in the wagon if you were scared?"

"Well, I probably should have" she said looking at Dave "but I wanted to be a member of the club and I wanted the combination to the chuck box."

"It's 1277," he said, "Same as our box at the post office."

She jumped up and went to the chuck box and spun the dial. 1277 worked. She hi-fived Jim and Dave both and said, "What you say we get some breakfast going?"

"How about pancakes and sausage?" Jim asked.

"Sounds good to me, I need a working man's breakfast. I've got a lot of work to do today planting the rest of those plants."

Dave said, "I'll light the burner." And Jim said, "OK, but I'm doing the cooking."

"OK bud, you're on."

Jim hopped up in the wagon and opened the icebox and handed down milk, a tube of patty sausage, a tub of butter and two eggs. Molly loved watching Jim cook. He enjoyed it so and she was learning some of their tricks. He made patties and cooked the sausage first.

Next he made the batter by adding two eggs and milk to the mix. He added a couple of capfuls of vanilla and stirred it all together and added a tablespoon of grease he salvaged from the sausages. Satisfied with the batter's consistency, he ladled six pancakes on the grill.

Molly joined Dave at the fire and said, "Regular little Chef Boyardee you've got there."

"Yeah" he said, "He does a good job."

All of a sudden, Jim started singing without reservation,

"Aunt Jemima pancakes without her syrup,
Is like the spring without the fall,
But there's one thing worse, than this verse,
And that's no Aunt Jemima's at all."

Molly gave him an ovation and Jim took a small bow.

Dave had found a chuck wagon dinner triangle at a flea market and had put it in the chuck box. Jim pulled it out and gave it a ring and said, "Come and get it while it's hot, boys."

Molly went first and Jim piled three pancakes and two sausages on her plate and his dad got the same. "You'll start" he said, "I'll get the next batch. Here's the butter and the syrup." Molly noticed that the syrup was of course, Aunt Jemima. After everyone was full, he cooked a couple more for the dogs and poured the sausage grease on top. "Makes their coats shine" he said. Molly swore that the dogs were smiling by the time they got through.

Jim rolled up Molly's bedroll while she and Dave put out the fire. Molly asked Jim if he would help her again today and he said he would and started up the path with the dogs.

Dave and Molly followed and on the way she said, "Thanks for making me look good back there. I liked that part when you said you saw the smoke coming from my fire."

"Partners in crime, I'll tell you a secret if you'll never tell."

"Cross my heart."

"Well, last year when he was doing his campout initiation I went down to check on him about midnight and guess what?"

"What?"

"He was in the wagon and Slick was under the wagon."

"You're kidding!"

"Nope."

"Why that little stinker."

Dave laughed and said, "Next morning he pulled the same little stunt you did. Probably the only secret he's ever kept from me."

"Thanks for sharing that with me, makes me feel better."

Dave started laughing and she asked, "What's so funny."

"I just thought of a good headline for a newspaper story."

"What?"

"Baskerville hounds climb Adirondack ladder and kill woman sleeping in covered wagon."

Molly laughed so hard she cried.

Dave left shortly for the orchard. Molly stripped the beds, emptied the hampers and started a load of wash. While the wash was going Jim helped her tackle the planting project and by noon everything was done on the porches. The hanging baskets looked a little skimpy but Mrs. Perkins said they'd grow fast if watered well. She had bought a showstopper at the nursery, a fuchsia Bougainvillea. The person waiting on her at the nursery said not to water it too much, that they liked stress conditions. She said that if you really want them to bloom their heads off not to look at them when you walked by and spit on them.

She knew that Dave would be coming back to the house shortly for lunch and she sent Jim to the orchard to tell him that she was bringing a picnic lunch. She had seen the orchard from a distance but wanted an up close look. She made tuna fish sandwiches and cut up some fruit, which she put, in a Tupperware bowl. She got forks, paper plates, napkins, a bag of chips and a large thermos of iced tea.

In the wash room she had spotted a blue and white checkered tablecloth and she packed it. Perfect, she thought. She put a few dog biscuits in a baggie for the dogs because she figured the pancakes they'd had this morning were wearing off. She fluffed her hair and put on a little lipstick and she was off.

She found the boys in about the middle of the orchard. They were doing what Dave called orchard KP which was chipping fallen limbs.

Dave turned off the chipper when she came up.

"How about some lunch?" she asked.

"Yes ma'am!" Jim answered.

"Hope you all like tuna fish?"

"One of our favorites," Dave replied.

Dave had a gallon of water on the trailer and he and Jim washed their hands and faces.

Molly spread out the cloth and they all sat down. Pudd'n and Slick had never seen a blue and white tablecloth on the ground and thought it was for them and Molly said, "Shoo!"

Dave told Slick to "Lay!" which he did and Pudd'n followed suit.

Jim was thrilled with the picnic. "This is fun!" he said.

Dave poured drinks and Molly handed each of them a plate and said to "Dig in."

Jim picked up a sandwich and said, "Where's the crust?"

"Your birds were looking hungry so I gave them a treat."

"These are better than yours, Dad!"

Molly doled out a few dog biscuits and everybody was happy.

"This is the first time I've ever been in a pecan orchard. It doesn't look that big when you're looking at it from the house, but when you're in it it's huge."

"It's pretty big" Dave said, "Twenty acres of anything is big."

"What are you all doing today?"

"Just cleaning up. We try to do a little each week so we don't get too far behind. There are always limbs down or sometimes lightning hits a tree and we have to take it down. Sometimes ice storms take branches down and sometimes the limbs get so heavy with pecans they snap off."

She couldn't help but notice that the place was immaculate. "Tell me about your trailer. Is it one of your inventions?"

"Well, I don't know if it's an invention but it's kind of my idea out of necessity. The generator gives us electricity for the saws and chipper. We saw up big limbs for the fireplace or the campfire. Jim's even sold a few cords of pecan wood. The smaller limbs we chip for compost or use it to keep weeds down. The generator is much quieter than a chain saw so there is less noise pollution. The electric saws are much quieter, safer and easier to use. We've got a twenty foot ladder and a ten foot trim saw if we need to prune up in the trees."

Jim said, "Pecan wood is real good for fires and cooking on the grill. It burns real clean and doesn't smoke too much."

"How do you keep track of where you are in the orchard?"

"That's a good question!" and he took her over to one of the trees and at the base of it was a brick with the number 15 M. He explained, "This is row M and this is tree 15. Number 1 is that a way and number 16 is that tree right there" as he pointed. "There are twenty-four rows of trees in the orchard and there are thirty trees in each row. It took a while to paint the numbers on all the bricks but it was worth it. I always know where I left off or where to start. When I spray I try to do one row at a time, same for fertilizing.

Jim might come in and say lightning hit 22 R and I'd know right where to go. Or maybe I'll see fire ants by 19 B and I'll make a note of it and next time I'm out with ant poison, I'll pay them a visit. The rows are A through Y." He went to the truck and pulled out a loose-leaf notebook, which contained the history of each tree for the past several years. He could tell the age of each tree. He had recorded fertilizing dates and the dates he had sprayed for webworms. He had harvest dates.

"Very neat!" she said, "I'm impressed."

"One reason I've wanted a computer was to be able to make these sheets and tables each year and to have a new book each year. I've been carrying this one for so long it's getting ratty and I'm running out of room."

"I'll help you when it comes in. That's why computers were invented, to keep track of data. I doubt that most pecan growers have put this much thought into their orchards. I could help. I could pull the limbs and put them in piles and all you'd have to do is drive through and stop at each pile."

"You're my kind of woman." He said laughing and he winked at her. "You just keep the picnics coming. Jim and I will haul the limbs."

He did it again. He unnerved her and she lost her train of thought.

"I've started keeping track of yields like Excellent, Good, Poor and I've got a few trees that haven't done so hot and if they don't perk up this year they're going in the fire place. I really believe this year is going to be a great harvest. Look at all those pecans!"

Molly did and he was right. There were jillions of little pecans like little bunches of bananas.

Jim came running up all out of breath and said, "We got a squirrel!"

Dave went to the truck and pulled out a double barreled 20 gauge and loaded it. He handed it to him and said, "Be careful!"

"Hold the dogs." He said.

Dave told the dogs to "Lay" which they did and Jim took off.

"I'll go with you," said Molly.

"He was around S 15," he said in a low voice.

As they got closer Jim started using the trees for cover and sure enough there he was about T 16. The squirrel was on the ground and not much afraid. Jim crept one tree closer and started to aim. Just as he was about to pull the trigger, Molly shouted, "Run squirrel run, Jim's going to shoot you!"

The squirrel seemed to understand and did a quick disappearing act and Jim who was about to become a hero was suddenly reduced to a zero. He was upset and told Molly, "I'm never going to take you hunting with me again."

"Good!" she said and she went back to the picnic area.

"Thought I heard a scream?"

"You did. It was me. I screamed and scared the squirrel away. Jim's really upset with me."

"He'll get over it. You know, a squirrel in your orchard is like termites in your house. Hard to believe a little ole termite can hurt you but they can.

They get you right in the pocket book. That's the way squirrels are in an orchard and they breed like rats"

Molly picked up the leftovers and headed for the house. About half way there she heard a shot and she knew what had happened. A four-legged termite had bit the dust.

The men came back to the house about four. They had buried the evidence and no mention was made of it. They brought in a good load of chips for the compost piles, which would be a chore for Jim in the morning. When they came in the house Dave saw that the house was spotless. Molly could tell he was pleased.

Molly said, "I've done the wash, changed the beds, mopped the floors and done the bathrooms. I would have vacuumed the carpets but I couldn't find the vacuum cleaner. Do you have one?"

Jim said, "Should we show her?" And Dave answered, "OK with me, I think she's an honest genie. I think we can trust her."

Molly looked puzzled and Jim led her over to the World board. At the end of the board was a bookshelf about five feet wide that faced the hallway. Jim said, "Watch this!" as he grabbed the edge of the carpet runner and pulled it back. Then he pulled on the edge of the bookshelf and it opened into a secret closet. The closet was about five feet wide and ten feet in length. She stepped inside for a look and Jim switched on a light. So this was the linen closet. They did have extra sheets. There was a row of beautiful monogrammed towels and sheets. "I was looking for these earlier," she said.

"Jackie made me buy all of those, like to broke me."

There was the vacuum cleaner in the corner. There were boxes of Kleenex, paper towels, toilet tissue, light bulbs and air conditioner filters.

"Very neat, I like!"

"I wanted a place to hide the duct work for the AC and the electrical boxes so I came up with this idea. Works pretty good and also gives us a place to hide all our mess."

Molly pulled out the vac and Jim said, "I'll do that. That's one of my jobs."

"You da man" she said and gave him a rub on the head.

Jim closed the closet and said, "Look over here!" Opposite the bookshelf was a matching bookshelf of the other side of the hall. It was at the end of the wall that separated the front hall from the den. He flipped back the throw rug and opened another secret closet. She went inside and turned on the light. There was a gun rack on the wall that held Dave's guns.

Jim said, "Look at this! We got silver! We're rich!" as he opened a silver chest.

"Well, I'd say you are rich. It's beautiful. It's King Edward."

"It was my grandmother's" Dave said, "No girls to leave it to. My brother and I flipped a coin. He got most of the furniture."

"You should use it!"

"Wouldn't that ruin it?"

"No silly, the more you use it the better it looks. Its silver, it's going to last forever. My mom uses hers every day and it sparkles like new. It would make your grandmother proud if you used it. It would make you think of her every day."

"Wouldn't it kind of be flaunting it?"

She answered, "If you'd bought the silver yourself, it would be, but you didn't. It was a gift and you would be honoring your grandparents if you used it. When people ate a meal at your house they'd know you were serving them with your very best. You could use all your old stuff for picnics and camp-fires. You know, I bet the silver in this set was mined right here in the U. S. Probably from the Rocky Mountains."

"I'll sleep on it," Dave said.

"Well, your Korean stainless is nice. Your guests will like it too."

"We don't have many guests," Jim added.

"Well, you're fixing to! We've invited the Neels, the Perkins, the Beauchamps and the Phelans. As much as they like you and your dad, I'm sure they'll accept the invitations."

There was a buffet in the closet and several boxes were on top. Jim opened one and said, "We got a bunch of old plates too." And he unwrapped one and handed it to her.

"Was this your grandmother's china?"

"Yep, she had a bunch of it."

Molly turned the plate over and looked at the markings. "This was made in England. It's Spode, probably worth more than the silver. How many settings?"

"I think ten, but I can't remember for sure."

"You should....." and he interrupted her saying, "Don't even think about it!" and he continued saying, "I'm going to watch the weather. It was plenty dry today and if the weather looks good for the next few days, we'll probably cut some hay tomorrow."

Molly said, "I've been thinking about the bell. Could we have a discussion about it."

"Sure!" Dave said, "What's on your mind?"

"Well, I don't think the bell should be a bell just for bad news. My grandfather used to have a camp on a river. It was only accessible by boat and we used to go there every summer for two weeks. All my aunts and uncles and cousins would vacation there every summer. Getting everyone to the dinner table at the same time was a real chore. My grandfather had a bell and ten minutes before we were to eat he would let one of us kids ring the bell one time. It was called the ten-minute bell. Everyone knew that they had ten minutes to wash up and get ready. Ten minutes later he would let one of us ring the real dinner bell two times. It was an honor to ring the bell. Whenever my brother or I would invite company he would always make it a point to let them ring the bell. My friends are still talking about the bell. It was a "happy bell". I'm not suggesting that you have a dinner bell because there are just the two of you." She continued looking at Dave, "Maybe you could have a certain ring and Jim could have a special ring. Say you two were at the lake and I wanted Jim. I could ring two times, wait ten seconds and ring two more times. Maybe your ring could be 3 quick rings, wait ten seconds and three more quick rings. It would be fun, kind of like Indian smoke signals but with a bell. The emergency bell could continue like it is now, just something to think about."

"I like it" said Jim, "Kind of like Indian drums."

"Me too!" said Dave, "Let's brainstorm this idea. Jim and I always have a contest each year to see who spots the first Martin on the house. What do you say five quick rings, wait ten seconds and five more quick rings."

"A Martin ring!" said Molly, "That's happy, I like it."

Jim added, "Dad always goes bananas when he sees geese fly over. We could have a goose ring. It would mean, "Stop what you're doing and look up, winters on the way." They had fun kicking ideas around.

Molly suggested that since Dave might be on the tractor sometimes that his ring should be three loud rings, wait twenty seconds and give three more loud rings. They went out to the bell and practiced. Dave liked the idea of a dinner bell and they decided that a single ring would mean that dinner would be served in thirty minutes. If they were in the fields, that would give them thirty minutes to get to the house. Jim's ring was to be one long and two shorts and repeated one time a few seconds later. The bell put everyone in a good mood. It wasn't just a bell of doom and gloom anymore. It had new life.

"Thanks Jess," Dave said, "That was a good idea."

"You're welcome, Clancy!" she responded laughing.

Jim asked, "What's your ring?"

"Well, I don't really need one since I'm only going to be here a couple of months."

"Nope!" he said, "You have to have one."

She thought a minute and went over to the bell and grabbed the rope tied to the clapper and gave three quick rings.

"What's it mean?" Jim asked.

"It means, I love Molly!"

Jim jumped up and rang the bell three quick times and Molly said, "Thank you Jim, *that* made me feel good," and she gave him a hug.

Molly smiled and looked at Dave and asked, "You want to try it?"

"Maybe later," he said smiling.

The dogs didn't know what was happening with all this bell ringing but they liked it. Maybe it had something to do with Pavlov's Law that was in their genes.

They started back to the house and Molly asked Jim, "When are you going to introduce me to your Molly?"

"Right now, I was just fixing to feed them. Come on!"

The dogs wanted to come but he told them to "stay" which they did. "Dogs make them nervous," he added.

She had seen the chicken yard from a distance but hadn't seen it up close. She also hadn't seen the fruit orchard or the garden. Maybe she would see these tomorrow. As they approached the chicken yard she noticed the trailer from the orchard. The generator and the chipper were covered with a tarp. There was a good load of chips, which Jim said he would add to his compost piles in the morning. The chicken yard was a large circle that had been fenced and divided like a pie cut in eight sections. The compost area was in one of the sections. There were two posts at the entrance with a sign hanging between them that said, "Miracle Egg Farm." There were several large flowering bushes along the fence and she made the comment, "Your flowers are beautiful!"

"Yes ma'am, they're pretty but that's all. They're Lantanas. They stink!"

"Come on!"

Jim picked a small branch off and said, "Smell!"

"Wow! You're right! Phew!" She said pinching her nose.

At the small end of the wedge was a gate, which Jim opened and led them into an inner circle. Here was the hen house where the chickens laid their eggs and got protection from the weather. Next to the hen house was another small building that contained an icebox for egg storage, a feed room and a sink with a cold water hookup. There were two screened windows and a screen door. The overhang of the roof was large which kept it shady and the weather out. The smaller end of each of the wedges had a gate that opened into the inner circle. Each of these gates had a sign on it for each day of the week.

Jim explained how the chicken yard worked, "Today the chickens are in Wednesday and tomorrow I'll come out and close this gate and open Thursday."

"Neat!" she said, "This has been well thought out."

"Yes ma'am, it was one of Dad's ideas. Range chickens are supposed to lay better eggs and be healthier chickens. They're not supposed to be under much stress if they can run around and get fresh grass and catch a few bugs. By rotating them there is always some fresh grass and there is no smell. They can always get in the hen house if they get scared or need to get out of the weather. Here's where they get their water" and he filled the small tub to the top.

"Want to gather some eggs?"

"Yes!" she said excitedly, "I've always wanted to. Ever since I was a little girl but I've never had the chance."

Jim got a basket from the egg room and handed it to her. "We'll start with BABYFACE."

As they walked to the other side of the hen house they passed the front and she noticed a wooden door with a latch on it and in the bottom of the door was a little opening like a doggie door but it was for chickens. There was a sign above it that said, "No Roosters Allowed". Another sign said "Miracles Performed Here Daily" and another sign that read, "Varmints Keep Out." Molly made a note that she would take pictures later to send home.

On the other side of the house was a continuous row of eight nesting boxes. Each box was about two feet in length and had a sloped roof to keep the rain out. The boxes were painted white, as was the hen house. Neatly painted on top of the first box was the name BABYFACE in blue letters.

Molly asked, "You mean all your chickens have names?"

"Yes ma'am. Dad named them after songs that start with girl's names."

"Come on! Do you know the song?"

"A little, it goes, Baby face, you've got the cutest little baby face. No other one can ever take your place, baby face.....Something like that" and he lifted the hinged lid and there was an egg.

Molly picked up the egg and said, "This is fun. How many chickens do you have?"

"Thirty."

"So we'll get thirty eggs?"

"Sometimes, but most of the time I get twenty-six or twenty-seven."

The next box was SUSIE.

"Do you know this song?" and Jim sang, "If you knew Susie, like I know Susie, Oh oh oh what a gal. She's got long.....Something like that."

Molly got another egg.

DOLLY was next and Jim said, "This is from Hello Dolly by Louis Armstrong and in a low voice trying to sound gruff sang, "Well, hello Dolly, well, hello Dolly, it's so nice to have you back where you belong. You're look-ing swell Dolly.....Kind of like that."

MELANCHOLY BABY was next and she asked, "You know this one?"

He sang, "Come to me my melancholy baby, cuddle up and don't go way, Smile my honey dear, while I kiss away each tear or else I will be melancholy too."

"What does melancholy mean anyway?"

"Sad."

SLEEPY TIME GAL was next and Jim sang, "Sleepy time gal you're turn-ing leaves into gold, sleepy time gal.....I forgot the rest."

Molly put another egg in the basket.

BONNIE was next. She couldn't believe that he knew all these songs. Most kids his age would be embarrassed to sing in front of an adult but he wasn't. He sang, "My Bonnie lives over the ocean, my Bonnie lives over the sea, oh please bring back my Bonnie to me.... I just know the start. Dad knows them all though."

They were six for six on eggs.

"Here's MOLLY! I told you I had a Molly." She slowly lifted the lid and Molly was still on the nest.

"Oh my God! What do I do?"

"Just reach under her real slow and see if there's an egg, kind of rub her belly."

"Won't it scare her?"

"No ma'am, women like to have their bellies rubbed."

"I guess Mr. Know-it-all taught you that."

"Yes ma'am. He knows a lot of stuff."

She reached in and pulled out two eggs. She gently closed the lid and said, "Look! Two!"

"She's one of my best layers."

"I know you know this song!" and Jim sang it again. "Just Molly and me, and the baby make three, we're happy in my blue heaven. That's all I know."

The last nest on this side of the house was MATILDA and Jim sang "Matilda I cried and cried for you." That was all he knew but he had the tune down perfectly. They rounded the corner and the first box had LOTTIE LYNN YA on it.

"Come on!" said Molly, "I don't think there's a song called Lottie Lynn Ya."

Jim said, "You're probably right but these four chickens here are Mack the Knife's girlfriends. Dad likes that song." And he sang, "Lottie Lynn Ya, Jenny Diva, Sukey Tartrey and Sweet Lucy Brown and the line forms on the right dear now that Mack Heaths back in town." SWEET LUCY didn't leave an egg.

CHANTILLY LACE was next and she asked if he knew this tune.

"A little, it was by the Big Bopper. He was from Beaumont, Texas, and was killed in a plane crash. Uncle Dave liked him a lot. It goes, 'Chantilly lace and a pretty face, and a pony tail a hanging down, and a wiggle in your walk and a giggle in your talk, Lord it makes the world go round'… Kind of like that."

Molly said, "I believe this is the most fun I've ever had. Your chickens would be a good scene in a movie. And with your singing I'm sure it would be a hit. People would love to see this."

"Dad said he was setting me up in business and I was on my own. It's been a good business for me. I've got my own saving account. Dad says I'm not supposed to talk about money but guess how much I've got in my savings."

"How much?"

"Seven hundred and twelve dollars."

"That's wonderful, Jim. Not many nine-year-olds have a savings account. Let alone that much in it. I'm impressed."

"I'm almost ten. My birthday is next week."

Molly said, "You're not going to believe this, but so is mine. Maybe we can have a birthday party together."

"Cool!" he answered, "Mine's Tuesday."

"Mine's Thursday."

The next girl was MARIE and Jim sang, "'Marie the dawn is breaking, Marie my heart is aching'.... That's all I know."

Marie was a goose egg for the basket.

TOOT TOOT TOOTSIE was next and Jim sang, "'Toot Toot Tootsie goodbyes, Toot Toot Tootsie don't cry'.... I don't really know that one but we have it on the player piano."

FIVE FOOT TWO was next but she didn't leave a donation for the basket.

Molly said, "I know this one. I had to learn it for a play one time." She put the egg basket down and started dancing as she sang. The routine came back to her and she sang the song all the way through in flapper style with a few Charleston moves thrown in.

When she was through, Jim jumped up and gave her a hug. "That was good!"

"Maybe we'll be in the movies together," she said laughing and they high fived.

They turned the corner and the first lady in this row was AVA MARIA.

"Don't tell me you can sing this one!" she stated.

"Nah, no one can sing that one, it's in Latin. It's real pretty though. It's about Jesus' mother. They sing it at weddings sometimes and at church. It starts out, 'Ah va Maree e ah, deee de de de de de de de.... de deee de de de de de de deee ah'.... Kind of like that"

"That was good Jim. I believe you've got an ear for music. I used to could sing it in college. It was required in one of my voice classes."

"No way!"

"Yep!" she answered and at the same time she was glad he didn't ask her to sing it because it had been too long and she wasn't sure she could hit all the notes again.

146

"Who's next?"

"MARIAN."

"You sure there's a song called Marian?"

"It's from 'The Music Man.' Marian was the librarian. Dad loves that movie and we watch it all the time. The girl is real pretty and there's a lot of singing in it. There's a little boy in it that has trouble pronouncing and he's real funny. Dad thinks we should put Marian in the cooking pot because she's not a good layer. He's probably right but I like her. She's a pretty chicken and gets along with the other chickens and she tries hard. I could never eat her."

Jim lifted the lid slowly and she was still on the nest trying. Unbeknownst to Jim she palmed an egg and reached under Marian. She pulled out an egg and said, "Ta daah!" as she held up the egg.

"Dad will never believe this," he said excitedly.

"How does the song go?"

"It starts out, 'Mariannnnnn, the librariannnnn'…. That's all I know. Maybe we can watch it before long."

"I'd like that."

MY BLUE EYED JANE was next and Molly said, "I don't believe I've heard this one either."

"It's by Jimmie Rodgers, the Singing Brakeman, and the Father of country music. Dad's got all these old records called thirty-threes and they're this big around" and held up his arms in a circle big enough to go around a small wash tub. "I'll show you when we get back to the house. He's got a bunch of them."

"How does the song go?"

Jim sang, "'The sweetest girl in the world is my blue eyed Jane, We fell in love like turtle doves while the moon was shining low' …. We'll play it later, you'll like it."

THELMA was next.

"Where in the world did your uncle find all these songs? I've never heard of Thelma."

Roy M. Philp, Jr.

"Thelma was Jimmie Rodgers' girlfriend." Jim pinched his nose and with an amusing nasal twang sang "T for Texas, T for Tennessee, T for Thelma that girl that made a wreck out of me. De o de lady oh, de o de lady who.'"

Molly was in stitches by the time he finished and Jim said, "I've got to work on my yodeling.

JEZABELLE was next and left them a nice white egg. Neither could remember the tune but Jim commented she was in the Bible and he thought she was bad.

AMAZING GRACE was next and Molly said, "I believe your uncle messed up here. I don't believe Grace is a girl's name in this song."

"You're right, dad just likes this song. It's about the grace of God."

She was taken back by his answer and asked, "You know about the grace of God?"

"Some." he said, "I'm learning all the time. Dad and I are reading the Bible together. We try to read seven pages each week. We're on page 282 right now. There are 890 pages in the Old Testament and 261 in the New Testament so it's going to take us a long time to finish. Dad says that someday someone will ask me if I've ever read the bible, and I can say, 'Yes, every word.' He says that not many people can say that."

"Do you know the words to Amazing Grace?"

"Oh yes ma'am. I know the first four verses. It's on page 378 of the Methodist songbook. A man named John Newton wrote it in 1779. He was a ship captain who was from a good family but was doing bad things because he ran a slave ship. One time he was at sea with a load of slaves and got caught in a bad storm and his ship started cracking up. He got real scared and knew he was going to die. He prayed to God to save him. God made the winds stop and the sea got calm and he and his crew were rescued. It changed him and he became a preacher and preached until he was an old man. He became blind and they told him he'd have to stop preaching but he told them he still had his voice and if they'd lead him to the altar he'd keep preaching until his voice gave out. He wrote the song about being saved by God's grace."

148

The song was one of Molly's favorites also and she and Jim sang it together, with much more meaning now. When they finished she said, "Jim, you amaze me. Maybe someday you'll be a preacher like John Newton." AMAZING GRACE also left two eggs. Fitting! She thought. God was pleased with young Jim's recount of something that happened a long time ago.

K K K KATY was next and left a beautiful white egg. Jim sang, "K K K Katy, beautiful Katy. You're the only G G G girl that I adore.... I get mixed up on that one."

ROSE was next and Jim sang a few bars with even an Irish accent.

CLEMENTINE and SUNSHINE were next and Molly joined him in a few bars of each. She also picked up two more eggs.

BEAUTIFUL DREAMER was another goose egg but Jim nailed the song. "We have this on the player piano" and he sang, "Beautiful Dreamer, queen of my song. List while I woo thee with soft melody. Songs of the rude world heard by the day, lulled by the moonlight have all passed away."

"Good job!" she said.

SWEETHEART was next and she asked, "Is this from 'Let Me Call You Sweetheart'?"

"No, but we have that one on the piano. This one is from one of Dad's old college songs. It kind of goes.... "She's the sweetest girl in all the world; she's the fairest flower that grew. She is my sunny southern sweetheart; she's the sweetheart of Sigma Nu."

"What's a Sigma Nu anyway?" he asked.

Molly was in stitches and answered, "It's a men's club in college. They call them fraternities." She wished again that she had a recording of this. She would never, never forget it.

ROCK A BY BABY was next and in Al Jolson fashion he sang, "'Rock a by my baby to a Dixie melody, Sing soft and low but don't you know you've got me in your spell. A million baby kisses I'll deliver, the moment that you sing the Suwannee River'"...Kind of like that."

"Thank you Al, that was nice!"

ROY M. PHILP, JR.

They were by the door to the hen house and she asked if she could look inside. She wanted to see how the chickens got in the laying boxes. Jim opened the door and she took a peek inside. There were little ramps that ran from the floor to each of the boxes. There were wood chips on the floor and the smell wasn't bad at all.

Jim said, "I put new chips in each month and new hay in their nests about every other month. We leave a light on all the time because it makes them lay better."

"How'd you come up with the name, Miracle Egg Farm?"

"Well, it's kind of a miracle that a chicken can eat some grass, a few bugs, some corn, some maize and a few scraps of food and produce a beautiful snow white egg. And they're so strong you can't break 'em with your hand."

"Come on?"

"Yep!" and he picked one up and held it sideways. "If you hold it like this and squeeze it, it will break, but if you hold it like this (he turned the egg long ways in his hand), you can't break it."

Molly said, "I can."

"Bet you can't!"

"How much?"

"Twenty-five cents!"

"You're on!"

He handed the egg to Molly and showed her how to hold it.

"Try it!"

She squeezed with all her might but she couldn't break it. She changed hands but that didn't work either. "I can't believe it!" she said.

"See, it's a miracle! You owe me a quarter."

The last hen was MEG RYAN and Molly said, "No way! There's not a song called Meg Ryan."

"You're right. Dad is crazy about her and said anybody so pretty had to have a spot in the hen house. You know that movie, "Sleepless in Seattle?" We got it. Guess how many times he's seen it?"

"Six!"

"Nope, fourteen. Besides Annie being so pretty, he says she has good sticks"

"What are sticks?"

"Legs! You know, like drumsticks. Know what?"

"What?"

"He says you got good sticks."

"Oh he does, does he?"

"Yes ma'am! He likes to watch you when you run. He says that you make him so tired that he has to take a cold shower just to wake up."

"Oh he does?" she said laughing.

"Yes ma'am! And he hates cold water. Sometime I just can't figure him out."

She was enjoying this conversation and asked, "What else does he say about me?"

"Well, I don't know if I should say it"

"Come on Jim, you don't keep secrets from your buddy."

Jim thought a minute and said, "He says you got movements like a fine Swiss watch. I don't know if that's good or bad."

"It's good! What else, Jim? Talk to me!"

"Well, I think it's a secret. I don't think I should tell."

"I'll tell you a secret if you'll tell me."

"What secret?" he asked.

"Promise you won't tell your uncle?"

"I promise."

"Well, the night I camped out, the coyotes scared me so bad I slept in the wagon."

"No kidd'n?"

"Do I have to do it over again?"

"No." he said, "I did the same thing. I won't tell."

They both laughed and high fived.

"I swear they were wolves!" she said and asked, "What else does he say about me?"

"What's a whammy?"

"I don't know! Why?"

"Well, I heard him say he'd like to put the whammy on you, so be careful."

"OK, I will and thanks for sharing that secret with me." She loved gleaning these tidbits of information from him. She knew Dave would die if he knew some of his secrets were out of the bag so to speak. She thought back to one of her history courses when she had read, that "loose lips sink ships," and she thought they do indeed!

Next, Jim took her to the egg room as he called it and she watched him wash and scope the eggs.

"What are you looking for when you scope the eggs?"

"Red dots!"

"What's a red dot?"

"I don't know exactly. That's what dad calls'em. I think they're drops of blood. He says nobody likes to see them when they crack open an egg. If we get one, we put it in the compost." He put the eggs in cartons. They'd gathered twenty-eight. "Dad takes me to town on Friday mornings and I sell them. I usually sell fourteen dozen each week. I donate eggs for our use and I pay dad back ten dollars each month for the wire and the post. He doesn't charge me interest."

There was a large onion sack hanging in the corner and Molly asked, "What's in this sack? It looks like dried flowers."

"They are. They're marigolds. We grow them."

"What for?"

"Secret!"

"Thought you and me weren't going to have any secrets."

"I forgot. You can't tell anybody though. Dad says it's a trade secret."

"Cross my heart."

Jim got out a handful of the flowers and put them in a bucket and rubbed them in the palms of his hands. He got a couple of scoops of chicken meal and dumped them into the bucket and mixed them up with his hands. They went outside and he poured the mixture in a small feeding trough and the chickens ran over and started devouring the meal.

"You mean they eat the flowers?"

"Yes ma'am. The flowers make their yolks a pretty orange color like the marigolds. Lots of people talk about my eggs and how pretty the yolks are."

"Where in the world did you learn that?"

"Dad researched it. He said they do it in China. It works!"

They were just about to finish up when they heard the bell ring one time. They looked at each other with a surprised look on their faces and Jim said, "Supper in thirty minutes!" and they high fived.

"Happy bell!" she thought and another bond was made. He had no idea how much he was pleasing her and making her happy.

Jim gave her a coffee can of chicken scratch to feed the miracle workers and he closed the Wednesday gate.

As the chickens swarmed for their treats, Molly said, "I've always wanted to feed some chickens. This is even more fun that I thought it would be."

"One more thing" he said. "Sometimes people come by to buy eggs and I keep some money to make change." He opened the icebox and pulled out a cigar box. "This is what I call my cold cash. I keep about fifty dollars here. If ever I'm not here when they come, maybe you'd sell them for me. I get a dollar twenty-five a dozen. It's a little more than the store, but they're better eggs and people know they're fresh. You know, there's a bunch of ways to fix eggs. There's hard boiled, soft boiled, poached, fried, scrambled, hard fried, soft fried, sunny side up, eggs benedict, over easy, eggs in the hole, golden rod eggs, egg omelets and that's not all. People love eggs. They're easy to cook and they're good for you."

"Well thank you Forrest!" she said. "You're making me hungry. Let's go see what that dinner bell was all about. I got so carried away with your miracle workers, I forgot what time it was. I'm hungry."

When they went into the kitchen, Jim said, "We heard the dinner bell! Cool!"

"Guess what?"

"What?"

"Marian laid an egg!"

"You sure?"

"Yes sir! I've got a witness."

Dave looked at Molly and she gave him the Scout Sign with the wrong hand.

"How'd you like his chicken operation?"

"I think it was the most fun I've ever had. I'd give a million dollars to have had a video recording of it. Jim gave me an academy award tour. And I learned a lot!" she said laughing. "I learned that people don't like to eat eggs with red dots in them, that you were a Sigma Nu, that John Newton was a ship captain that witnessed the grace of God, (she pinched her nose) that Thelma was Jimmie Rodgers' girlfriend, (she unpinched), that Meg Ryan has good sticks, that Miss Molly is one of Jim's best layers, two eggs, (and she gave a little curtsy), that Lantana stinks, that Mack Heath has four girlfriends, and that women like to have their bellies rubbed. And that's just some of the things. Oh my God, I learned so much!"

She opened her purse still laughing and gave Jim a quarter.

"You don't have to pay me."

"No, a bet's a bet."

"What was the bet?" Dave asked.

"Egg trick. I didn't even have the strength to break a silly egg."

Dave laughed and said, "Better watch him. He's got several more egg tricks."

"What's for dinner?"

"Chicken pot pie. Not much but it will fill us up."

CHAPTER 9

HEY PECAN MAN

They went to the breakfast table and Dave had set three places. Each place had "good silver" a fork and a spoon.

Molly looked up and he was smiling at her and said, "Nothing but the best for my guest."

The chicken pot pies were the old style in the little tin foil pans. The crust was golden brown on top and they were delicious. He had baked them in the oven for forty-five minutes. Maybe he was right about microwaves. She knew that microwave bacon wasn't that hot. He served the pies with crisp slices of apple and milk that was so cold it made your teeth hurt.

"These are pretty," Jim said holding up a fork.

Molly replied, "Yes, they are and they'll last you a lifetime with a little care. You can't dig with them in the garden. My mom made a rule that we could never put silverware in the disposal side of the sink. For all I know we only had one accident and that was when my dad fed the disposal a spoon."

"That's a good rule. Let's us do that, Bud." And Jim shook his head yes.

"What's the spoon for?" Jim asked.

"Surprise!"

When they were all through, Molly cleared the table and then came back to the table and sat down. "We're ready for the surprise now."

Dave got up and got three glasses and the Blue Bell. He put two scoops of vanilla in each glass and then added three Lorna Doone cookies. He added two teaspoonful's of raspberry extract and filled the glasses to the three-quarters mark with milk. He brought them to the table and said, "This is what

I call "Big Dave's Raspberry Doone Special." He handed each of them a glass and said, "You have to goulash it up a bit. I got the idea from Molly."

"Dad's a nut about raspberries. He says they eat them in heaven."

While they were all goulashing Molly said, "You know, they make Hawaiian Punch extract. Maybe Jim could make a Hawaiian Punch Special someday."

"Cooool!" Jim said, "I'm going to do it."

It was so cold it hurt to eat it too fast.

Molly was quiet for a minute and Dave said, "I can hear those wheels turning. What are you thinking about?"

"Maybe you could come out with a line of extracts and all you'd ever have to buy was vanilla ice cream. You could add your favorite flavoring and invent your own specials. Maybe you could call them "Imagination Extract Flavors.""

"By Molly by Golly!" Dave added chuckling.

"I like it!" she said. "Deal me in!"

"Me too!" Jim said and added, "This is good."

"It is!" said Molly, "It really, really is. Next time I might serve you all a Blueberry Animal Cracker Special."

"Cool!" said Jim and he asked, "How about a game of World to see who does the dishes?"

Molly said, "I'll play! What's the target?"

"Bull's-eye state!"

"What state is that?" she asked.

"Rhode Island."

"I get it." she said laughing, "It's the smallest state."

Dave lost and Molly said she would dry.

When they were just about through, Dave thanked her for getting them to use the silver. "It did make me think about my grandmother and I think she was pleased. If you would, I wish we had one of those silverware dividers for the drawer and maybe you could bring out what you think we will need."

"I'd love to. Next time we go to town I'll look around. No need to bring it all out."

There was a pause in the conversation and Molly said, "Some night just for the fun of it and there's just the three of us, I'd like to make a formal setting. It would be a way to show Jim a few etiquette rules. Not to show off, but it would be good to know if he ever goes to a real fancy restaurant or gets invited to the White House."

"Good idea! Maybe you could refresh me a little bit, too."

"You know what I'm going to dream about tonight?" She realized the second she said tonight that she had left herself wide open but it was too late.

"Me!" he said laughing.

"No, Mr. Smarty pants! I can't stop thinking about your ice cream idea. It's really got potential."

"Thanks!" he said. "I was kind of joking but it dawned on me that it probably would fly. Some ice cream czar might put a horse head in your bed if you tried it. I'll think some more on it, too."

After dishes they all went to the den and Dave got in his favorite chair and watched the weather. Conditions looked good for several rain free days. He had already booked several orders and was anxious to get them filled.

Jim asked Molly if she'd watch "The Music Man" with him. He wanted her to meet Marian, the librarian, and hear the little boy sing. She said she would but she wanted to freshen up first and she went upstairs.

While she was gone Jim got Dave's camera and asked, "Is this thing loaded?"

"Just put a new roll in a few days ago; you going to take some pictures?"

"No, but I want you to when she comes back, you just have it ready," and he went to the piano and loaded "Five Foot Two." "Dad, you're not going to believe it. She can sing and dance. She's good! Take a bunch of pictures."

Molly reappeared in white shorts, a pink V-neck cotton sweater with three-quarter sleeves. Fresh lipstick, freshly combed hair and a little foo foo water for effect. She saw Jim sitting at the piano and he said, "You've got to sing one song for dad."

"Which one?"

"Five Foot Two!"

"I'd be too embarrassed."

"You made me sing thirty songs for you, I'm just asking for one. Please."

"OK!" she said "Just one."

Jim pushed the button and the song started. She took a deep breath and began. On a wood floor and with the music she did a much better job. She sang, she shook, she shimmied and used all the moves of the twenties she could think of. She flashed her eyes and she poo poo pe doo'ed. Just when she thought it was over the song repeated itself and she did it again with even some new moves that she didn't know where they came from. She caught Dave aiming the camera one time and she stuck out her tongue at him. He recorded it for future generations. She sang, "Five foot two, eyes of blue but oh what those five feet could do. Has anybody seen my girl? Turned up nose, turned down hose, never had no other beaus. Has anybody seen my girl? Now if you run into a five foot two, covered with fur, diamond rings and all those things, bet cha life it isn't her. But could she love, could she woo, could she, could she, could she coo. Has anybody seen my girl?" She ended with eyelids fluttering, the back of her hand under her chin and the other on her knee. He also got this pose on film.

They both gave her a hand and Jim jumped up and gave her a hug.

"I believe that song was made for you." Dave said.

"Well, I am five two."

"Do it again!" said Jim.

"I already did. I didn't know it repeated, you stinker."

She enjoyed watching "The Music Man." It was so wholesome, so romantic, and full of hope and happiness. It made her like Dave even more knowing that he valued this movie. Jim was watching from the floor, she was lying on the couch and Dave was in his Archie chair.

She glanced at Dave maybe ten times during the first forty-five minutes of the movie and each time he caught her. She was having trouble concentrating so she propped a pillow beside her head so she couldn't see him.

Shortly, Dave got up and said, "I'll be at the shop."

She enjoyed the movie and Marian, the librarian was everything Jim said she was. The little boy from Gary played a great part and the barbershop singers inspired her to appreciate music even more. The "that's my boy" line even brought a tear. When it was over Jim said, "Did you like it?" as he pushed the rewind button.

"I loved it! It was one of the best movies I've ever seen."

Molly and Jim retired to bed after the movie. She was beginning to like her new routine. She wasn't used to going to bed so early but they got up a lot earlier so time wise it was a wash. She enjoyed seeing the sunrise, this was new for her and she liked it. Her last thought as she fell off to sleep was, I wonder what he's doing in the shop.

She awoke to Jim's version of "The Sun is Up" which wasn't quite as loud as Dave's but still plenty audible. She got dressed in a hurry because she wanted to try a new recipe on them. Jim was just finishing the bacon when she came down.

"Morning sunshine" she said and gave him a rub on the head and asked, "Mind if I try a new recipe."

"No ma'am! Can I help?"

"Sure, I'll need a skillet with about a quarter inch of oil in it."

She got down a bowl and put in one egg, one-half cup of milk, one-half cup of flour, a pinch of salt, and a teaspoonful of baking powder. She whipped them into a batter and Jim asked, "What'cha making?"

"My Aunt Sue's Chicken Fried Toast. She's famous for it. Our family has been making it for years. I think you'll like it. It's bound to be good, it's got a miracle egg in it." Next she got eight slices of white bread and cut it diagonally.

While she was waiting for the oil to get a littler hotter Mr. Dave appeared and she poured him a cup of coffee, one lump.

"Molly's cooking something new for us. She learned it from her Aunt Sue." Jim stated.

She dipped the bread into the batter and laid them gently in the hot oil. In almost no time they turned a golden brown and she turned them over to do the other side. She cooked four pieces at a time and let them drain on a paper towel. She served them with Aunt Jemima syrup and in a small bowl a mixture of powdered sugar with cinnamon as an option. The men devoured them and asked for seconds. She could tell they liked them and knew her Aunt Sue would be pleased when she told her.

They had coffee on the east porch and watched the sunrise and listened to the Martins. Dave looked handsome in his white shirt, Wranglers and Redwings. He was on a high. It was a hay day. He had a plan. She had heard of the term "hay day" and wondered what its meaning was. She made a mental note to look it up. Maybe it was "hey day" instead of "hay day."

Dave said he would start in the Indian pasture as it was now called and would work his way down the hill. He hoped to cut at least twenty acres today and would probably cut 'till dark. Molly made sure he had his cell phone with him and fixed him a large thermos of iced tea and said she would have lunch for him at the chuck wagon at noon.

"Deal!" he said. He wasn't used to being pampered but he liked it. He left for the field and she went with Jim to watch him open the proper gate and feed the chickens.

The parameter fence was covered with roses and she went to take a closer look at them. She recognized several as old-timey varieties, the kinds that seem to thrive on neglect. She remembered one time driving with her parents and seeing an old farmhouse that had burned to the ground many years before but the roses the original owners had planted were still blooming their heads off with total neglect. She remembered her mom's comment; "Now that's a rose I could raise." These were the same types.

There was a railroad tie border around the rose beds about two feet wide. In this space were growing a ring of marigolds and more zinnias than she had ever seen before. The view was breath taking. Compost and wood chips kept the weeds down. Her mind started racing. This was probably the only chicken yard like this in the United States. People would love to see it. What mom wouldn't want to bring her son or daughter here to see this? To gather eggs, to feed the chickens, to scope the eggs and to walk out with a dozen eggs that their child had gathered, and to hear Jim sing his songs. Oh my God! She thought. She would brainstorm this idea and bring it up at later date. She had never had eggs that tasted so good before. Maybe there was something to this range chicken experiment of theirs. The yolks were definitely a beautiful color. They were definitely premium eggs. Grade A triple plus however the grading system worked.

When she went back inside the chicken yard she found Jim sitting on a stool cracking up oyster shells on a large cement block with a hammer.

"What in the world are you doing?"

"Dad read somewhere that chickens need extra calcium to make strong egg shells. Every once in a while I bust up some oyster shells and they peck on the pieces, must work because we never have any broken eggs."

"Yeah it works! It makes them hard as rocks. I couldn't even break one." And they both laughed.

When they got back to the house Molly got the binoculars and took a look to see if she could see Dave cutting hay. She spotted him and thought something was wrong and called him on his cell phone. He answered and she asked, "Are you OK? Are geese attacking you? I can see white birds flying all around you."

"No!" he said laughing, "Those are cattle egrets. They're after bugs."

She asked if it would be OK to take the truck to town. She had a few things she needed.

"OK by me."

"Is it OK to take Jim? He wants to sell some eggs."

"Sure."

"We've got the short list, is there anything you can think of?"

"Nope, you all be careful."

"One more thing, Is it OK to take your credit card?"

There was a pause and he said, "Sure! It's on the top of my chest of drawers. Oh, and before you leave, check and see how my perfume is holding out," and he hung up laughing.

She got the card and the short list and they were off. Jim brought twenty dozen eggs with him because the camping trip had put him behind on his deliveries. She parked the truck at the town square and they agreed to meet at Allison's Jewelry store at ten. She found two dresses and a pair of shoes that would go good with either dress. She was ready for church. She had a dress.

Jim was at the jewelry store when she arrived. Mr. Allison came over and asked if he could show her anything. "No" she said, "I just came in to find young Matthew."

Jim introduced Mr. Allison to Molly and told him that she was going to be his nanny for the next two months. He said, "Call me Will. I've known Dave since he moved out here and I consider him one of my best friends." They made small talk for a few minutes and Jim said, "Measure her ring size, I might want to buy her an engagement ring someday."

His comment got raised eyebrows from Molly and Will at the same time. She went along with him and Will measured her finger. "Size six." He said.

She ended up buying a small sterling necklace with a dove of peace. It would add a little sparkle to her new outfits. Jim liked it too.

They went to the truck and Jim said he'd forgotten to tell Mr. Allison something and he would be back in a minute. At the jewelry store he made a purchase and paid Mr. Allison forty-five dollars in cash. It was the biggest purchase he had ever made. He didn't flinch or hesitate a second when he heard the price. One of his helpers wrapped it for him in a small box and he put it in his pocket. He was ready for Molly's birthday. He was proud.

They stopped at the grocery store and picked up the items on the short list. She sashayed through the cookie department and picked up a few items for future "Specials" and also picked up another gallon of Mr. Vanilla Blue Bell.

She had planned to fix sandwiches for lunch when they got back but on the way out of town they came to a chicken place and she decided this might be more of a working man's lunch. She got a ten-piece bucket with biscuits and some cream gravy on the side.

162

As they approached the Indians, they could see Dave on the tractor. She pulled over on the shoulder and gave a few long honks and he waved.

At the house they unloaded and Jim went to hook up the travois. She strapped on a small Igloo and a new thermos jug, which she had filled with water. She was sure he was tired of iced tea by now. She had Jim ring the dinner bell one time as a test to see if he could hear it while the tractor was running. About a minute later he gave it three quick rings and ran to meet Molly on the path.

"Did I hear my ring?" she asked.

"Yes ma'am!"

"Thanks" she said and gave him a quick hug.

At the chuck wagon Molly helped Jim move the chairs to the shady side of the wagon and they waited for Dave.

He made one more pass around the field and drove the tractor to the wagon.

Molly said, "Glad the birds didn't get you."

"Yeah, me too. Did I hear the dinner bell?"

"Yes you did! Did you hear the Molly ring?"

"No."

"Well, Jim gave it to me, made me feel good."

Molly pulled out the chicken and fixed each of them a plate. While they were wolfing it down Molly said, "Sure would be nice to have a picnic table out here. Maybe you could build one on a rainy day."

"Yes'um Miss Scarlet" he replied smiling.

It was a great lunch. Dave was still on a high. He would get to cut more than he thought he would today. The dew point was low and the warm breeze was drying the hay fast. Not having to go to the house would give him more time.

Molly asked if she could drive the tractor after lunch. He said he would give her a lesson and if she didn't grind the gears too bad he'd let her make a round or two.

"How'd the shopping go? Did I buy anymore perfume?"

"No, Mr. Smarty Pants! I did buy a dress and a necklace at Allison's but I used my own card." She showed him the new thermos she had bought him and he was pleased. "I also got you some bananas. They're supposed to be good for your potassium."

After a little rest, Dave started the tractor and took Molly for a shake down. He explained the gears and the proper speed. She learned how to raise the cutting arm and to put it in neutral. They went through some safety dos and don'ts which he made her repeat to him. She was a little jerky at first but in a short time she had it down. After the first round she told him to get off that she wanted to make a round by herself. He bragged on her that her touch was easy on the tractor and he knew the tractor would appreciate it. He stressed the rpm's. "The tractor will run a lot faster but this is the best speed to make the cutting blade work best" and he pointed to a little mark on the tachometer.

"I wish you had your camera. I would love to send my dad a picture of me driving the tractor. He comes from a long line of farmers and I know he'd get a kick out of it." She drove off with Dave scratching his head and Jim giving her the thumbs up.

The feel of the tractor was sensuous. Maybe it was the same feeling that women who ride Harleys get. The sound of the powerful engine, the feel of the leather, the fresh air, the smell of the freshly cut hay, the grass hoppers fleeing the monster and the egrets swarming all put together made it exhilarating. She stopped once when a doe jumped up out of the tall grass and ran a few yards and stopped to look back at her. She put it in neutral and did a walk around and about twenty yards in front she found a fawn bedded down that was afraid to move. She guessed its mother had given a signal not to move or maybe it was just born and couldn't walk yet. She lifted the cutting bar and went around.

After a few more rounds she saw Dave and Jim coming. When they got close she saw that he had his camera.

"You missed a spot over there" he said pointing.

"Don't you dare cut that? There's a fawn bedded down. Prettiest thing I ever saw. Big brown eyes, she didn't move a muscle."

Jim said, "I want to see!" he told the dogs to stay and he took off. Dave went to see the fawn and got a couple of pictures. He also got some of Molly on the tractor. She talked him into sitting on the motor cowling while she made one more round. She wanted a picture of her driving with the egrets flying in the background. She took a picture of him sitting backwards on the tractor hood while she drove. He looked so ridiculous that she just had to have it. He dropped her off at the wagon and suggested that she and Jim take a swim.

"Great idea, but all my swimsuits are in Ohio."

"Well, no skinny dipping in front of Jim" and he drove off smiling at her.

"You be careful with my tractor!" she snapped back.

"Yes ma'am."

Jim had told him she had a birthday coming up and he made a mental note to treat her to a bathing suit as a birthday present. A string bikini would be nice and he slapped himself across the face. "Dirty old man," he thought and he slapped himself again.

Dave was true to his word and came in right at dark. He cleaned up and they had lasagna and a super salad Jim had picked from the garden. She topped off supper with a dessert she called, Maraschino Doone Cherry Blue Bell Special. The men inhaled it.

"Kind of takes your breath away." Dave added.

"Yes, you do," she thought but answered, "I take that as a thumbs up."

"Yes ma'am!" Jim said, "That was good. I never had cherry ice cream before."

They returned to the study and Jim brought out the Bible and turned to his marker. They read ten pages that night since they had another reader. They discussed what they had read. She was inspired by their routine. Jim asked some good questions and they did the best they could. She was glad they let her participate and it made her feel at home. "Samuel is a tough read no matter what your age," she thought.

Jim retired shortly and she and Dave went to the porch and watched the moon rise over the lake. He told her that the weather still looked good and he would cut again tomorrow. She wanted to help and he said he had a smaller tractor with a hay rake and he would teach her how to drive it in the morning.

"With conditions right, you cut hay one day, rake it the next and bail it the next. A rain on the already cut hay can cause it to mildew and you'll lose that cutting."

She was in bed at 9:30 and couldn't believe it. If it was a "hay day," shouldn't they be dancing and celebrating somewhere? Wonder what a "hay rake day" would be like? As she was about to drift off, her mind raced. She needed to get back home to find another roommate to help defray expenses or move out of the apartment and back home until she got her finances back in order. She needed to talk to the insurance company about her car.

She had a couple of thousand in her savings but her rent times two would wipe her out in no time. It was a godsend that she had chosen to receive her salary over twelve months instead of nine. That would help. Maybe after the first baling she could go home for a week to get her affairs in order. Maybe she could take Jim with her. It would be fun and might widen his horizons a little. She'd sleep on it.

She awoke to the music of the Martins. It was so peaceful; one would have to experience it to describe it. She pulled the covers up for a couple of extra winks before the in-house songfest began. Whoops, too late. The birds that sing must be on the wing and she popped out of bed. She was excited. It was a hay rake day and she'd have her own tractor. She had seen it. It was red.

The bacon was almost finished when she came down. The men wanted her to make Aunt Sue's toast again. She said she would and Dave watched her as she mixed. He wanted to make sure he could duplicate it. The breakfast was another success. Jim volunteered to do the dishes and Molly fixed water jugs for each of them and they left the house for a lesson in hay raking. Dave was patient with her and after one round she was making nice little windrows as they were called. The windrows were just the width of the bales and all the baler had to do was to follow the rows.

Dave insisted that she wear one of his white shirts to protect her from the sun. He found an old straw hat that somewhat fit and made her put sun block on her hands and face. Before he left her he said, "If you don't get burned out after today, I'm going to get you some work clothes and a better hat."

It would be Jim's job today to watch Molly for safety reasons. He was also to fix lunch and bring it to the wagon at noon.

The Massey Ferguson tractor wasn't nearly as powerful as the John Deere, and it didn't have a sunroof. On a break, Jim brought out the water jug and they had a chat. She was already tired of the sun and was glad he insisted on the hat, which was none too flattering. They got on the shady side of the tractor and Molly leaned against the wheel as she drank and rested. She enjoyed chatting with Jim. He told her that his Dad calls this tractor the "Little Red M F" and she had to bite her lip to keep from laughing.

By noontime the sun was taking its toll on her. It wasn't near as much fun as when she began. There were no egrets following her either. She heard the thirty-minute bell and immediately turned the tractor towards the wagon. She even beat Jim there. Dave pulled up a few minutes later.

"Looks like you got the hang of it," he said. "You're doing a good job."

"Thanks!" she answered, "Raking is a lot faster than cutting. I ought to be through in a couple of hours."

Jim opened the cooler and brought out potato chips, large purple plums and baloney sandwiches. He had cut the crust off the bread and cut them diagonally. "Hope you like baloney? Me and dad do. Dad says don't ever read the label on baloney or you'll never eat it, but it's healthy and not too fattening."

"You should say Dad and I instead of me and Dad. One of my jobs as a nanny is to help you with your English."

"Yes ma'am." Jim answered.

She enjoyed the lunch and when she was just about finished, she asked Jim if he would get her one of the pads out of the wagon. She wanted to straighten her back a little.

Jim climbed up in the wagon and said, "You want one too, Dad?"

"Yeah buddy!"

"A pillow too!" said Molly.

"Make it two, Bud."

Molly lay on her stomach in the shade of the big tractor and pulled the pillow under her head. Dave put his pad beside hers and lay on his side facing her.

Molly said, "I've got an idea."

"What?"

"When we start back to work, why don't you drive the Little Red M F'er and I'll drive the John Deere. I'm more of a John Deere type."

"Sorry about that." He said laughing. "I've been meaning to get an umbrella for it. We'll switch."

"And I want a Stetson hat, just like yours."

"You got it."

"And Red Wings!"

"What size?"

"Don't worry about the size; just lend me your card."

Dave got up and said, "I've got to get back to work. I'm going broke taking a break."

Molly laughed and got up too. "Good lunch, Jimbo! I'll give you an A on that."

Jim halved the last sandwich with the dogs. Slick wasn't used to so many noon time treats. He was sure Molly had something to do with it and he decided she was his new best friend.

Dave completed the raking about four and went to relieve Molly. "Why don't you go to the house and get cleaned up and take a power nap? I'll be in about dark and we'll go to town and eat a steak."

"I'd like that," she answered.

"Sometimes Jim and I go bowling on Thursdays and they have a good restaurant. It's a dry county but their steaks are really good."

The thought of getting cleaned up and going out was exciting. It was kind of like a date but she knew it wasn't.

The bath she took was probably the best she'd ever had. Maybe it was the bath beads he'd bought her that made her feel so good or maybe it was an honest day's work. The brief sleep did wonders, and she was bright eyed and bushy tailed when Dave came in.

He was in good spirits and said that they had cut fifty acres in two days and raked thirty. "Tomorrow we'll bale thirty and rake twenty. I'll get John to help me with the baling."

Molly treated herself to a pre-dinner glass of wine and waited for Dave to get ready and for Jim to get back from tending his miracle workers.

She wore the pink sweater again but with khaki linen pants. She got a "hubba hubba" out of Jim who always made her feel good.

"I wonder what Mr. Dave will wear tonight?" She thought as she was enjoying her wine on the front porch. She had a hunch and when he appeared, she was right: a fresh pair of Wranglers and a white Brooks Brothers "no iron shirt." He looked exactly like he did this morning when he climbed on his tractor. Only difference was he was wearing his dress brown Red Wings and a nicer belt.

Jim called shotgun and they were on their way.

About the third light into town they pulled up behind a convertible. The girl driving had the music on loud and was kind of dancing with it. As they got closer Molly could see she had a bumper sticker and as they got a little closer she could read it. It read: Wrangler Butts Drive Me Nuts.

"Oh my God!" she said, "I believe this girl's right down your alley."

Jim laughed and said, "That's Jolene! We know her."

Jolene happened to look in the rear view mirror about that time and recognized the truck but Molly doubted if she could see that Dave had passengers because the truck was so high.

When the light changed she quickly changed lanes to the left and let Dave pull up beside her. Dave looked out the window and gave her a little wave.

Jolene said in a sultry voice, "Hey, pecan man, when you gonna show me them nuts of yours?"

Molly couldn't believe what she had just heard and in a reflex leaned across Dave and gave her a look of disapproval. Jolene was surprised by

Molly's sudden appearance, and hit the passing gear and was out of there. She gave a sheepish little wave as she changed back into Dave's lane.

Molly said, "I believe she's got the hots for you."

"What are you talking about? She's only seventeen or eighteen years old. That's Will's daughter. Will is one of my best friends."

"Well, all of her hormones are working. I believe she's right down your alley."

"Well, you're wrong. Taking advantage of her would be kind of like clubbing a baby seal."

"Well, next time I see her I'm going to wash her mouth with soap."

"Did she say a bad word?" Jim asked.

"It was the way she put the words together Jim. It wasn't lady like."

And then Dave just had to make the smart little statement; "Maybe you're a little bit jealous."

Molly looked up at Dave who had a little smirk on his face and she gave him an elbow to the ribs and said, "In your dreams, you big pecan man."

"Ouch! That hurt," and they drove in silence to the bowling alley.

The atmosphere at the bowling alley was fun. Everybody knew everybody. Dave made contact with several of his hay customers and handshake deals were made. Not too many women here: it seemed mostly a guy hang out. Dave was glad to see John and asked him if he could help him bale in the morning.

"You already cut?" he asked.

"Yep, got me a new hand, she's easy on the equipment and doesn't eat too much," and he put his arm around her and gave her a little hug.

John told Molly, "You got yourself a new best friend at our place. That letter you sent Caroline really perked her up. She sleeps with those hair things you gave her and little Rudi thinks he owns the place. He spends more time in people's arms than he does on the ground. Shelley said she was going to call you all tomorrow. She's finished the jelly and wants you all to come over Saturday night for burgers on the grill."

"Sounds like fun to me," said Molly, "Better ask Pecan Man here, he's the boss."

"We'll be there, and I'll bring a tiger watermelon."

The lanes were pretty crowded so they decided they'd bowl another night and went to the restaurant to order. Dave was right, the steak was delicious. Maybe because it was Black Angus or maybe the company. Several men stopped by the table. Dave seemed to be a popular guy but he knew some of them were just coming by to get a better look at Molly. One even had the gall to ask if they were a number. Dave was about to throw out an answer of some sort when Molly said, "No, I'm just Matthew's nanny for a couple of months."

"No kidding," he said excitedly, "Maybe you'd like to go dancing sometime."

"Sounds like fun! I only have weekends off though."

"Good deal! I'll be calling," he called out as he tipped his hat and left.

She looked at Dave who was in some kind of shock and said, "Wow! Talk about a hunk."

"You can't go out with him."

"Why not?"

"He's a sleaze ball. That's why."

"Afraid he might club me?"

"Exactly!"

"You don't think I can take care of myself?"

"Well, it only took me about four minutes to have you in my bedroll," he said smiling.

"Maybe you're a tiny bit jealous?" she answered back.

The thought of her going out with someone else was killing him. He was dying. He looked into her eyes and said, "Maybe I feel responsible for you."

"Maybe you'd like to eat a little crow for dessert?"

Before he could answer, the waitress came over and asked if they'd like some dessert.

"Yes ma'am!" Jim answered, "I'd like a piece of apple pie with a dip of vanilla on it."

"Make it two" Molly chimed in.

The waitress looked at Dave and asked, "How about you Dave?"

"I'd like a little crow."

Molly laughed and Dave said, "Make it three."

The waitress looked at Molly who was making a little twirling motion with her finger next to her ear and pointed to Dave.

The waitress nodded yes to Molly and left with the order.

Jim said, "Next time we come we'll have to bowl."

"I'd like that" she said, "Maybe we can have a contest, you and me against your dad and his partner."

"That'd be like taking candy from a baby," Dave replied.

"Might be another time to eat some crow! Big Boy."

The boys didn't know it but she had bowled all her life with her dad and her brother. In the wintertime in Ohio the only games in town were bowling and pool. She even took bowling in college for her required PE. She made a note that if she did get to go back home for a visit she might bring back her own ball and shoes. Might even bring back her own Q Stick. She was good at both. Her brother was a perfectionist and had learned the proper techniques, and she had learned the basics from him. She decided to keep her little secret and that he would eat a little more crow at a later date. It would be fun.

CHAPTER 10

BUZZ BURGERS

John showed up right after breakfast and had a cup of coffee with them before they went to the field.

Molly was fascinated by the baling operation. Dave and John worked well as a team. There was not a wasted motion. She could see that they needed the John Deere because of its extra power so she took Little Red. She knew she could do it. Heck, only twenty acres to rake!

After lunch, Molly finished with the raking about two, and she and Jim went over to help the men. Dave unhooked the hay rake and hooked up a custom-built low boy trailer to the tractor. He had an order for one hundred-and-fifty square bales and he wanted them stacked in three rows of ten bales each and five bales high. "When you all are through with that one, we'll load up another one with fifty bales."

Amazingly, by dark they had done it. One hundred and fifty bales on one trailer and fifty on another and a little over one hundred four foot round bales in the field.

She knew she would not run today. She felt as if one of the tractors had run over her. Seeing the fruits of their labor on the trailers and in the field was exhilarating. It wasn't even her land but she felt good about it. She imagined that Dave was feeling the same good vibes but even more.

"How about that beer now," Dave asked John.

"Thought you'd never ask."

Jim said he was going swimming and climbed up in the wagon to change. He wanted her to come in but she didn't have a suit. "Next time we go to town, I'll have to get one."

Molly passed on a beer offer but stayed and listened to the men hash over the day's progress and the plan for tomorrow. They would bale the other twenty acres tomorrow in round bales, make a few deliveries, and stack as many of the round bales as they could. Time permitting they would make a trip to town and get Molly some Wranglers, a hat, and a couple of pairs of work gloves. Her hands were a mess after lifting all those bales. It took Jim and her both to lift them. She thought back to Jolene's bumper sticker and laughed to herself. His was definitely driving her nuts. Wonder if it works both ways?

Back at the house Dave went to turn on the weather channel and Molly said she would fix supper.

Jim wanted to help and she told him to get six eggs and scramble them in a bowl with a little milk and while he was doing that she got the skillet out and put in a pad of butter and melted it. She told Jim to pour in the eggs and when they became fluffy she poured in a small can of ranch style beans and larger can of Wolf Brand Chili. She turned the heat up a little and told Jim to stir.

She got down three bowls, three spoons, poured three glasses of milk and put come crackers on a plate. "Call your dad" she said, "We're ready."

Dave came to the kitchen and said, "Wow! That didn't take long."

They all dug in and Molly said, "It's one of my brother's camping recipes; easy but good, better around a campfire when it's cold outside. In restaurants, I believe they would call it huevos rancheros but my brother's name for it was goulash. Sometimes he might throw in an onion or dice up a potato. One time he chopped up a jalapeno and threw it in.

"I like it!" Jim said, "Next time I want to do it."

"Maybe we'll call it Jim's Goulash." Molly threw in.

"One time he made it and he was out of chili, and he used a can of Ireland's Bar B Q Beef. It was good too."

THE HOOT OWL MAN

Dave told Jim to write down a couple of cans of each for our camping chuck box and a couple of cans for the chuck wagon box. The boys did dishes while she went to get cleaned up.

She came down in her robe with wet hair and a towel wrapped around her hair. She hoped her new look wouldn't scare them too bad. She couldn't look her best all the time and she knew she wasn't far from going to bed.

She came into the den and did a little twirl. "How do you like my new look?"

"Cool!" said Jim but she got no reply from Master Dave.

The boys were watching a baseball game. Barry Bonds had just hit one to Timbuktu and they were watching the replay.

"Maybe we'll watch "The Natural" before long." Jim suggested.

"Can I interest you boys in a Surprise Special?"

"Yes ma'am! I'll have a surprise."

"Me too," Dave answered.

She fixed Jim a Pecan Banana Doone Blue Bell Special and for Dave and herself a Courvoisier Blue Bell Special with two Doones on the side.

She passed them out and got an immediate "Alright!" out of Jim.

She watched Dave's face for his reaction and saw his eyebrows go up and he asked, "What's this called?"

She said, "I call this a W T M Blue Bell Special with a side order of Doones."

"Not bad, I think I lov"...and he stopped short.

"You think what?" she asked with ears perked up.

"I forgot what I think. This is freezing my brain!"

"Well slow down, you're supposed to sip it."

When he was through he said, "That was good, I believe you've got something there."

Dave fed the dogs and said he was going on a short walk. Molly told Jim she was going to bed but he talked her into one song on the player piano and they sat down together.

"Which one?" she asked.

"Want to hear Dad's favorite?"

"Which one is that?" and he put on "You're Nobody 'til Somebody Loves You."

"This is his favorite?"

"Yes ma'am. He says it's his theme song. I tell him I love him but he says it has to be a woman."

He pulled the rinky tink pull and pushed the button.

They sang together but Molly's voice was so pretty and strong that he stopped singing and just listened. She set the tempo just right and hit all the words just at the right spot. The song repeated itself and she sang it again;

"You're nobody 'til somebody loves you,
You're nobody 'til somebody cares,
You may be king,
You may possess,
The world and all its gold,
But gold won't bring you happiness,
When you're growing old,
The world still is the same
You'll never change it,
As sure as the sun shines above,
You're nobody 'til somebody loves you,
So find yourself somebody to love."

"That was good! Jim said.

"What else does he like?"

"He plays this one a lot" pointing to "Heart of My Heart," "but this is probably his next favorite" and he pulled out "Anytime."

"Let's do that one and then call it a night." Jim pushed the button and they sang;

"Anytime you're feeling lonely,
Anytime you're feeling blue,

Anytime you feel down hearted,
That will prove your love for me is true,
Anytime you're thinking 'bout me,
That's the time I'll be thinking of you,
So anytime you want your baby back again,
That's the time I'll come back home to you,"

When the song was over, they high fived and headed off to bed.

Dave had several low-boy trailers he had customized for hauling his hay. Unless he had an order for large round bales, he preferred the four-foot round bales. He tried to keep five of his trailers loaded with fourteen round bales on each. Two rows of four on the bottom and two rows of three nested on top. He didn't charge for the use of the trailers if they had them back by the next day. He got thirty dollars per round bale if he had to deliver it but would knock off five dollars per bale it they picked it up. They would still get the discount if they used his trailer. It was a little niche that he had come up with and his customers liked it. Dave provided tarps and tie downs and kept his trailers in good repair.

Round bales were good deals for volume hay users, because one man with the right equipment could handle and feed a lot of stock single-handedly which helped keep labor cost down. Each round bale was equivalent to fifteen to seventeen square bales depending on how tight they were rolled. Dave rolled his tight and his customers knew it.

Square bales took more labor and time to handle but were more profitable. They stored better and suited his smaller customers. He got three dollars per bale and didn't discount these, but he would let a customer use one of his trailers for no charge on an order of one hundred bales or more. He had a large hay shed with a tin roof and a concrete floor. The north and east sides had walls to keep out the weather; the open sides made for easy loading and unloading.

His next cutting would be all square bales. They stacked and stored well, and he hoped to have several thousand bales stored before winter got here.

His agreement with John was that John would use last year's hay first for his own use. He worked for free but got paid in hay. Last year he used about one hundred round bales for his own cattle operation. It was a good deal for both of them. John could raise more stock and didn't have to tie up his own land for haying and purchase his own baling equipment.

The hay operation was growing, and he was constantly trying new ideas and the hard work was beginning to pay off. He had put together several sets of rollers on wheels that could be wheeled around to help him load his customer's trailers and trucks with a minimum of lifting. He had one trailer that had a motorized conveyer belt that would lift bales from the trailer to a hayloft. He charged extra for this trailer but his customers said it was worth it. It was so popular that he decided to build another one in the near future.

After another great breakfast Dave and John hit the fields and started baling the remaining twenty acres. Molly brought them lunch to the field and they kept working while they ate.

They were determined to beat the rain. They finished about three and John went home. Dave hooked the spear on the John Deere and a low-boy to the Little Red. Dave did the spearing, and Molly pulled the trailer to the bales in the field. By dark thirty they had loaded two trailers with fourteen round bales each and taken them to the hay shed. They were working on the third when they felt the first drop of rain and they ran to the house.

"Thanks for your help. We made a good team."

"That was fun. Maybe next time you'll let me spear."

"You bet. We've got one hundred and ten more acres to cut, and then we'll repeat the process two more times. Then it will be pecan time. Cold winters we make some hay, warm winters we eat some hay."

"If you don't mind me asking, how much did you make off the hay last year?"

"Thirty-four thousand, my labor was zero because John and I did all the work and we don't draw a salary. My new baler cost twelve thousand, but I can depreciate it. I've got an accountant helping me but I probably miss some deductions. The more improvements we make, the less we have to report as income. I fertilize to make better hay. I send a sample each year to A & M to have it assayed and graded. I've done what they say each year and my protein count is 15.7 which is just as about as good as hay gets. Horse farmers only buy the best grade for their horses. A & M told a big racetrack about my hay and I've got a verbal order for an eighteen wheeler-full later this fall. Things are picking up. This year we ought to make a killing, because I've got a genie working for me." He said laughing.

He continued, "Jim is getting stronger and is going to be a real help in the future. Sometime we're going to cut a real fat hog on the pecans. They're our ace in the hole. I'm sure we'll have some bad years but we plan to have a lot of irons in the fire."

She was enjoying this conversation and asked, "Tell me about these irons in the fire."

"Blueberries, plums, peaches, apples, blackberries, dewberries, figs, mayhaws, kumquats, peppers, pickles, lettuce, tomatoes, watermelons, cantaloupes, strawberries, a line of jellies, jams, marmalades. Firewood, pecan wood, compost for sale, flowers for sale, gourds, iron work, wood work, paintings, greenhouses, and that's just a few." He said as he took a breath.

He continued, "Right now we sell all of our pecans in bulk. What if we had a line of pecan candies, pralines, shelled pecans, and gift baskets? Maybe even a website. And catfish! That lake has more catfish than you can imagine. Before long I'm going to let Jim start harvesting some of them. Most of them are around three pounds right now. He could easily catch twenty-five each week and I know of a catfish place that will pay a dollar twenty-five per pound for live catfish. I believe he could pay for his college education with catfish. Twenty-five per week wouldn't hurt the population at all. Twenty acres is a big lake. And what about a Bed & Breakfast cabin on the lake? A family could bring their kids and enjoy the lake like we do. They could fish, campout, canoe, swim, enjoy the wildlife, see Jim's chickens, pick berries, gather pecans, pick peaches, whatever. Maybe you could go down some morning and fix them Aunt Sue's chicken fried toast or mix their old man a W T M Blue Bell Special with Doones on the side. I guarantee they'd be back next year."

"Wow!" she said, "You do have some ideas."

"Sorry about that. I get carried away about the potential of this place." And he started again, "And maybe fishing clinics for kids, or fly fishing clinics. A place to have kids' birthdays. A place that caterers could use for rehearsal dinners or family picnics, a place to have Bar-B-Q's or fish fries, maybe a place to have weddings."

And Molly threw in, "And don't forget the Imagination Flavor Extracts."

"Right, they'd go good in gift baskets."

"Sounds like you and Miss Jackie are going to be busy."

"I don't know? She hates this place."

"I know you're kidding."

"Nope, that's the truth," and added. "She's coming for a visit in a few days; she called yesterday."

There was a long silence and Molly could almost feel his predicament. This might be a good time she thought and said, "I've got an idea I'd like to run by you. I need to get back home for a few days to get my finances back in some kind of order. I've got to find a roommate or move back home. I can't afford the rent all by myself. I also need to get squared away with what to do about my car. I need to meet with the insurance company. I was thinking, maybe I could take Jim with me. Might widen his horizons a little. I'm sure my brother or dad would take him fishing or arrowhead hunting. It would give you and Jackie a few days together and maybe you wouldn't get killed because I was here. I believe those were the words you used."

"Yeah, I kind of believe they were. That's not a bad idea. Sure you wouldn't mind taking Jim?

"Are you kidding? It'll be fun."

Dave said, somewhat relieved, "I'll buy the tickets if you promise to come back."

"Deal!" she said but added, "If you promise not to do anything crazy."

"Like what?"

She paused a bit because she knew she was pushing it and said, "Well, like flying to Las Vegas to hear chapel bells."

"Would that upset you?"

"Maybe," she said and rolled her big eyes at him and added, "About this much" and she held up her thumb and forefinger about a quarter of an inch apart.

He laughed and said, "That didn't look like very much."

She held them up again but about three inches apart this time.

"I promise." He said grinning.

"I'll make the arrangements and ask Jim if that's OK?"

"Sure, but I know what he's going to say when Jessica asks him."

The next morning after breakfast Dave said he needed to go to town to get diesel fuel for the tractors and to buy a watermelon for tonight. Molly asked him to pick up a roll of film for her camera.

When he left, she invited Jim to Ohio and he was on cloud nine. It would be his first time on an airplane. They went to the World board, and he had her show him exactly where they would be going. He was journey proud and they weren't even off the ground. He got out the *Britannica* with Ohio in it and started reading. Molly found a good book from Dave's collection and curled up on the couch. It was hard to concentrate because Jim asked so many questions. "My God!" she thought, "he knows more about my own state than I do."

Dave came back about noon and after lunch and they all retired to the den. Jim told his dad about Molly's invite to Ohio and asked if it was OK. Dave gave the green light and Jim gave him a history lesson on Ohio. When he was finally through Dave got a book and settled in his chair and started to read.

Molly asked Jim, "Well, what are you and I going to do before we go to the Phelan's tonight?"

"Would you like to play blocks?"

"You bet!" she answered not knowing what she was getting into.

Jim pulled the bearskin rug to the side and slid out the block set to the center of the rug in front of the fireplace. She was instantly impressed with the block set. It was a square box with all sides open. Each block size had its own compartment. "Very, very neat!" she thought.

"Weighs thirty-two pounds." Jim threw in.

"Who made these?"

"Uncle Dave."

On top of the box painted in blue letters was IMAGINATION BUILDING BLOCKS.

"What does it mean?"

Jim explained, "You have to have an imagination to use them. Do you have an imagination?"

Molly glanced up to Dave who was watching and enjoying the moment and answered, "I think so!"

"Good! But before we start, you have to know the rules. When we're through you have to put all the blocks back in the box. OK?"

"OK."

One corner of the box had a hinged lid and was locked with a padlock. "What's in here?"

"Top secret!"

"You can tell me."

"Nope, if I tell you I'll have to kill you."

"I promise I won't tell. Genies don't break promises."

"OK if you promise, but you won't believe it."

"Try me?" And he rattled off without taking a breath: "9 cars, 12 trucks, 5 boats, 200 marbles, 11 airplanes, 2 helicopters, 4 horses, 2 dogs, 2 Harleys, and a 4 wheeler."

"No way, tell me again," she said thinking he was pulling her leg and he repeated the inventory verbatim.

He explained how the key was hidden. "See these two blocks here, they're fake. Behind them is a key. See!" as he pulled out a key which was hidden on a retractable string. He unlocked the lock and started taking out his treasures. "Now do you believe me?"

"Awesome!" she answered, "I believe your uncle has an imagination of his own."

"What do you want to build?" he asked

She studied the pile of toys and said, "An airport. Will you help me?"

"Sure!"

"I'll start with the control tower," she said.

She tried to make the blocks stand up on the crocheted rug but they kept falling down.

Jim could see she was having trouble and said, "A building is only as good as its foundation" and he showed her how to put a foundation on top of the rug so the blocks wouldn't tip over.

"You are so smart. Where did you learn that?"

He said, "Well, it's in the Bible. You should build your house on a rock, not the sand. The rug is kind of like the sand."

Molly glanced up at Dave who was taking all this in and he winked at her. "Damn!" She thought, "If he only knew what that did to her."

They built a hangar, the tower, and runways and let their imaginations run wild. Molly really got into it and let her inhibitions fall. She took a plane and walked around the room making buzzing noises like a jet. She buzzed Dave a few times and then made a nice landing.

Dave enjoyed watching them play so much that he had gotten his camera and took several pictures of them but mostly of her. He used to play blocks with Jim for hours when he was little but now that Jim was getting older, Jim had new games and worlds to conquer. The block set had been a great time to get to know Matthew and was a bond between them. Any kid would love to have a block set like that, and he made a mental note to make a set for young Jackson.

Jim got his dad to take a picture of the final project and they started putting the blocks up. As they were putting them in the proper compartments she asked, "Why are some of these different colors?"

Jim answered saying, "These blocks here are walnut like they make furniture out of. It's a hardwood. Real slow growing and expensive. These are pecan. These are oak which is real strong. They make railroad ties out of oak. These are from a cypress tree. They grow in the water and are good for building boats because they swell up and won't rot or leak. And look at these,

these are long leaf yellow pine." And he picked up a piece and showed her the grain on the end of the block. He counted the rings and said, "These trees were real slow growers. This little block is twelve years old and probably came from a tree that was this big around. Think of how old that tree must have been. Dad got some of the boards out of an old building they were tearing down."

As the blocks were being slid back to their resting spot Molly said, "That was fun, Jimbo!" and they high fived.

"You should see dad build a suspension bridge sometime. It's really neat."

They left shortly for the Phelan's and when they got to the front gate, all three of the girls were standing there with a bouquet of flowers in their hands for Molly.

"I was afraid of that" laughed Dave.

Caroline was mad at her sisters because Molly was her friend. They weren't supposed to give her flowers. Dave disarmed all the tension with a few peppermints. Jackson brought out Rudi Kazuti and the race was on. Molly got a few pictures of each of the kids, trying not to show favoritism. Shelley took them inside. She wanted Dave to see the "Jelly by Shelley," and she had finished Molly's quilt and was anxious for her to see it.

Dave was pleased and bragged on her. After visiting a few minutes, he went outside to see if he could help John with the fire and to talk cows and hay.

Molly was thrilled with the quilt and stayed in the kitchen to help Shelley. After a few minutes of girl talk, Molly couldn't stand it any longer and pulled out her own jar of jelly.

"Look!" she said proudly, "and with my own label."

Shelley read the "by Molly by Golly" and asked, "Did Dave think it up?"

"You know he did! It took him all of twenty seconds."

"I love it!" she said. "I told you he had an imagination. Your label will go with anything, pickles, jams, jellies, peppers, anything. Jelly by Shelley only goes with jelly. Very clever, I like it."

There was a pause in the conversation and Shelley asked, "I think I see a little more sparkle in your eyes. Any sleep walking going on over there?"

"Not yet!" she said laughing, "But I'd be lying if I told you I didn't think about it."

Shelley laughed and Molly said, "Something's got to be wrong with him. He doesn't curse, he reads the Bible, he cooks, he works like a Trojan, he writes letters, he's got a dozen hobbies, and he's a model father. What's wrong with him?"

"Honey, the only thing wrong with him is in his head. That big city girl with those silk blouses has messed up his mind. She's a looker though but probably can't even cook an egg and I'd bet money she doesn't do bathrooms."

"She's coming next week to the farm."

"I'd love to be there when she sees you for the first time. Maybe we'll have an old fashioned cat fight."

"I'll be gone. I'm going back home for a few days and taking Jim with me."

"Oh my gosh, she'll have him all to herself."

"Yeah, I thought about that and I got him to promise he wouldn't do anything crazy while I was gone. I think he knew what I was talking about. Maybe you could call him every five minutes to make sure they aren't in the sack. Or maybe John could call him and tell him his prize bull got out and he needed help. Maybe you could invite them over for supper one night. All's fair in love and war, isn't it?"

They both had a good laugh and Shelley changed the subject and said, "Thanks for sending the note to Caroline. It was her first letter and boy is she proud of those barrettes."

"I didn't mean to show favorites. I've got to get back in Morgan's and Isabel's good graces."

"You wouldn't possibly know of a good sauce for burgers? I've been experimenting but haven't found the one I want."

"Matter of fact I do" Molly answered, "My Aunt Sue has a recipe she calls "Buzz Sauce" and we call the burgers "Buzz Burgers." It's really good; our whole family uses it."

"What'll we need?" And Molly called out the ingredients; Stick of butter, half cup of ketchup, 2 tablespoons Lea & Perrins, 1 tablespoon liquid smoke, 1 tablespoon white wine vinegar and 6 tablespoons brown sugar."

Shelley had everything and put them in a small saucepan and melted them all together. She got a small basting brush and took it to John. She repeated the instructions Molly had given her and told him to start basting the patties after they had been seared and to cook them over a low fire. Molly had made the patties a little thicker than Shelley was used to saying that the thicker patties worked better with the sauce.

Everyone loved the Buzz Burgers. They went on and on about them and John called it a Blue Ribbon sauce. Molly said, "I believe the beef had something to do with it. Is this some of your beef?" she asked John.

"Yes ma'am, it's Angus."

"Well, it's excellent. It tastes like I remember beef should taste. Some of the beef you get in the store now days is terrible."

She had a new best friend; John was real proud of his Angus cows.

Jim asked Mr. Phelan if he'd take Molly for a ride in his truck through the cow pasture. He wanted her to see how friendly his cows were. He agreed and Molly and Jim rode with him. Jim was right. The cows swarmed the truck and some did stick their heads in the window to get some rubbing and sweet talk from John. Once when she was watching John give # 47 a head rub, a cow stuck her head through Molly's open window and cold nosed her on the neck. Molly let out a scream that scared everybody including the cows.

"That's the first time I've ever been "wet willied" by a cow."

They all had a good laugh and John handed her a rag to wipe off the drool.

Over watermelon, Jim recapped the story of the cow licking Molly on the neck and the kids loved it. They made her tell it again in her own words. Molly exaggerated the story and said the cow's tongue was this long and held up her hands about ten inches apart. The kids squealed with laughter.

Molly got several more pictures of the kids and after lots of hugs they went home.

Shelley's last words to Molly were that she and John would keep Dave sidetracked the best they could. "We're on your side," she said.

As they drove off Molly said, "I like the Phelans; they're real people."

"Me too, I've got this feeling that someday we'll be in business together. I've thought about some sort of co-op. Maybe Shelley could run it and we'd go halves. I'd furnish the products and she and her girls would furnish the labor."

"They're just kids!" said Molly.

"I'm thinking about the long haul. Those kids have a future and I want to be a part of it. Together, we'll all succeed."

"You're a good man Clancy, I can hear those wheels a grinding."

Sunday morning Molly was up first and took about a five-mile-run. She got back to the front gate just as the paper man dropped off the Sunday paper. She cooled down on her walk back to the house. The dogs were glad to see her. They had learned to stay when she told them to. Slick learned in a hurry that trying to keep up with a two-legged gazelle was not all fun and games.

Dave had made coffee and was frying some patties of pork sausage. Jim was buttering some English muffins, which he was going to brown in a skillet. They had already cut up a bowl of fruit.

"How was the run?" Dave asked.

"Good and bad!" She said as she opened her purse and pulled out a five-dollar bill and a one-dollar bill. The boys were watching her every move. She signed each of the bills and dropped them in the cuss box.

Jim was first to speak and said, "You used the Lord's name in vain?"

"Yes, and on a Sunday to boot."

"What else did you say?"

"One of the F words."

"What made you do it?"

"While I was running this big black snake was crawling across the highway. He was about half way across and I ran to the left to keep away from

187

him. I was just about even with him when another one came out of the grass like it was following the other one. I stopped and turned around and there was another one crossing behind me. It scared me so bad I let out a couple of bad words."

Dave said, "It's mating time for snakes. I've seen them do that before. How about a cup of coffee Miss Potty Mouth?"

"Jim said the cuss box was an honor system. I hope you jokers are playing as honest as I am."

Jim was figuring with a pen on a piece of paper and said, "Wow! You could have said twenty-four twenty-five cent words for what you just put in."

"Thanks for sharing that information with us, Jimbo. I really appreciate that." And she gave him a little knuckle rub on the head and they all had a good laugh.

Molly met lots of new people at church; too many to remember all their names. First thing she did when she sat down for the service was to pick up the *Methodist Hymnal* and turn to page 378 and sure enough, there it was just like Jim said it was, "Amazing Grace." She looked up in the corner and sure enough was "by John Newton, 1779." He was right, the kid was amazing.

The sermon was about angels. Preacher Bob made several mentions of biblical angels and read several passages. She couldn't figure out where he was going with the sermon and her mind started drifting. All of a sudden he asked the congregation, "How many angels have you seen this week?" He paused a few seconds and then said, "I've seen three." Now he had her complete attention and he continued. "The first one I saw was at Kroger's. There was a young mother pulling her grocery cart with one hand and pushing a wheel chair with the other. In the wheelchair was a young girl probably about eight years old. The child was nicely dressed. She was well groomed and had ribbons in her hair and was smiling. Her mom was giving her 100 percent of her attention and she also had a smile on her face. They were by the cereals and the girl's mom was showing her the pictures on the boxes. The mom held up two boxes and let the child choose the one she wanted."

"Think about that young mother. She takes care of that child twenty-four hours a day, 365 days a year. She bathes her, feeds her, loves her, takes her shopping, tucks her in, lets her make choices, and even has time to tie ribbons in her hair. And she does it with a smile on her face. Now, I ask you! Is that young mom an angel? I think she is! And I guarantee her daughter thinks she is."

His other two angel stories were also good and he ended the sermon with the question, "How many angels have you seen this week?"

She thought to herself and quickly came up with the answer. Three! One man angel, one boy angel and one canine angel.

The closing hymn was "Open my eyes, that I may see" Bob's wife played the piano and everyone sang. The words seemed to jump off the page at her. They were beautiful words and just the ones she needed to hear. As the song ended she closed her eyes and said a little prayer, "Dear Lord, open my eyes, open my ears, open my mouth, open my heart, illumine me and thank you God for bringing me here today."

After the service they had a visit with the Perkins on the front steps of the church. Mrs. Perkins thanked Jim for the thank-you note and bragged on his penmanship. Dave said he was going to cook some ribs for supper and asked them if they'd like to come out to the farm for supper. "I want you to see what Molly did with those plants you gave us."

Bob said, "Never met a rib I didn't like!" and Mrs. Perkins chimed in, "We'd love to. What can I bring?"

"Nothing," said Molly, "Just yourselves."

"We'll bring potato salad! Won't take no for an answer. What time?"

"Fiveish."

As they drove off, Jim said, "We should have told her to bring some cookies."

Molly laughed and said, "I'll take wagers that she brings cookies."

The Perkins visit was fun. Dave had gotten Molly to make some Buzz Sauce for him to use on the ribs.

During the meal Bob commented that they were the best ribs he had ever had. Dave agreed with him but didn't say so. But he added, "I think it has something to do with the sauce. It's an old recipe that's been in my family for years." He glanced at Molly who was listening and had her eyebrows raised and her hands on her hips not believing what she was hearing. "I've been thinking about bottling it and trying to sell it." He looked back at Molly and winked at her and said, "Might make Molly my partner," which got a smile out of her.

"Well, I'd buy it! Best I ever had"

Mrs. Perkins brought cookies just as Molly thought she would and Jim had Molly make them all a Perkins Chocolate Chip Blue Bell Special. It was a big hit and Bob asked for seconds.

After supper Jim wanted Mrs. Perkins to hear Molly sing and talked her into one song.

The two ladies sat down on the piano bench together, and Mrs. Perkins played and Molly sang, "Just a Closer Walk with Thee." When the song was over Mrs. Perkins said, "Honey, God has given you a voice that a choirmaster dreams about, and believe me, I know what I'm talking about."

"Thanks!" she answered "I'm a little out of practice but I love to sing."

"She can play too!" said Jim.

"Really, I'd love to hear you play."

"Jimbo, you're embarrassing me."

"One song!" he said, "The one you and Dad played."

She looked at Dave and gave him a little come on gesture with her finger.

Dave reluctantly sat down at his drums and Molly started her boogie piece again which was her rendition of Katie Webster's, "Black Satin." Dave did a much better job this time because he knew what to expect. The piece started off tenderly and then exploded into some real swamp boogie. They got a standing ovation when they finished and Jim commented, "That's boogie woogie!"

Later, after the Perkins had left, Molly got a call from Theresa inviting her to her house for a bread making session tomorrow and to take Brad to the

Neels to pick up a puppy. She asked Dave if she could use the truck and he said she could if she promised to bring home a loaf of that bread.

The weatherman said it looked like no rain for the next three days and Dave made the decision to cut twenty acres in the morning.

The next morning Molly fixed Dave a jug of water and a goodie bag and said they'd be back by one and would bring lunch. She got his card and they left for the Beauchamps.

Theresa was a good teacher and had the patience of Job. While the bread was rising, they went to the Neels to get the puppy. Herschel said he had one left.

Brad was on top of the world and when he saw the puppy he asked Mr. Neel if the puppy had a name. Mr. Neel said, "Well, this pup's mom is called Belle and this pup has a little star on her forehead so I named her Belle Star, but I shortened it to Star. She seems to like it."

Brad said, "Here, Star!" and the puppy ran right to him. Brad liked it and Star was her official name.

After the Neels, they stopped at the grocery store and Theresa helped Molly pick out yeast and flour she would need for future loaves and also a couple of pans that Dave didn't have.

While the bread was baking she went shopping and got white shirts, Wranglers, Red Wings, a straw Stetson and three pair of leather work gloves. Dave had told her he wanted her to have a pair of gloves for each of the tractors and one for the truck. She hoped he had beefed up his card because she had hit it a lick. She laughed to herself; she would be the spitting image of Dave only shorter and maybe a few more curves.

She picked up Jim and the bread and they started home. It was a happy time. Belle Star was plenty happy with all the new attention and young Brad was ten-feet tall. Those fish that Dave gave away were still working and the bread was hot.

CHAPTER 11

AND HOW DID
I IMAGINE?

When they got back to the farm Dave had already cut the twenty acres and was sitting on the front porch. There were four large boxes on the front porch. They were Holstein colored and had green writing on them. The Gateway computer had arrived. As she went up the steps, she said, "Mooooooooo."

Dave laughed and said, "Think you can set it up?"

"We'll have you Yahooing by dark."

She had thought ahead and already had the right phone line for an AOL connection and had purchased a super duper surge protector. After lunch the men wanted to help and she let them unpack the boxes and she explained each part as she hooked it up. She installed the software one by one. She hooked up the HP printer and scanner and installed their software. She hooked up the Bose speakers and put in a Patsy Cline CD for a test. Patsy never sounded better. They played a game of Solitaire and then she went to Word and wrote a short letter misspelling a few words, which the boys caught. She hit spell check and showed them how it worked. "No more misspelled words!" she said. After the corrections were made she hit "Print" and the printer spit out a beautiful black-and-white copy of the letter. She put in the encyclopedia disc and asked Jim to pick a topic.

Jim said, "Chickens."

She typed in chickens and hit the "Enter" button. Page after page of information came up and she showed him how to scroll through them. "Neat!" he said.

Next she hooked up the modem and installed AOL. Up until now she had done everything on her own password. She told Dave he would have to come up with a password of his own. She suggested pecanman@aol.com and laughed so hard she hurt. She e-mailed her brother a note saying she was coming home for a visit and bringing Jim with her. Maybe they could work up a fishing trip. She sent the mail and added him to the address book. Next she wrote in Webster.com and when it came in she typed in the word Chicken. The word came up with the definitions and she said, "See this little red megaphone. If you don't know how to pronounce a word, all you have to do is click on this megaphone and the computer says the word." She clicked on it and the computer said, "Chicken!" which got an "Unbelievable!" out of Dave for about the tenth time.

Molly was having fun showing off and said, "Watch this!"

She went to e-Bay and typed in fishing lures.

"Look!" she said, "There are thirty-seven pages of old fishing lures for sale with twenty lines on each page. What was the name of the fishing lure Mr. Neel gave you?"

"Pumpkinseed Spook!"

She scrolled through several pages and bingo, there it was. "Look! Someone has one for sale and the price is thirty-five dollars with two days still left on the bidding." She clicked on the picture and made it larger. She hit the print button and a color picture of the plug came off the printer. Dave said, "Holy smoke!" this time.

She got off e-Bay and hit Massey Ferguson on Yahoo and hundreds of sites hit about dealers, parts, attachments, etc. "You can shop for a part by mail if you have to. I'm going too fast but you will pick it up in no time."

"Watch this!" she said and she typed in weather.com and zeroed in on Texas weather and the five day forecast for their county. "This site is open 24 hours a day so you won't have to run to the TV at a certain time." She showed him Doppler radar and clicked on one of the little blue dots over Ohio. "There's the weather where we're going Jimbo. Better pack a rain coat."

"Later we'll make our plane ticket reservations on the computer, but I want to show you one more thing before I turn it over to you. Watch this!"

She got on a map site and said, "What's our address at the farm?" and Dave called it out and she typed it in. "What's the zip?" and she entered that. "What's the Perkin's address?" and she entered that and their zip code. She hit "Enter" and up popped a map with directions to their house from the farm. She hit print and out came a map. She looked at the map and said; "Shortest route to their house is 23.2 miles. This might help you with your hay deliveries."

Dave let out another "Holy Smoke!"

The boys wanted a turn and Jim went first. He had been using computers at school so he was pretty much at home with it. Dave finally got his turn and went back to the weather and read the forecast and looked at the highs and lows and commented, "This weather information alone is going to be worth the price of the computer."

Molly said, "I'll bet the computer can be a business expense. You need it for billing, for delivery routes, for weather, for business letters. I'll bet you could even deduct this room. It's your office. You paint, you draw, you keep books, and you read your trade journals."

Dave added, "I'll talk to Larry about it. I need every deduction there is. I have to pay my own Social Security and my own health insurance."

"I'll bet you can even deduct your AOL bill each month." She said.

"You make it sound like I'm making money just sitting here," Dave laughed.

"You are! Like those uniforms you bought me today; those can be a business deduction. Maybe you should pay me a few bucks each day and claim me as a migrant farm worker. Maybe I could pick up a John Deere part you need in Ohio and you could deduct the price of the plane tickets as an expense."

"Maybe you could come visit me in Alcatraz?" he laughed.

194

"It's called Creative Accounting. Listen!" she said, "Those fat cats in Washington have pensions, retirement plans, health insurance for life and perks you can't imagine. They don't even have to pay Social Security because what they have is so much better. Lots of them retire and go to work for private industry and retire again and collect Social Security also. It's called double dipping. Farmers all over the country are going belly up because they weren't creative. You've got to look out for yourself. You need to talk to my dad. Lots of his best friends used to be farmers."

Molly's comments really started him thinking. He knew there was a lot of truth to what she was saying and he needed to get creative.

After some struggle he finally came up with an e-mail address of Shepherdfarms@aol.com. Molly liked it and said it would be good for business and would look good on a business card.

Supper was on the west porch, sliced apples, green grapes, Swiss cheese and Molly's bread with butter on the side. Dave thought the bread was better than Theresa's and she did too but she knew it was just the pride of making it herself that made it taste so good. Jim had water and they savored a couple of glasses of wine.

After supper she got on the computer and made their reservations. The tickets were too high but she knew it was because of the short notice. The airport in Tyler had a shuttle to Dallas at 8:15 on Thursday morning. There was a direct flight to Ohio and they would pick up a car at the airport. She made all the arrangements on the computer.

The next morning Molly came down in her new work clothes. She even wore the hat for effect. As she entered the kitchen she said, "Howdy Podnas."

"You look nice!" Jim commented.

"Thanks!" she said. "I forgot to get a belt but I don't think they'll fall off."

"How do the boots feel?" Dave asked.

"Funny! They make me feel like I can kick a little A. Is that normal?"

"Yep" he laughed, "You're a couple of inches taller. Did you get some gloves?"

"Yes, just like you said, three pairs."

"Save those receipts. I might be deducting those uniforms."

She winked at Dave and said, "Now you thinking, cowboy!"

Dave hooked up the John Deere for her because it had the sunroof. She would make wind rows and he would make a few deliveries. Jim would do his chores, start the wash and keep an eye on Molly.

Jim had told Dave that Thursday was Molly's birthday and Dave came up with the idea that since Jim's was Tuesday, they would have a joint birthday celebration Wednesday night. They would have a fish fry at the wagon and Molly would have to catch the fish. There were to be no presents. The airline tickets would be their presents. They all agreed and thought the fish fry would be fun. Molly told Dave in private that she thought it would be nice if he picked up a small cake for Jim, which he agreed to do when he went to town.

Molly finished with the raking after lunch and by day's end, Dave had delivered three trailers and reloaded four. It was a good day's work and one to be proud of. Tomorrow's plan would be for Dave and John to bale and for Molly and Jim to load and stack.

That evening before supper Molly came down in her running gear and sat down in a kitchen chair to tie her shoes. The boys were in the kitchen and while she was tying, Jim asked, "Want to play a game of World?"

"Sure! What's the target?"

"Kiss-a-me!"

"Excuse me?"

Jim went to the map and said, "See this river right here" and he pointed to a spot in Florida. "This is the Kissimmee River. It flows into Lake Okeechobee right here."

"Pretty small target, what's the prize?"

"The winner gets to kiss the loser on the mouth."

Molly glanced at Dave who was all ears and smiling and eyebrows raised.

She said to Dave, "Do you want to get in on this game?"

"How could I lose?" he said laughing.

"No!" interrupted Jim, "He can't play, just you and me."

"OK Mr. Hooking Bull, I'll play but the kiss has to be on the cheek."

"OK!" Jim replied but a little less enthused.

"Who goes first?"

"You do!" and Molly aimed and fired a shot into the Gulf of Mexico.

Jim's shot was about one half inch off target and Molly bent down and Jim gave her a kiss on the cheek.

"Want to play again?" he asked and Molly said, "Yes, but not Kissimmee. Let's play Gary, Indiana and the loser cleans up the kitchen"

"OK!" Jim said and added, "Uncle Dave, you can play this time if you want to."

Dave hesitated and Molly said, "Pluck, pluck, pluck," which was a new line she'd picked up from "The Man from Snowy River."

Jim researched the target and when he located it he said, "I'll go first."

He threw and Molly said, "Looks like you hit the windy city, mate." and added, "I'll go last."

Dave verified the target, took aim and fired, which was a direct hit on Lake Michigan.

"Hope you brought your life jacket old boy!" she said laughing.

Molly took aim and started singing, "Gary Indiana, Gary Indiana, My home sweet" she threw and there was a thud "home."

Her dart was a quarter inch off Gary, Indiana.

Jim and Dave looked at each other in amazement and Molly added some more Snowy River talk. "I'm studying to be a supervisor you know. I'll be back to check on your work. I think I'll take a little jog while you boys are working. How about it Slick, you want to run with Jess?"

Slick was so excited he was about to wag his tail off. He jumped up and licked Molly right on the mouth. Molly hugged him back and said, "Well, I love you too! "And she trotted out of the house with Slick and Pudd'n right beside her and singing "Gary, Indiana."

"Lucky dog," Jim said, "He plays a better game of Kissimmee than I do and he can't even throw a dart."

Dave laughed and added, "That's a pretty clever little game you thought of, bud. I'll have to remember that one."

They all went down to the lake about four-thirty. Jim loaded a few things on the travois including some towels for when they went swimming. Molly had gone down earlier and snuck the cake into the icebox in the wagon because she wanted it to be a surprise.

At the lake, Jim armed Molly with a Zebco on a light rod and tied on a chartreuse Beetlespin.

They all got in the boat and Jim said he was going to be the guide, and he ran the troll motor over near the island where there was some deep water. Dave had brought his camera and said he was the official photographer. Molly had never had so much attention and she was loving it.

"What are we after?" she asked.

"Sakalet!" Jim answered.

"What in the world is that?"

"White perch, in Louisiana they call them sakalet. In Texas we call them crappie or white perch. Sakalet means, "sack of milk" in French."

Molly glanced at Dave who was enjoying hearing his student recite the little tidbits he had been teaching him. He gave her a thumb up.

"Cast over there!" and Jim pointed to a little cove in the island. "You'll probably catch everything but we're after about ten white perch."

On her first cast she caught a small bass and was excited. Jim let the fish go and Molly said, "Hey! What about our fish fry?"

Jim laughed and said, "This time after your plug hits the water, count to ten and start reeling real slow, the white perch are deeper."

She did and bingo, she had one. As she was reeling it in Jim said, "Reel real slow. They have tender mouths and if you pull too hard the hook will tear out."

Jim netted the fish and put it on the stringer. "Nine to go!" he said.

In less than an hour she had caught her ten. She had also caught and released several bass and bream. Once she had her hook straightened by King Kong whom they never saw. Jim said it was bound to have been a catfish by the way it pulled.

Dave had a blast taking pictures and when they got to the dock he had her sit in the front of the boat and hold the stringer close to the fish while it was still in the water. He aimed the camera at her and told her to lift the stringer out of the water real fast. He wanted to try and capture the droplets of water coming off the fish. He had her do it a couple of times to make sure he got a good one and got another of Molly and the guide holding the stringer together.

Dave said that he would clean the fish and suggested that Jim start a fire. Molly said she would get everything ready for the fish fry. When Dave went to the chuck box to get his filet knife he asked Molly if she saw that snake swimming across the lake when they were fishing.

"No!" she answered, "Did you see one?"

"Yep!" and he went to the dock to clean the fish.

She asked Jim, "Did he really see one?"

"Probably not, it means he wants to rattle some ice. You know, Snake Bite Medicine."

She walked down to the pier and said, "You know, I think I did see that snake. Was he black with a yellow belly?"

"Yep, that was him."

"Would you like a bourbon and water?"

"Hey, that sounds good."

"At your service, Obi Wan," And she gave a little bow.

Back at the wagon she said, "You were right, he wants to rattle some ice."

She fixed them each a drink and went back to watch Dave finish cleaning the fish. She was impressed with the ease and skill he showed filleting the fish. Not much mess and the waste went into a bucket, which he said he would bury later.

Dave put a small pan of water on the burner and had Molly dice up an onion in tiny pieces while he was waiting for the water to boil. He put some cornmeal in a small bowl and added the onion and some salt and pepper. When the water was scalding he added a little to the mixture and made a thick mixture like cookie dough.

"What are you making?" she asked.

"Hush puppies."

"Don't believe I've ever had one."

"It's kind of a Southern thing. They're easy to make. The secret is that the water really has to be hot when mixing, or the puppies will dissolve when they hit the hot grease."

When the grease was the right temp he spooned in some dough and cooked the puppies.

When they turned a golden brown and were floating he put them on a brown paper sack to drain. Molly sampled one and said, "They're delicious!"

"Should be, the cornmeal probably came from corn grown in Ohio. Maybe even off your daddy's farm."

"You're full of it!" she said laughing. "I'm going to make a batch for mom and dad when I get back home. They'll love them."

The fish fry was a success and Molly went on and on about how good the fish tasted.

Dave said that in his book white perch were the best fresh water fish next to walleye, but since we don't have walleyes in Texas, white perch are the best, then catfish and then bass, the smaller the bass the better.

"I like them all!" said Jim. "Bream fried crisp are good too. We even eat the tails."

"Come on!"

"Yes ma'am. They taste like potato chips but better."

The campfire was fun and Molly was full of herself. She was still the center of attention and she loved it. She recapped most of the fish she caught one by one and of course old King Kong who got away because Jim had set the drag too tight. Jim taught her to say "Rabbit Rabbit" if the smoke started blowing her way and doggone if it didn't work most of the time.

After a while she climbed up in the wagon and brought out a cake with ten candles burning. Jim was excited. Uncle Dave didn't make much of birthdays and having Molly here made it special. They sang happy birthday to Jim and when they were through he made them sing it again, but this time to Molly.

Dave said, "I know I said no presents but I did get a couple of things" and he went to the side box of the wagon and pulled out a large sack. He told Jim, "Your big present is the plane ticket but I got you a bag for traveling and a doppkit." Jim opened the doppkit and there was toothpaste, a toothbrush holder, a Speed Stick, a comb, a hairbrush and a small bottle of mouthwash. "Maybe Molly will help you pack your bag, might be colder up there than it is here."

Jim wasn't at the bashful stage yet and gave him a hug and said, "Thanks!"

Dave reached back in the bag and pulled out a leather belt with a silver buckle and said, "This is for you."

Molly stood up and tried it on. "Perfect!" she said, "How'd you know my size?"

"Well, I kind of went snooping in your room and looked at a couple of labels. Here's one more present. I bought two and the lady said you can take them back or exchange them if they don't fit." He handed her the sack and she looked inside and there were two bathing suits.

She said, "Men don't buy women bathing suits."

"I know it. Talk about feeling funny in the store. Ladies were staring at me."

"They're one piece. I haven't worn a one piece in years."

"Well, they looked good in the pictures. I wasn't going to buy you a bikini."

"Thanks! She said, "They probably won't fit and I might be taking them back. This one has possibilities."

Jim reached in his pocket and pulled out his present and gave it to Molly.

"What's this?" and she looked at Dave who gave her a I don't know move.

She opened it and it was a ring, a James Avery sterling ring with a small cross in it.

"It's beautiful Jim! It's just like yours and your dad's isn't it?"

"Yes ma'am. Dad gave me mine after I did my overnight at the wagon and since you did your overnight, I wanted you to have one."

He went on, "If you wear it with the long part of the cross pointing away from you it means you want Christ-like things to be coming out of you. If you have a special need or prayer and want Christ coming more into your life, you wear it pointing toward you. Three or four times a day I happen to look at mine and it reminds me to try harder to be a better Christian. Me and dad wear ours pointing out most of the time."

She slipped it on pointing to the more Christ-in position and said; "Thank you!" and she gave him a big hug, "This is the nicest and most meaningful present I've ever gotten. I'll never take it off."

Dave was touched by the sincerity and tenderness of the moment, thought to himself, "Why didn't I think of that? Wow, what a kid."

Jim got the three of them to touch their cross rings together for good luck.

"This is too expensive of a gift for a ten year old to give."

Jim said, "You should thank the Miracle Workers; they're the ones who really bought it."

She thanked him again and went to the wagon and returned with a small box she had wrapped. "This is for you."

Jim unwrapped it and inside was a perfect arrowhead. It wasn't one of those maybe-it- was and-maybe-it-wasn't-arrowheads. This one was perfect.

"I found it in my dad's cornfield when I was about fifteen. Dad had plowed the rows and it rained a few days later and washed the dirt off. Dad thinks it's probably a Shawnee point. It's plenty old. I've been carrying it ever since for good luck. I want you to have it."

"This is the best present I've ever gotten" and he jumped up and gave her a hug.

Dave gave it a look over and said, "This is really special bud, maybe I'll make you a little box to keep it in, can't believe Molly is giving you her good luck charm!"

"Got me a new one!" she said pointing to the ring and she gave each of them a touch with hers.

"Let's go swimming!" Jim said.

"I'll go." Dave said.

"Me too if my suit fits," Molly replied.

Jim jumped up in the wagon and pulled his suit out of the barrel and changed. He took off with the dogs and they heard his splash.

Dave helped Molly pull her boots off and she climbed up in the wagon to change. She asked Dave if she could borrow his knife because there were some little plastic things in the suit and she wanted to cut them out. She also asked him to hand her the lantern. He went to the chuck box and got the lantern and handed it up to her and said, "There's a hook in the top if you want to hang it up." It was plenty dark and the moon wasn't up yet. The lantern was a battery type with a florescent bulb that threw out a pretty good light. He had bought it because he thought it would be safer than a Coleman lantern around all the canvass. He refreshed his drink and sat down by the fire to wait his turn to get dressed.

When he looked up he couldn't believe what he saw or maybe what he couldn't see. She had hung the lantern in the top of the wagon and was silhouetted. She didn't have on a stitch of clothes and he could see every detail: her hair, her nose, her arms, her breasts. "Oh my God!" He thought, "I shouldn't be watching her," but he couldn't stop. He wasn't really seeing her was he? It was probably the most sensuous sight he had ever witnessed. "I've got to get a picture of this" he thought. "I might paint it someday." He opened his lens to 1.4 and took the picture using no flash. He took two more and was out of film. "No way will those come out" he thought, "they would be too perfect."

Finally she had the suit on and turned off the lantern and climbed down.

"Fits pretty well!" she said, "Might let you do all my shopping."

Jim hollered, "When yawl coming?"

"Be there in a minute" she answered.

Dave told Molly to sit where he was; he had something he wanted to show her and he climbed up in the wagon and turned on the lantern. He slowly took off his shirt and hammed up a few muscle flexes like the body builders.

"You big ham!" she said.

He turned off the light and finished dressing in the dark and climbed down.

Molly said, "Don't tell me you could see me like I was seeing you?"

"Yep, but I really didn't see you, did I?"

"I kind of believe you did."

"I don't know what I saw but it looked good."

"Maybe you're a dirty old man. How many little Jolenes you pulled that trick on?"

"You're the first."

"Well it won't happen again!"

Dave laughed and said; "I only saw your imagination."

"And how did I imagine?"

"About a seven!" he said laughing and took off for the lake.

She was right behind him and made a nice little dive into the water. After the initial shock of the cool water she said, "This is nice, I might start doing this all the time."

"What took yawl so long?" Jim asked.

Molly laughed and said, "Ask Charles Atlas here, he can explain it better than I can."

"Well," Dave said, "Molly couldn't figure out which suit to wear. She tried on one and didn't like it so she tried on the other one. She didn't like that one so she put the first one back on again."

Molly started laughing. He could see me! That was exactly what happened.

"Your dads full of it Jim, it just takes women longer to dress" and she put her hands on Dave's head and gave him a good dunking.

Jim said, "Know what? Sometimes I've seen dad when he gets real hot drive his tractor down to the lake and go skinny dipping."

"Probably scares the poor fish!" which got a good laugh out of Jim and a dunk for herself.

After a little KP at the wagon they headed back to the house in their bathing suits and wearing their boots. Dave wished he had more film in his camera.

Molly wearing her bathing suit and in Red Wings was cute. Actually it could probably be used for a Red Wing commercial. Maybe it could read, "I love my Red Wings so much I even wear them to the lake when I go swimming."

He thought to himself, "How could someone look so ridiculous, silly and sexy at the same time? She'd even make a strait jacket look good. Hell, even her shadow looked good" and a rigor went through his body.

After cleaning up, Molly helped Jim pack his new bag for the trip to Ohio and they all got ready for bed. It had been a great day for everyone.

Dave was nervous the next morning. He didn't want them to go. He already missed them and they weren't even gone. He had a thought that she might not come back but she had to; she had his son and he had her dog. Jackie's coming also had him a little upset. Until Molly entered the picture he was fairly content with his relationship with Jackie, but now all he could think about was Molly. Maybe Jackie was coming to tell him she had found somebody else. There was urgency in her voice when she called. He remembered her saying, "We need to talk."

On the way to the airport he made sure that they would call him when they got there. Molly made him a list of phone numbers and e-mail addresses in case he wanted to try his first e-mail. In the airport he slipped her some money for expenses and insisted she take his credit card in case of an emergency. As they were about to go through the security check he gave them both a hug and said to Molly, "May the Force be with you."

As the plane took off, he said a little prayer for their safety. He didn't have much use for flying and had the philosophy that you could never die in a plane crash if you never got on a plane.

He felt lonely on his drive back to the farm. Jim hadn't been out of pocket in a long time.

When he got to the farm John was waiting for him and they started loading and stacking the square bales. They broke for lunch and finished up about three. John took a loaded trailer home with him of last year's hay, which cleaned out the hay shed.

Later, Dave got a call from Jim. They were there and it was beautiful. The phone connection was bad and he said they would call back later when they got to Molly's mom and dad's house.

Dave took the dogs to the lake and gave them what Jim called a trick bath. He had them each retrieve a stick and then lathered them up and had them retrieve it again. Jackie hated smelly dogs, and he wanted her to like them.

Next he fed Jim's chickens and did a few other chores before he got cleaned up himself.

Jackie's flight was direct to Dallas where she would rent a car and would call him when she was on I-20. He tried to read but couldn't concentrate. He went outside and watered Molly's plants, which probably didn't need watering, but he had to burn off some of his nervous energy. Just as he was finishing the watering his cell rang and it was Jackie.

"Where are you?" he asked.

"I'm in New York."

"What?"

She explained that one of the partners in the firm had a slight heart attack at the office and her boss had dumped some of his important clients on her and it would be impossible to get away. She would be working long hours and weekends until he was back on his feet. She was sorry and hoped he wouldn't be too upset with her. They made small talk for a few minutes and he told her that Jim and his nanny had gone to Ohio for a few days. Jackie said she felt worse now that she knew it would have been just the two of them all alone for a long weekend.

After they had said their good-byes he felt the pressure being lifted off immediately. He had gone through about ten mood swings in the last couple of days. Jackie not coming made him feel like he was being true to Molly. "Wow!" he thought, "This is why they write all those country songs. Maybe this one could start out:

I'm sad that you're gone
But glad that I'm true
Because my real girl couldn't come.

Bound to be a song somewhere in this scenario," He laughed and thought, "It's funny but it isn't funny."

He had so much new energy that he decided to go jogging. She seemed to enjoy it so much, maybe there was something to it, and if she kept serving him all those Blue Bell specials he was going to have to burn a few more calories. Maybe I could add these lines to my new song:

Because my real girl couldn't come
I went jogging tonight
To get my mind off of you.

"Maybe I'll just jog off to the funny farm and admit myself" he said out loud.

He surprised himself on the jog. He did much better than he thought he would. Muscle wise he was in excellent shape because of all the farm work but he was lacking in wind power. He had read several running articles since Molly came and they all said that the wind power would come quickly if you ran on a regular basis. He set a personal goal to jog three times a week. He would try to run on Sunday, Tuesday and Thursday. Once he got some wind power, he would try to shave some minutes off his time. A three-mile run and a three-mile walk back were bound to be enough for a good cardiac workout. One article said that if you could run two miles in sixteen minutes three times a week you could eat and drink anything and never have to worry about diet or the extra ring around the middle. That might be a long-range goal. A two mile run and a two mile walk back sounded better than a three and three.

On his walk back to the farm his cell rang and it was Shelley. They talked a few minutes and she asked, "How's Jackie?"

"She didn't come!"

"How come?" And he explained.

Shelley started laughing and Dave asked, "What's so funny?"

Shelley said still laughing, "Well, I'm just doing my part."

"And what's your part?"

"Well, you've got Miss Ohio pretty shook up. She wanted me to call you every five minutes to make sure you all weren't in the sack."

"Really?"

"Yes, and she wants John to call you in the morning and say that his prize bull got out and tore down a lot of fence, and tomorrow night I'm supposed to call you and ask you all over for supper."

"This is interesting. I appreciate you calling."

"Well you big dope, if you mess this up I'm never going to speak to you again. This girl was made for you and you know it. Don't you just love her?"

"Well, she's got my attention. Last night I fell in love with her shadow."

"What does that mean?"

"I don't know. She's got me pretty shook up."

"Don't you dare tell her I called?"

"I won't, and thanks!"

Just as he reached the road to the farm the phone rang again and it was Jim. They were at Molly's home and her mom was cooking a pot roast. Her brother was there and they were going fishing on Saturday. Her dad was cool and showed him five more arrowheads he had found over the years. Her dad said he could walk the rows tomorrow if he wanted to and look for points. "Molly wants to talk."

"Hi!" she said.

"Sounds like you made it OK."

"Yes!" she said. "Jim's a big hit. That "yes ma'am" and "yes sir" of his is paying off. How's Jackie?"

There was a long pause and Dave thought about saying something cute like he had just got a call from John and that his bull had gotten out but he couldn't do it. "She didn't come," and he explained why.

There was a fairly long pause and she said, "I'm glad."

"Me, too." he answered.

There was another long pause and each of them knew they had let their guard down.

"Pudd'n misses you! I don't but Pudd'n does. Slick too!"

The both laughed and Molly ended the conversation with, "We'll dance when I come back. I still owe you fifty-nine."

"Deal!" he said, "I'll see you all on Tuesday."

He spent the next couple of hours on the computer and reading his best companion, *Windows 98 for Dummies*. He was fascinated by the accuracy of the weather channel and decided that tomorrow would be a shop day of some kind. The barometer was falling and the wind would be from the east.

When he got ready for bed he noticed that there was a little bouquet of flowers on his bedside table. A closer look revealed that they were buttercups, common little old buttercups and they brought a smile to his face. One of Molly's trademarks was that she had little vases of flowers all over the house. She picked most of them on her cool down walks back to the house. She brought back flowers he had never seen before and he lived here. Where in the world does she find them all? He wondered and she was constantly raiding the Zinnia patch out by the garden.

He pulled back his comforter and pitched his big reading pillow on the floor. On top of his pillow was a piece of paper. He picked it up and there were the words, "Be Good," which brought another smile. He lay down and reached over and turned off the light. He stared at the ceiling a few minutes and then reached up in the air and closed both of his arms around a five foot two female shadow and pulled her in. The last thing he thought before he drifted off was "Be Good" and he went to sleep with a smile on his face.

CHAPTER 12

THE 13ᵀᴴ HOLE

The next morning after breakfast Dave went to the hen house to open the Friday gate for the chickens and to gather the eggs since he hadn't done it yesterday. He sang as he went and when he opened the MOLLY nest he saw that there were three eggs. "Way to go girl!" he said and he picked them up. One of the eggs had a "Smiley" sticker on it and Dave said laughing, "I should have known."

When he came to FIVE FOOT TWO'S nesting box he thought, I bet she's doctored up these eggs for sure and sure enough she had. There were five eggs in the box. One was normal; one had a Chiquita banana sticker on it, another Granny Smith 4139 sticker, another Washington Red Delicious 4015 and another with a Sweet Vidalia Onion 1015 on it. He chuckled to himself and thought how clever she was. He wondered if he could ever do anything as clever as the stickers on the eggs. Premeditated wit! She was the best no doubt about it.

All the other nests had normal yields except for MARIAN. In her nest were seven unmarked eggs. He laughed and said, "I'm not believing this Marian!" in a loud voice as if the chickens could hear and understand him. "Show and Tell will be tomorrow. I'll be back to check on your work."

When he was finished with the eggs he decided to go to town to drop off his film. He had three rolls and most of them were of Molly. One roll was from the camping trip and the others were all taken at the farm. He remembered seeing one of those 1 hour photo places and was anxious to try it. He still took slide pictures because he had a projector that he could impose a slide on a canvas in case he wanted to paint it. He could make the image larger or smaller simply by moving the projector backward or forward. He found the photo place and ordered prints of each in addition to the slides.

Next he hit the post office, the hardware store, a boat dealer, got a haircut, ate lunch and did some grocery shopping. He also delivered twelve dozen eggs for Jim since he was gone.

His last visit was with Will at the jewelry store. When Will saw him come in he said, "That boy of yours give that girl the ring yet?"

"Yeah buddy! He's got a new friend for life."

"Not every day a kid that age comes in and plops down that kind of money. I gave him a discount but it was still a lot."

"Well, he was mighty proud. Hell, I'd bought it if I knew it was going to make her that happy."

"Boy's got good taste in picking his women I'd say," Will chuckled.

Dave invited Will and his wife to come out to the farm next Saturday for a fish fry.

"Sounds like fun."

"How old is young Phillips?" Dave asked.

"He just turned four."

"Well, bring him along too. We'll set him on the pier and let him do some perch jerkin. Don't need to bring a thing. I've got the poles and plenty of worms. You might want to bring a cooler to take some fish home. Might want to bring your bass rod and you and I might slip off and get lucky. I'll have Molly call Lauri and work out the details."

"Man, I can't wait!"

Dave picked up the pictures on the way out of town and couldn't believe how good they were. She was the most photogenic person he'd ever photographed. She was fantastic and the silhouetted pictures of her imagination were probably the best he'd ever taken. He might show them to her at a later date but for the present he'd have to hide them. When he got back to the farm he couldn't stand it. The pictures were so good he wanted her to see them right now. He decided to scan them and try to e-mail them to her parent's house.

After reading the directions several times he decided to try it. He scanned a picture of her in the hammock, one of her holding up the stringer of fish, one of her and Jim loading square bales on a trailer, one of her driving the tractor with the egrets in the background, one of her standing on the front porch with the new plants, another of her pouring mayhaws into a five gallon bucket, and one of himself sitting backward on the hood of the tractor. He figured her dad would get a kick out of that one. Boy did he look ridiculous. He sent them to Ohio one by one and the computer said they were sent so he guessed they were.

He put each of the slides in the projector and blew them up on the screen. They were so good he was inspired to paint. There were several he liked but he finally narrowed it down to two. One was of Molly singing "Five Foot Two" and it was priceless in his book. It was silly, cute, uninhibited, flirty, and of course, she was beautiful. The one he decided on was one of her playing blocks with Jim. She was on her knees and holding a small silver airplane in her hand and playing like she was flying it. Her back was straight, her head was cocked a little and her eyes were on the plane. He could almost hear the buzzing sound coming out of her mouth that she was making that day. She was an adult but in this picture she had slipped back to her childhood.

It was clouding up and he decided to jog before he started his painting project. He'd be on a crash-jogging program until they got back. The better his wind power was the less he would embarrass himself if he ever ran with her.

After the run he went to the lake and took a swim. They kept a bar of Ivory in a plastic soapbox on the pier and it had become a ritual to take a lake bath whenever he went swimming. After the swim he went back to the house totally relaxed. He had fruit for lunch and worked himself into a painting mood.

Time got away from him and it was dark before he knew it. He completed the sketch and it came out better than he thought it would. He hadn't drawn in a couple of months but it quickly came back to him or maybe because it was a labor of love. The hard part was finished; tomorrow he would start applying the oils and bring the sketch to life. Also tomorrow he would start on building a picnic table for the campfire area per Miss Ohio's request. He decided to make it twelve feet long and would put a couple of holes in it for a couple of beach umbrellas.

Before turning in he decided to check his e-mail. There was a message from Molly that read:

"Thanks for the pictures. Mom thinks you're good looking and that your house is beautiful. Dad says he's never seen anyone ride a tractor like that. My brother wants to come fishing in your lake. You did a good job with the scanner. I'm impressed. Jim is having a good time. You'd be proud."

Thanks for letting us come,
Chiquita

The next morning he was up with the chickens and started painting. He broke about noon and went to work on the table. He kind of had a reputation for overbuilding and the table was no exception. The benches and the table were all one piece, and he couldn't even lift it. He had copied it the best he could from a picture in a magazine. He used galvanized screws and bolts and after sanding it down real good stained it with a redwood stain. He decided that on Monday he would turn the table upside down and put some runners down and pull the table on a lowboy with a come-along. With the treated wood and the waterproof stain it should last a long time.

The big iron bell had a few rust spots and he decided to take it down and clean it up. He wire brushed the old black paint off and put a primer on it. Tomorrow when it was dry, he would paint it with a silver rust proof paint. It was a "Happy Bell" now and needed a face lift. He tied a new nylon rope on the clapper and painted the pole the same color as the house.

On the World board, he hung a brass galley bell he had purchased from the boat dealer. It would serve as their ten-minute bell. After it was hung he gave it a test ring and had the thought that her granddad would be pleased knowing that one of his traditions was being carried on. Really it was a pretty good idea and he knew Molly would like it and making her happy made him happy.

Molly's table idea inspired him to build another small table for cleaning fish. It would be much easier on the back and he wondered why he hadn't thought of it before. He used a scrap piece of Formica for the top, which would make for an easy clean up.

He replaced the American Flag on the front porch with a new one that was a little larger. It looked good and reminded him of how proud he was living in such a great country.

The weatherman hit the nail on the head with the afternoon shower but starting tomorrow it would clear up for several days. He would cut hay on Monday depending on the dew point.

He painted, jogged and piddled away the rest of the day. Sunday he churched it by himself and everyone wanted to know where Molly was, especially the men. On the way home from church he stopped by a Sam's store and found a matching pair of pool umbrellas. They would picnic in style.

He finished the painting and couldn't wait for her to see it. It came out so good he got fired up and starting sketching the other one of her singing. Later he jogged and had a salad for supper. He could tell his wind power was getting better and it was probably just in his mind but he seemed to have much more energy. Finishing each run gave him a feeling of accomplishment and the cool down walks seemed to be a good time for thinking and he was getting new ideas.

The next morning he got the ten-ton table loaded and took it to the lake. He positioned it east and west thinking that would get more shade from the umbrellas and also both sides of the table would get a view of the lake. He stuck the umbrellas in the holes for a test. They looked good and he took them down and stored them in the wagon and went to cut hay. By dark he had cut close to thirty-five acres. Tomorrow he would rake until it was time to pick them up at the airport around three.

He couldn't wait for them to get back. It wasn't fun eating by yourself and life on the farm wasn't near as much fun without someone to share the experiences. The wine wasn't quite as sweet and he hadn't had a Blue Bell Special in several days. The dogs were going bonkers. They had decided that it wasn't as much fun without Molly and they were missing those little snacks she slipped them during the day.

He called Shelley and invited the whole clan including Rudi Kazuti to come to the farm for hot dogs and swimming Tuesday afternoon. It would be kind of a welcome home party for Jim and Molly.

Shelley said, "We would love to. The kids need an outing. What can I bring?"

"Bring that cow puncher of yours and your guitar."

"Say, doesn't Jim have a birthday coming up?"

"It was last week. Molly's too! I bought a little cake from the grocery store."

"Well, I'm going to make him a real cake."

"That'll be swell, you all come any time after four."

The next morning he raked hay and ate a quick lunch and got cleaned up. He left the house an hour early because he wanted to pick up all the hot dog fixings and some soda pop for the kids. He put the perishables in a cooler in the truck and headed to the airport. He was at the gate when they got off the plane.

Jim was grinning ear to ear when he saw him and Molly looked even better than he remembered. He got a hug from each. He swore that Jim had grown two inches in the short time he'd been gone. He was about to ask him how the trip was but Jim spoke first.

"Dad!" he said, "You should see their farm. Mr. Goodson raises corn, and pigs, and apples. Their topsoil is two feet thick. He gave me some buckeyes and I'm going to plant them. They bring you good luck. We'll have good luck forever. I went fishing with Hobbs on the Stillwater River and we caught small mouth bass. Man can they fight." He paused and pulled out a sack of buckeyes and a sack of seed corn. "Look!" he continued, "I'm going to plant some corn. They live near Bradford in Darke County. I'll show you where it is on the map. It's where Annie Oakley is from. Mrs. Goodson fixed us chicken fried toast just like Molly."

"Hold on, Bud. Take a breath. Let's pick up yawl's bags" and they went to the conveyor.

Molly left for home with a small carry-on bag but returned with two suitcases. She pointed them out and Dave picked them up. They were plenty heavy and he was glad. It meant she planned to stay a while.

"What you got in here, a bowling ball?"

Molly laughed and said, "Funny you said that. That's the same thing the porter said at the airport when we checked our bags."

On the way to the farm Jim started to tell him about her brother, Hobbs' idea but before he got started, Molly said, "Let's talk about that later when we can sit down and 'think tank' together."

"Yes ma'am!" Jim said, "That'll be cool."

"Did you take care of my chickens?"

"Yeah, buddy. Put the money in your cigar box and guess what?"

"What?"

"Marian laid seven eggs!" he said looking at Molly.

"No way?"

Molly said, "I only put five in."

"You lie!" Dave said laughing. "And guess what else? She didn't lay a single egg for the next four days."

Molly laughed and said, "Maybe she was tired."

Dave told them he had invited Shelley and the kids over about four-thirty for swimming and hot dogs and he asked Jim to help by being a lifeguard. He wanted them to use the buddy system.

The dogs started prancing when they saw the truck drive up. Jim and Molly gave them some good hugs and there was much tail wagging and a few figure eights were run.

When Molly stood up she turned to Dave and said, "You got a new bell?"

"Nope, just a little paint."

Dave picked up her bags and they started to the house.

"New flag?"

"Yep, the other one was getting a little dingy."

She saw the fresh flowers on the hall table and commented, "And fresh flowers?"

"Yeah, yours died, so I put in some new ones."

"They look nice! Makes me think you missed us."

She looked at Dave and he held up his thumb and forefinger about one-half inch apart, which got a laugh out of her.

She immediately saw the galley bell and asked, "What's this?"

"Ten minute bell."

She gave it a little ring and said, "I like!"

Dave took her bags upstairs while she did a walkthrough of the house. On the way down he heard her scream from the study. She had discovered the painting.

He entered the room and she said, "I love it! You make me look prettier than I really am."

"I don't think so; you're pretty easy to paint. I've started another one," and he showed her the sketch.

"I'm flattered! Thank you!"

"Well, they're not yours. I'm painting them to remember you by when you're gone but you can come look at them anytime you want," he said smiling.

She laughed at him. She loved this game they were playing.

"That's my picture. I'll steal it if I have to."

He showed her the rest of the pictures on the projector and she said, "Wow! I might let you take all my pictures."

Jim hollered from the front door, "They're here!"

They all went outside to greet them and there was lots of hugging. Dave played with Rudi a few minutes and called the other dogs over to let them know that Rudi was his friend and they weren't to hurt him. The kids already had their suits on and Molly took Shelley up to her room so they could put on their suits.

Shelley noticed the flowers on Molly's nightstand and said, "Don't tell me Dave put these flowers here?"

Molly said, "I guess he did."

Shelley went over to the bed to admire the bedspread she had made and said, "The spread looks good."

"I just love it!"

Shelley noticed a note on Molly's pillow and picked it up and took it to her. "What does this mean?"

The note said, "I was"

Molly laughed and told her about the "Be Good" note she had left on his pillow.

Shelley laughed and said, "I'd have a heart attack if John put flowers by my bed, but I'm not complaining. He's plenty good in the sack. One button undone and he's ready. One thing about farmers staying at home is that they think the bedroom is their office. I dread it when all the kids are in school. He'll be chasing me all day."

Molly laughed and at the same time a rigor went through her. "What a problem to have," she thought.

Dave and John went to the hay shed and lined a lowboy with bales of hay which they stacked two bales high. They made an inner ring one bale high for everyone to sit on. They would have a hayride to the lake. He pulled the tractor and trailer to the front gate and he and John went inside to put on their suits and help the girls get ready.

The hay was sticky on the kid's legs so they put their towels on the bales and they were off. Hearing all the laughter made Dave feel good: happy healthy kids! What a blessing, he thought.

Dave watched Molly as she went over to inspect the new table. She rubbed her hand across it and looked up and gave him an "OK" with her thumb and forefinger.

"You like?" he asked.

"Like it more if it had an umbrella."

Dave went to the wagon and pulled them out.

"Blue OK?"

"Perfect!"

Molly pulled out the checkered tablecloth and she and Shelley started getting everything ready. John said he would get the fire going for the dogs and Dave took the kids to the lake.

Dave had the kids line up on the pier and he jumped in about chest deep and asked, "Everybody that can swim raise their hands." Everyone raised their hand except Isabel.

Dave asked, "Jackson, can you swim?"

"Yes sir."

"Well jump in and swim to me."

He jumped in and just as he thought, he sank like a rock. Dave had him up in a second and Jackson looked pretty relieved when Dave put him back on the pier. He had the other kids jump in one by one and swim to him and then back to the ladder for an assessment.

Jim went first and swam like a champ. Caroline and Morgan both made it with a lot of dog paddling. Dave explained the buddy system to them. Jim and Jackson were to be buddies and Morgan and Caroline were both to be buddies to Isabel. There could be no running on the pier and no jumping on the right side of the pier or swimming under it because there were brush piles there. He had purchased two small life jackets in anticipation and fitted one to Jackson and one to Isabel.

He told Jackson to jump in but he was afraid. Reluctantly he decided to try it and was pleasantly surprised to find himself bobbing like a cork. Isabel took to the water like a little duck. He also had a pair of Floaties for Morgan and Caroline, which they didn't want to wear. Later Caroline decided she wanted to try them and she left them on. He had also bought two blow-up rafts for Molly and Shelley and he had marked the swimming boundaries with a yellow rope. No one was supposed to go outside the ropes.

The breeze was from the south which tended to blow the rafts down the lake but the girls held on to the north rope and soaked up some rays, did some serious talking and a lot of laughing. Dave and John got in the water with the kids and tried to wind them down.

Molly had brought one of her Miss Ohio two piece suits with her and was not hard to look at. Shelley also had on a two piece suit and one would never know that she was the mother of four.

After the swim they cooked the dogs. The kids had a blast and the table was a big hit. Shelley pulled out the cake and while she was getting her guitar out of the case Molly lit the candles. Shelley played and they all sang happy birthday to Jim. Shelley said the cake was Jim's present but she also had another present for Molly from all the kids.

Molly opened the present and there were four bandanas. A red, a pink, a green and a light blue. She gave each of the kids a hug and thanked them. She took one and tied up her hair with it and called Pudd'n over and tied the pink one around her collar. The kids loved Pudd'n's new look. The scarf added instant class and Pudd'n seemed to know it and liked the new attention.

While they were cleaning up Shelley told Molly to be careful when she wore the bandanas and Molly asked, "Why?"

"Bandanas drive cowboys' nuts" she said laughing. "You be careful. I've been married eight years and four of those I was carrying a baby. That's fifty percent of the time."

"Are you going to have anymore?"

"Lord, no. Last time I told that doctor to tie a double half hitch on those tubes of mine. Isabel is the caboose."

They sang a few songs and Molly was impressed with Shelley's playing and the kids singing. They sang "She'll Be Coming around the Mountain," "Do Lord," "Jesus Loves Me" and "Jacob's Ladder." Molly wished she had a movie camera and could have recorded it. It was a perfect example of family love and devotion. She could easily see why Dave loved them so much.

When they got back to the house Jim took the kids to see his chickens. Molly took Shelley into the study and showed her the painting.

"Oh my God!" she said. "That's unbelievable. I'd pose nude for him if he'd paint me like that! Just like that girl in Titanic."

220

"Shelley!" Molly said, "Are you being bad?"

"No honey! I'm just telling the truth," she said laughing. "I believe you've got him just where you want him. All you have to do is put that little brass ring in his nose to lead him around. Anyone looking at that picture can tell that the painter is in love with his subject."

"Come on!"

"I just might get Matthew to come visit us for a few days to let you birds be alone."

"Don't you dare?" Molly said laughing.

When they went back outside the kids were just returning from the chicken yard and had two dozen eggs that they had just gathered. John was ready to get back to check on his cows. Rudi was ready, too. Running with the big dogs was tough. John said he'd be over in the morning to help with the baling. Jim thanked Shelley for the cake and Molly thanked the kids for the bandanas.

As they drove off Jim said he was going to feed the dogs.

As he ran off Molly said, "I'm crazy about Shelley."

"Me, too!" Dave answered and added, "She didn't look too bad in that swimsuit either."

Molly gave him a big frog on the arm and said, "You big pig. I won't tell you what she said about you."

"What'd she say?"

"Nope!" she said, "Not telling! And I'd like my wine now."

"Yes ma'am, coming right up."

Jim joined them on the porch and asked if he could tell her brother's idea now. Molly said it was a good time and they all went to the study.

Jim saw the painting for the first time said, "Wow, Dad, this is your best painting ever."

Molly added, "Wasn't that nice of your dad to paint that for me?"

"Wrong! That's for us son, to remember the Genie by."

"Good!" he said, "We can hang it in my room."

"Now what's this thing you want to tell me?"

And Jim started, "Dad, her brother is real smart and has a degree in marketing and knows how to make things sell. One night me and him and Molly sat down at the kitchen table and did this thing called a Think Tank. He said that Think Tanks work best on round kitchen tables so since we've got one let's go to the kitchen."

"OK by me" Dave answered and they all went to the kitchen and sat at the table.

"I told him everything about my chicken business and how I sold my eggs. Molly added a lot of stuff that I hadn't even thought of before. She told him about all of your ideas and some that you hadn't even told me. We drew pictures and what were those things called?" he said looking at Molly.

"Diagrams" she answered.

"Yeah, diagrams and look what he came up with" and he opened up a folder and pulled out some papers and drawings.

He showed him a drawing and said, "This is a new egg carton design. It's called the Bakers Dozen Egg Carton. A long time ago bakers used to give you an extra donut for free if you bought a dozen. Regular egg cartons only have twelve holes. This one has thirteen holes. The 13th hole is in the middle and is for advertising or good will. If I put an extra egg in it, it's good will and advertising for me. It says, 'Thanks, you get a bonus and I appreciate your business.' It leaves a good taste in their mouth that I'm trying to please. This is good for my business."

Dave looked at Molly who was enjoying Jim's enthusiasm.

"Now look! Say blue berries are ripe and ready for picking. I put a small cup of blue berries in the 13th hole and a note that says the blue berries are ripe. You pick or we pick. Bring the kids. Six dollars per gallon now I'm advertising. I sell one dozen eggs but because I advertised, the people come out and pick two gallons of blue berries for twelve dollars. The 13th hole could be a small jar of jelly, pecans, mayhaws, seeds, flowers, a peach, a tomato, blackberries, tangerines, a pumpkin, or even a small plant."

Molly said, "It could be salted pecans, sugared pecans, pralines, or candy. Whatever was in season?"

THE HOOT OWL MAN

"What do you think, dad?"

"I like it! Your business helps my business and my business helps yours and word of mouth helps us all. Where can we get some of those egg cartons?"

"Hobbs said he was going to try and patent the idea. If he gets it maybe we can all be partners. He's going to have some... What's that word?"

"Prototype" Molly answered.

"Yeah, he's going to get someone to make some and if he does he's going to send me a thousand of them which would last me about a year. Little egg people like me might like to buy them or maybe a big egg company would pay big bucks for the idea. What do you think?"

"I love it! Great idea! We'll be partners" and he and Jim shook hands.

"And Molly too" Jim said, "A lot of the ideas were hers."

Molly said, "I'll take the painting for my share."

"No way" Dave said smiling, "We'll have another Think Tank later. One question though. How are you going to get a pumpkin in the 13th hole?"

"A miniature pumpkin, oh yeah, that's another thing Mr. Goodson says I should raise.

Each year he plants an acre of pumpkins. A week before Halloween and a week before Thanksgiving he loads a bunch on a trailer and goes to a busy highway or a shopping mall and sells them. Two dollars and fifty cents for one or five for ten dollars, most people buy five. Five hundred pumpkins is a thousand dollar bill. He says its work and you have to have a trailer, but it only takes a couple of weekends. He says just sow the seeds and trust in the Lord for the harvest. We've already got the trailer. It'll take my chickens a long time to make that much money. Mr. Goodson says that what he doesn't sell he feeds to his pigs. He says they eat them with a smile on their face."

"What else did you all talk about?"

"Well, Mr. Goodson sat down at the Think Tank and Molly drew him a map of the farm and he asked what we were doing with the woods behind the lake. I told him nothing and that there were lots of deer and wild pigs. He said you could probably lease the land to deer hunters, but I told him you didn't want anybody shooting. He said you could lease it to bow hunters. He said that bow hunters have a better appreciation for the land than most hunters do and that they would love to have a lease like that with no pressure from guns. The lease would only be for a couple of months each year and it would help control the deer population. He said you could probably trap some hogs and make some mad money. Might even put hog wire fence around it and raise some hogs. All those acorns would make for real fat hogs and you could sell some each fall after the acorns were gone."

"And look at these. We went to a tractor show and Molly got all these brochures and catalogs. She ordered you something."

"What?"

"An umbrella attachment for the Little Red M F. Forty-five dollars plus shipping."

"I probably could have built one."

"Well, Mr. Smarty, I wanted you to have a receipt so you could write those two plane tickets off."

He looked at her and said, "You're good."

"Thanks!" she said and at the same time holding up her empty wine glass and added, "And I'd like for my new tractor umbrella to be red and white."

"Yes ma'am" he said laughing and at the same time thankful that she hadn't said pink. He'd feel funny driving a tractor with a pink umbrella.

After the Think Tank was over Dave said, "Well, you all have given me several new ideas to sleep on. I think I'll hit the hay. I'm glad you all are back."

Molly got a load of wash going and said she had some unpacking to do and maybe a little ironing.

The next morning Dave was first up and decided to jog before breakfast. The sun needed to burn off the dew before they stated baling so he had plenty of time. When he got back to the house they still weren't up and he guessed they were exhausted from the trip.

Molly came down first and poured herself a cup of coffee and went looking for Dave. She found him on the computer reading about planting corn and pumpkins. He was making notes and had several printouts.

"Morning" he said when he saw her, "Hadn't thought about pumpkins. That's a good idea for Jim. Shouldn't be too hard and we've still got time to plant."

Molly saw the sweat on Dave and noticed the new jogging shoes and asked, "Have you been jogging?"

"Yeah" he said, "Chugged out about a mile, liked to killed me."

"Maybe you'd like to run with Jess sometime?"

"Maybe!" he said smiling.

"I forgot one thing that we talked about at the Think Tank. Mom sat in for part of the time and was fascinated by Jim's chickens and the girl's names on the nesting boxes."

"What did she think?"

"She said that you should tell the schools that they could make field trips to the farm. The kids could learn about chickens, or pecans, or hay farming, or orchards, or gardening, all kinds of stuff. She bets that the kids would tell their moms about it and their whole families would want to come out and pick. Next year there would be a new batch of kids and in a few years you'd have more customers than you could shake a stick at."

"Wow that might be the best idea yet."

"She had one more idea, listen to this. She went bonkers over the may-haw jelly. She said that jelly making was becoming a lost art. For a fee, say thirty dollars, you could teach young girls or newlyweds how to make jelly. You furnish the fruit and the jars and each jelly maker would go home with twelve jars of jelly they could give as gifts. The kids would be proud of their accomplishment and their parents and grandparents would be double proud. Once you did it a couple of times, word would spread."

Dave said, "I'd feel funny doing that but maybe Shelley could do it."

"Maybe a home economics class could make a field trip and gather the fruit and make the jelly and sell it for a fund raiser. You could have "Jam by Pam" or "Jelly by Kelly" or "by Holly by Golly" you big jerk" she said laughing.

Dave got up and said, "I'll have one of those dances now."

He caught her by complete surprise and she said, "At eight o'clock in the morning?"

He put on Patsy Cline's "Crazy" and they danced. He held her further away and did much better. When it was over he said, "Fifty-eight."

John came over about ten and their plan was to work 'till dark. Jim was going to be the official water boy. Molly wanted a try at the baler and Shelley would come over about one and bring lunch.

Molly added the green bandana to her uniform to match the color of the John Deere. Shelley ragged on her when she brought the lunch and asked her if she was still "Being Good."

They finished just before dark and John went home pulling a low-boy with fourteen round bales for himself.

Thursday was a load and stack day and they went to the lake for a light lunch and a cool off swim. Jim and Molly had no trouble cooling off. Molly had put on another of her ten times hot bathing suits that short circuited Dave's cool down system. At lunch Jim asked if they could go to the bowling alley tonight and he got a green light. Molly said she'd go and wanted another one of those steaks.

That night when they got to the bowling alley Jim went on in and as they were walking in Dave asked her if she wanted to bowl. Molly said she did but she hadn't bowled in a long time and made him promise not to laugh at her.

Dave promised and Molly said, "I do better if I gamble."

Dave laughed and said, "What would you like to bowl for?"

She thought a minute and said, "My painting! If I win I get the painting."

"And what do I get if I win?"

Molly paused a minute and said, "Well, if you win you get to keep the painting and you get to paint me in the nude."

"What?"

"You know, like the girl in Titanic."

"Are you serious?"

"Haven't you ever painted someone in the nude?"

"Well yes, but that was in an art class and the subject was a guy."

226

"Well, this is your chance. If I lose, you get to keep both pictures but you have to promise me you won't show it to anyone."

Dave shook at the thought of painting her and asked, "What would your parents say?"

"How would they know? I'm over twenty-one, you know."

The temptation of sin was too great and he said, "You got a bet."

Molly said, "Three game series, total score."

"Deal!" he said and they shook hands.

Jim and Molly both rented shoes and she finally found a ball that would fit her. It was a twelve pound piece of junk in any bowler's eyes.

The first game scores were Jim 114, Molly 158, and Dave 169. Dave bragged on her and said that 158 was a good score for a girl. Inside he knew his 11-point lead wasn't that great and he had to stay on his toes.

Before they started the second game she asked if she could borrow the keys to the truck. She had forgotten something. Dave offered to go but she said she wanted to get it.

When she returned she was carrying a 14-pound blue bowling ball that had the name MOLLY engraved on it and she was carrying a pair of shoes that just happened to be her size.

"What's all this?" he asked.

"Well, I saw you go to a locker and get your own ball and shoes before the game so I decided I'd use my own. I brought them from home."

The next game was a little different. Jim bowled a 109, Molly a 172 and Dave a 174. He still had a 13-point lead, but he was worried.

The third game Molly started off with back-to-back spares and Dave started off with back-to-back strikes. She struck the third frame and as Dave was picking up his ball off the rack she said, "I think red satin would be a nice background for the painting. Don't you?"

Dave lost all concentration and hit the head pin dead on leaving him with the worst split possible in bowling. Needless to say he was left with an open frame. Molly struck her next two frames and when she returned to her seat she mumbled, "Gobble, gobble, gobble."

Dave recovered nicely but Molly was too good. Final scores on the last game were Jim 121, Dave 181 and Molly 201. Dave's three game total was 525 and Molly's was 531. She had won by six pins.

He had lost his painting. He was a little humiliated and somewhat shook up. To top matters off, Sleaze Ball appeared and started talking to Molly.

"Hey" he said, "I called you last week but Dave said you'd gone back to Ohio. The dog didn't tell me you were coming back. How about this weekend? Saturday night."

Molly got rid of him and they went to the restaurant to order.

"What did he want?" Dave asked.

"He wanted me on red satin" she said laughing.

"I'm going to kill you when we get back home."

"Don't worry, he won't be calling anymore. I told him I was dancing with you now."

By the end of the meal Dave was almost out of his bad mood. He wouldn't be making anymore bets with Molly. No telling what else she had in that suitcase.

The next day Dave and Jim came in for lunch after marking out the future pumpkin patch. They were on a high. Dave had read that the secret to making a good pumpkin crop was to make sure that the roots were moist. Since pumpkins were about ninety percent water that would be a must because summers could get awful hot during the pumpkin growing months. The best way to assure proper moisture was a drip irrigation system. He had wanted to learn how to set one up and this would be a good time to learn and if he did the work himself the supplies would only run a little over three hundred dollars. Weeds would be the biggest problem so he decided to Round Up the patch and then plow it up and make the hills. They would plant the second week of July and trust in the Lord for the harvest. They would plant just a little over an acre. Dave had talked Jim into including Shelley as his partner because he would need people to help man the pumpkin booth and to help chop the weeds. They would need help harvesting and hauling the pumpkins and John and the girls would be a big help. They would keep a list of expenses and pay him back before they split.

He thought the patch might produce five or six hundred pumpkins but one article said that one acre well irrigated and with proper weed control might produce three to four thousand pumpkins. "Surely this was a misprint," he thought. Shelley was enthused and got John's blessing and he said he would help her.

Over sandwiches Molly said, "Do you want the bad news or the good news?"

Dave answered, "I want the good news."

"Well, the Neels are coming for a visit. Mrs. Neel wants to see what we've done with the plants and Mr. Neel wants to see your lake and go fishing. He's going to bring his tackle box and wants to see if his old lures still work. They're coming Friday afternoon. Mrs. Neel is going to drive."

"What's the bad news?" Jim asked.

"She can't drive at night so I asked them to spend the night. She doesn't think that climbing the stairs would be good for Herschel so I gave them your room for the night. You all will have to be up in the Martin room with me."

"That's not bad news!" Jim said, "It'll be fun."

Dave said, "Thank you! I've wanted to get them out here for some time but didn't know how to do it. We'll fish in the afternoon and if he's up to it, we'll fish again in the morning. I want Jim to get to know him better. No bad news here Miss Molly, all good news."

"You don't snore do you?" she asked.

"Sometimes he does." Jim said. "I throw a pillow at him and he shuts up."

CHAPTER 13

I TOLD HIM I WOULD

Friday afternoon about three, the Neels arrived. Herschel's two beagles quickly let the two labs know that they weren't going to take any bull from them and a little man pecking order was quickly established. Molly gave Mrs. Neel a tour of the house and then took her outside to show her the plants.

The new plants seemed to like their new surroundings and the TLC that Molly gave them. Mrs. Neel was pleased with Molly's effort and gave her several more ideas to think about. She had also brought a trunk full of new goodies to plant and a large orange sack of yellow jonquil bulbs that she said she just had to have. She said that jonquils were kind of like blue birds. They make everybody happy when they see them.

Dave took Herschel to the study and showed him the computer. It was the first one he had seen up close and in operation. Dave got on e-Bay and brought up the old fishing lures. Herschel was a walking almanac and knew almost every one of them. When they came to the Pumpkinseed Spook, Dave showed off. He enlarged it and they read all the sales pitches and Dave printed it out. Herschel couldn't believe it.

"How many of those do you have in your box?"

"Probably seven or eight."

"Well, seven or eight times thirty-five dollars is a lot of money."

Herschel loved the website and wanted to read them all. Finally Dave said, "Let's look at this again tomorrow. What you say we go and try and catch some bass?"

They went to the lake in the truck so Herschel wouldn't have to climb the hill on the way back. Dave said he would work the troll motor and put Herschel in the back of the boat and Jim in the middle. He brought his own rod and reel but didn't plan to do a lot of fishing himself. Herschel had brought his twenty-five pound tackle box and his own rod and reel. The old rod was stiff as a board and the reel was the famous 1924 Shakespeare Direct Drive. The line on the reel was probably thirty-pound test braided nylon. His first cast didn't go very far and he said, "Guess my old reel is kind of like me, all stove up." He gave it a shot of oil, which helped a little, but his distance was limited.

Dave said, "Use my rod. It's just like yours but you have to push this button before you cast. This is a Garcia 5000. I think you'll like it. You still have to keep your thumb on it when the line's going out."

On the way over to the honey hole, Herschel caught two bass in the two-pound class and Jim had caught a couple of bream. When they got to the honey hole Jim said, "This is where the big boys stay. I've had my line broken several times here."

Herschel took the spook off and snapped on a Lucky 13 that really was as big around as a broomstick. Dave showed him how to adjust the knob on the left side of the reel to balance the weight of the heavier plug to prevent a backlash.

"What won't they think of next?" he commented and asked, "How deep is it over by those two logs?"

Dave said, "About five feet."

Herschel's fish talk was coming back to him and he said; "Now, Matthew, between those two logs is his bed room. I'm going to cast in there and see if I can wake him up."

He made a perfect cast and the plug hit the water with a big splash which Dave was sure scared every bass in the area away.

Herschel said, "You got to let all the ripples go away before you twitch it. He's looking at it right now and the little bass are probably scared off because it's so big." Probably a full minute passed and he finally gave it a twitch.

He waited a few seconds and gave it another, which produced a tremendous strike. He set the hook and maneuvered the fish out of the logs and then put his hand on his heart like he was having chest pains and said, "Matthew, take the rod, I can't do it."

Jim took the rod and the fight was on. Herschel looked at Dave and gave him a wink. Dave was instantly relieved. A second before he envisioned himself giving CPR in the boat. Jim landed the fish and they took pictures with the Lucky 13 still hanging from his mouth. Herschel told Jim to hold the fish straight armed toward the camera. "That'll add about two pounds to the fish," he said laughing.

They released the fish and he took the plug off and put it back in his box and Jim asked, "How come you're putting it up? You're one for one on it."

"Well" he said, "I just wanted to see if it still works. I can't use it anymore because it's bad for my heart."

Herschel looked at Dave who had a big grin on his face and was shaking his head.

"Jim tells me you got an illegal plug."

"Sure do! This is the greatest plug ever made. I think I've got six of them. This one is my favorite" and he pulled out a MudBug that had a green back and a pearl colored belly.

"You can throw this plug in two inches of water and twitch it out or you can reel it fast and it will go four feet deep. If you stop reeling it floats back up going backward and wiggling like a crawfish. Drives fish crazy."

All eyes were on him as he snapped it on. He studied the area for his next cast and said, "See that log over there that's barely under water? I'm going to throw over it several feet and reel up to it under water. Then I'm going to stop and let it float up and then I'll twitch it over the log and reel it fast back to the boat." Before he cast he asked, "Don't think there's any game wardens over there in the trees watching us, do you?"

"I doubt it. This is private property."

He cast and did exactly what he said he would and about the third crank after he twitched it over the log, he had one. As he reeled, the fish jumped half out of the water and tried to shake the plug out of its mouth. Herschel laughed and said, "Shake it but don't break it."

Jim netted the fish and said, "'Bout four pounds" and he released the fish. "We only keep fish that are under fourteen inches. We need to catch five or six like that," which they did in short order and Dave headed back to the dock.

The fish-cleaning table worked like a charm and while he was cleaning the fish Molly brought him a Weller and Water before he had even told her that he had seen a snake on the lake. Molly asked Herschel if he would like a drink and he said he believed he would. "Just like Dave's."

The campfire brought out the best in Herschel. He had been there, done that, and told story after story. Jim was soaking it all up like a sponge and asked all the right questions. Mrs. Neel got on him one time and said to let the other people talk some too.

Molly showed them the ring Jim had given her and Jim told them of the arrowhead she had given him and he would show it to them when they got back to the house.

It was a great fish fry and also a great night back at the house.

The next morning Herschel wanted to fish again and Dave asked him if he would mind just taking Matthew by himself. He said, "I always fish with him and I want him to learn how to fish with other fishermen. He knows most of my tricks and I think he can learn some new ones from you."

Herschel said that would be fine and he'd give him a good dose of B. S.

Dave laughed and said, "Speaking of B. S. that hand on the heart trick with the Lucky 13 scared the living hell out of me."

Herschel laughed and asked, "Mind if I use your rod again?"

"No sir, and if you get the backlash from hell there's another one just like it in the wagon. Catch a mess to take home. Jim knows where the white perch like to hang out if you want some of those. We need to take more fish out of the lake. There's another Zebco in the wagon that's good for throwing light plugs. An eighth ounce Beetle Spin seems to be about all they'll hit. I've got some chores to do, but I'll come down and check on you about ten and make us a pot of coffee and clean your fish.

The Neels' visit was great; they left after lunch with their dogs and a nice mess of fish.

"How'd you like fishing with Mr. Neel?"

"Man, it was fun. He calls small bass summer bass and a bass between two and three pounds a stud bass. Big bass he calls hogs. One time he caught a bass and stood up and held him high in the air and said, "Tell your friends you were eight feet out of the water and that you saw the sun," and then he let him go. Sometimes he would say, "Come to Poppa." When we started out he said, "Dollar on the first fish, dollar on the big fish, and dollar on the most fish." "I caught the first fish so he owed me a dollar and I caught the most fish so he owed me another dollar. He caught the big fish so I owed him a dollar. At the end he owed me one dollar. Almost all of his fish were big. He can really fish. He showed me how to work a top water plug called a Tiny Torpedo. It was clear plastic and the bass loved it. I can work it good. He had another plug called a Dalton Special that bobs in the water like a carrot standing straight up. I caught three on it. When he caught one on a MudBug he would say, "Candy from a baby.""

"Guess what?"

"What?"

"He says that when he dies and if I happen to go to his funeral, he wants me to put a MudBug in his coffin. He thinks they fish in heaven and he wants to have his favorite plug. Any color but he prefers the green one."

"What'd you tell him?"

"I told him I would."

"Know what else? You won't believe it but he swears it's true. One time he caught three bass on a Tiny Torpedo at the same time."

"How could that be? It's a small plug."

"Well he said he did and I believe him. Mr. Neel doesn't lie. Another time he caught a five pounder and a four pounder at the same time on a Lucky 13."

As Jim was rambling on, Dave's mind wandered. Old timers like Mr. and Mrs. Neel had such a vast knowledge of the past. Good things, bad things, things that work and things that don't work. Young folks could learn so much from them and he made a mental note to do a better job with older people. They were an untapped resource. Over the years he had heard "Take a kid fishing" several times. He might reverse it to "Take a senior citizen fishing." How many Mr. Neels are out there? Probably a bunch he thought.

Molly cleared the dishes and said, "Guess what, Jimbo?"

"What?"

"You got one more birthday present."

"Who from?"

"I'll go get it. I think you're going to like it."

She left the room and Dave and Jim looked at each other with a puzzled look. Molly returned with Mr. Neels wooden tackle box and placed it on the kitchen table.

"When you all weren't looking, he brought it in the house and told me to give it to you. He said he didn't have any kids to leave it to and he thought you would take good care of it. He said you need to get a rod and reel like your dad's or the hogs will eat them all up because your line is not strong enough. He hopes you will ask him to come fishing sometime."

Jim looked at his dad with a look of amazement and asked, "Can I keep it?"

"Think you can take care of it? That's a real treasure."

"Yes sir!"

"OK, Bud. You're a lucky young man."

Jim said, "I'm going to take it in the den and spread all the plugs out so we can look at them. I'll call you when I get them all out. We can count them and clean them up real good."

As soon as Jim left the room, Dave put his face in his hands and started crying. Molly left the room to let him be by himself. She came back in a few minutes and he had gotten himself pretty much back together.

"You OK?" she asked.

"Yeah, I'm a tough guy."

"You're a big wus!" she said with a chuckle.

"That old man just gave my boy part of his soul. I can't believe he did that. I can't believe that people are so nice to us."

"They're nice to you because you're nice to them. You've got those fish a working. Now get in there and help him discover his new treasure. Maybe you can get Jim to give him a call in a little while to thank him."

Molly curled up in a chair and watched them unbox and polish them up. Dave was probably more excited than Jim if that was possible. These were collectors' items and the original boxes even made them more valuable. Dave got out the brass polish and shined the brass fittings on the tackle box.

Dave asked Jim, "Do you think you'll ever sell any of them?"

"No way dad, these are Mr. Neel's."

Dave glanced up at Molly and she gave him a thumb up knowing he had just heard the answer he was hoping to hear.

"I feel the same way, Bud," and he gave him a head rub. "You're about the luckiest kid I know. Why don't you give Mr. Neel a call and thank him."

Molly thought back to their farm in Ohio. The routine was to plant corn, pray for rain, feed the hogs, grumble about the price of corn, grumble about the price of hogs, sell some apples and look at snow for several months. Dave's farm was much more fun, lots of irons in the fire and lots more potential. No price supports and hardly any grumbling. She thought back to Shelley's comment that a farmer thinks his bedroom is his office and a tingle went through her. Her mom and dad never seemed to grumble much about all those snowstorms. Maybe corn farming wasn't as gloomy as she thought it was and she laughed out loud.

Dave asked, "What's so funny?"

"Mom and Dad, they just got a lot smarter."

"What does that mean?"

"Maybe I'll tell you someday when a blue northerner rolls in and it starts snowing and all the roads freeze over."

On Friday Molly took Jim to town to sell his eggs. Friday was a better business day because more stores in the Town Square were open. She was going to try an experiment today and see if she could boost Jim's business. She had found an old wooden wagon in a garage sale and cleaned it up real good. She thought about painting it but decided that fresh paint would ruin its charm. She had cut twenty-four dozen Zinnias and made twelve bunches with two dozen in each bunch. She wrapped the stems with wet moss and wrapped them in tin foil to keep them moist and placed them in an Igloo cooler with about a half-inch of ice in the bottom. She figured the cooler would keep the flowers fresh and from being windblown on the ride to town.

When they got to town they loaded the wagon. She put the flowers in a wooden case like the old Coca-Cola cases but this one had deeper holes. She stood the flowers upright in the holes and they looked great. Molly's mom used to say that Zinnias put on a show of their own and she was right. Jim put his eighteen cartons of eggs on the wagon and twelve jars of Shelley's jelly. Molly had also picked a large bucket of tomatoes from the garden and told Jim to try and sell them five for a dollar. She included a box of Ziploc bags in case he made a sale. The Zinnias were to sell for two dollars a bunch. Molly waited at the truck while Jim made his rounds.

Jim's customers loved his enthusiasm and his entrepreneurial spirit and when he returned to the truck, his face was beaming.

"Look!" he said, "I sold everything but two jars of jelly. The ladies went bananas over the flowers. Mrs. Bullard bought four jars of jelly and three dollars' worth of tomatoes. I gave her a bunch of flowers and called it advertising. I could have sold more flowers."

Molly was almost as excited and he was and said, "Well, next week we'll bring more. The more you cut them the more they bloom. We can even make some bunches with shorter stems for smaller vases. There were a lot of those."

They stopped at Sonic for a cherry limeade and while they were waiting he counted his money. He had $128.50. "Wow!" he said, "Only $22.50 came from eggs. I owe dad two dollars for each jar of jelly. That's the best I've ever done."

Molly was pleased with the experiment and said, "I'll bet with a little help you could make that much every time you sell your eggs. By the time you're old enough to drive you can buy your own truck with your own money. Not many kids can say that."

"Know what? One lady named Mrs. Holtzclaw said she was having a party next week and asked if I could bring her six bunches of flowers next Friday. I told her I would."

"That's good Jim. We'll put some "blue" on them when we get home and water them real good. Maybe we can weed a little bit. Zinnias are pretty hearty and bloom a long time. Maybe you can try and sell some blueberries next week. Last time I looked they were starting to get ripe. Maybe you could even invite some of your customers out to pick."

Jim couldn't wait to tell his dad about the good luck he had with the flowers and the tomatoes. Dave was pleased and complimented Molly on the wagon idea.

Jim said, "Guess what? Mrs. Tyndall at the antique store told me that the wagon was valuable. She said that there are a lot of people that collect old toys. She offered me fifty dollars for it and said she could easily sell it for a hundred."

"Maybe we should enlarge the Zinnia patch a little. What do you think?" Dave asked.

"I think it's a great idea. I've saved some magazine articles about raising cut flowers for profit that really looked interesting. The article told some of the do's and don'ts of getting started and told which flowers to grow by zones. By having several varieties you can have longer harvesting seasons and more to offer your customers. The lady in the article did it with her daughters, but the business got so good that the whole family got involved."

That night Molly organized another "think tank" at the kitchen table to discuss Jim's business. She wanted him to become better organized and to have a plan. The meeting was fun and it was decided that Jim would carry a notebook with him when he made his rounds and record each transaction. He would make notes about future orders or comments or suggestions. He would keep a list of expenses and would start an address book of his customers and their telephone numbers. He would post a monthly planner calendar in the kitchen and write down things like the date the lady wanted the six bunches of flowers next week. She was depending on him and the calendar would help him not to forget.

Dave liked the monthly planner idea and said they would share the same calendar and help each other out.

Molly said, "It'll be a little trouble at first but it will get easier after a while. Later you might even make a list of your customers on the computer and maybe around Christmas time you might send them a Christmas card. Or maybe you and your dad might like to have a big Bar-B-Que at the farm and invite all your customers. Maybe you could make it an annual event around harvest time or Thanksgiving. Dad's been doing it for years and his customers and workers look forward to it, especially the wives. Farmers' wives are always looking for an outing. He says it's been good for his business and has helped build friendships. He even invites his suppliers. The feed man, his plumber, the propane man, the mailman, he invites them all."

"Let's do it, Dad! It'd be fun."

"Why would he invite the plumber?" Dave asked.

"Dad wants to be on a first name basis with everyone. You wouldn't believe the kind of service he gets. All he has to do is pick up the phone and they move him to the top of the list. Mom usually sends them home with a pound cake or an apple pie."

Dave smiled at Molly and said, "Good idea! The Bar-B-Que might be a fish fry but a good idea. Might get a blue grass band and have a little music. Hay barn could be the dance floor."

"Maybe you'll send me a plane ticket over the Thanksgiving holidays and I'll come down to the first Shepherd Farm's Hootenanny."

"Might just do that!"

The next couple of weeks were a whirlwind. The hay mountain in the shed was growing. Dave was running with Molly on a regular basis and feeling better than he could ever remember. They had gone from Samuel to Kings in the Bible which Molly was thankful for. Samuel was a tough read. Jim was doing well on his piano lessons, and she was sure he would be playing by ear before it was over. He had a gift for music and an excellent memory.

One weekend Frank brought Brad out for a fishing trip and while the boys were at the lake Theresa taught Molly how to make a new bread called "Monkey Bread." Each piece was dipped in butter and laid in the Pyrex dish and then put in the oven. They chatted while the bread was baking and when it was done they sampled it.

"Oh my God!" Molly said, "This in sinful. Where on earth did you learn this?"

"Before I married Frank I lived in LaMarque for a while next door to a man named Graugnard. I think his first name was Milton but his grandkids always called him Paw Paw and that's what I called him He used to have a bakery in Galveston but sold it when he retired. Everything I learned about baking I learned from him. I kick myself for not being a better student. There I was living next to a master baker and I only learned a couple of things."

When the boys came back from the lake, young Brad was hooked on fishing and Dave and Jim became hooked on monkey bread.

Dave started on a block set for Jackson who had a birthday coming up in a couple of weeks. Now a whiz on the computer, he was becoming a walking encyclopedia on pecan farming. He made the decision to build a building for drying and storing the pecans. He had only sold in bulk before but he was sure they could find a market for shelled pecans as well. He couldn't believe the price shelled pecans were going for in the stores and in the food catalogs. He had been on several chat rooms with other pecan farmers and had gotten several invitations to visit their farms. He contacted several companies about harvesting and shelling equipment. They were eager for his business and one company in Georgia offered to fly him there for a "hands on" demonstration and to take a tour of several pecan farms in the area. Dave accepted their offer and would be there the first week in August.

The umbrella attachment came in from Ohio, and Dave found a red and white umbrella as Molly had requested. Molly turned out to be a great farm hand and organizer and she was much prettier to look at than John was.

Jim planted the buckeye seeds Mr. Goodson had given him on the island in the lake. Dave had already planted several dogwoods, some Japanese cherries and a few plum trees on the island but there was plenty of room left for the buckeyes. Jim gave the island the official name of Buckeye Island. If they grew they would have good luck forever.

When Dave put the pencil to the drip irrigation system for the pumpkin patch it would be too much work. There would be too many hills and it was not practical. He found some sprinklers that would throw a fifty-foot circle and decided to make the patch one hundred feet wide and four hundred and fifty feet long. He would make sixteen tripods each six feet tall and would attach the sprinklers to them. There would be two rows of sprinklers, eight in each row and fifty feet apart. He would need sixteen cutoff valves and thirty hoses that were each fifty feet long. The system would be easy to set up and duplicate each year if it worked.

Hoses were cheap and the pressure from the well was good enough to run three or four sprinklers at the same time without a problem. He put too much time in the pumpkin patch, but he wanted it to be a success for Jim and Shelley both. If it worked it would be easier next year. There would be thirteen rows each four hundred and fifty feet long and the rows would be seven feet apart. The hills on each row would be three feet apart which meant there would be 1,950 hills. They would plant three seeds in each hill so that three or four thousand pumpkins per acre probably wasn't a misprint after all. John and Dave made scoops for each of the hills and put a couple of shovels of compost in each one. He could let the kids do the planting.

Shelley brought her brood out after lunch, and she and Molly supervised the planting. They finished late afternoon and decided to take a swim. They all suited up and headed to the lake but Dave and John lagged behind to enjoy a cold beer.

John said, "Hell man, I never thought I'd be mad at a pumpkin. I'm sick of them already and we haven't even picked the first one."

Dave laughed and said, "Me too, but it might be profitable and give Shelley some mad money so she won't have to beg from you."

"Yeah, that'd be nice."

Dave laid down on one of the benches to get the kinks out of his back. His sore muscles and the two beers had made him sleepy and he dozed off.

John joined the others at the lake and Molly asked, "Where's Dave?"

"You won't believe it! He's asleep. He laid down on the bench to straighten out his back and while we were talking he stopped answering. He's sleeping like a baby."

A few minutes later Molly went to check on Dave and sure enough he was sound asleep and gently snoring. An idea popped in her head and she went to the chuck box and got out Jim's carving box with the paints. She found a bright red nail polish and very gently started painting Dave's toenails. She was just about through when she saw Morgan and Caroline coming up. She put her finger over her mouth to shush them. When the girls saw what she was doing their eyes got big and they had to put their hands over their mouths to keep from laughing. Caroline ran back to the lake to tell the group the news. The rest of the group came to see just as she was finishing. Caroline had told them all not to make a sound. Molly put the paints up and they all went back to the lake and had a good laugh. Molly made them all promise not to rat on her and they were all sworn to secrecy.

Dave woke up a little while later and walked down to the pier. The kids were all looking at him and started laughing.

"What's so funny?" which made them laugh some more.

Isabel said, "Your toes" which got another round of laughter.

Dave looked at his toes and a look of astonishment came over his face. He turned almost as red as the polish. He bent down and tried to rub it off but it was acrylic enamel and had already dried.

"That's real cute! Wait till I tell the guys at the bowling alley you paint your toes."

John's comment put the kids in stitches again.

Molly's mind flashed back to the first time she had seen her mom pull the trick on her uncle at her granddad's camp on the river. It was just as funny today as it was back then. Maybe even more fun because she had all these witnesses. They would laugh about the time big Dave got his toes painted for years to come.

Dave did a big cannon ball off the pier that pretty much soaked the whole group. He hadn't been the victim of a good practical joke in a long time. He knew the kids were probably sworn to secrecy but he decided to add a little excitement to the moment by telling them what he was going to do when he caught the guilty party.

"When I find out which one of you little rascals did it, I'm going to take you out behind the hay shed and make you drop your britches and give you ten licks with my belt."

The threat brought more squeals from the kids.

"Or maybe I'll catch the guilty one sleeping and I'll cut off all her hair. How'd you like to be bald headed?" He looked at Molly who had an impish little smirk on her face and said, "I know it wasn't Molly because I helped save her life and she wouldn't do such a thing." His comment got more laughter.

Jackson said, "I'm hungry."

Shelley said, "Oh my gosh, the time got away from me. We need to go."

Jim asked if he could make goulash for everybody for supper. He and Molly went to the chuck box and they had the chili and the beans.

"You'll need two dozen eggs and there's a new gallon of milk in the ice box."

The kids were thrilled that they were staying for supper. Dave said he would go get what they needed from the house and Molly told him to bring a package of English muffins. She would toast them on the grill.

As Dave started up the path John said, "And put some socks on those twinkle toes of yours, you're embarrassing me." And there was another round of laughter.

Jim did good on the goulash recipe and retold Molly's story of how her brother invented it. They all loved it and there wasn't even enough left for the dogs.

Dave said it was supposed to rain tomorrow which would be good for the pumpkins and if it didn't, he would test the sprinkler system. He told them of the article that an acre of well-managed pumpkins might produce three or four thousand pumpkins. He saw a little smile come on Shelley's face.

"Wow!" she said, "I thought we were shooting for a thousand."

"We planted over five thousand seeds. No telling what we'll get"

After the Phelans left, Jim put on a movie and Molly went to take a bath and shampoo. Dave went to piddle in the shop.

Molly came down after about an hour and got a "Hubba hubba" out of Jim.

"Thanks!" she said, "Where'd you learn that?"

"Dad says it sometimes when he sees a pretty girl."

"Where is old twinkle toes?"

"He's at the shop."

"What does he do there? He goes there a lot."

"Plays music makes geese, all kinds of stuff. He's crazy about geese. Why don't you go there?"

"You don't think he'll mind?"

"He won't mind, but don't walk up behind him if he's using a power tool."

"How come?"

"Sometimes if you distract a person using a power saw they cut their fingers off."

"Who taught you that?"

"Uncle Dave, he's a nut about safety with power tools."

"I think I'll go check out his shop."

"Ask him to show you his pet mongoose. He's crazy about him."

"I thought it was against the law to have a mongoose as a pet in the United States."

"I think you're right, but he has one. It came from Calcutta, India."

"See you later."

She put on a dash of Chanel before she left for the shop, might be a good testing ground for her father's theory. It was about nine and very dark outside, but she could see a light coming out of the shop. There was a gentle breeze and it felt invigorating. She heard music coming from inside the shop.

She eased up to the door and peeked in. He had his back to her and he was sanding on a goose with a belt sander. The goose didn't have wings and was smaller than a real life size. He was listening to a Louis Armstrong CD.

The shop was awesome. It was like nothing she had ever seen. Interesting things covered the walls. Half-finished projects all over the place, odd pieces of wood, things hanging, standing, leaning, iron bins, wood bins, and power tools everywhere. Also the giant patterns of the Indians and their horses. She had a thought that this must be the same feeling that Willie Wonka got in the chocolate factory. There were several V's of Snow Geese hanging from the rafters of the shop. Some of the V's were larger than others, which made the formations appear to be flying at different altitudes. The effect was exciting. She had the thought, "I wonder how much someone would pay for one of these formations to hang in a den with a high vaulted ceiling. A bunch I bet." The bodies of the geese were in perfect proportions and the wings appeared to be made of tin and were bent in different positions that made the geese look like they were really flying.

All of a sudden Dave turned off the sander and grabbed the remote to the CD controller. He turned up the volume because he knew one of his favorites was about to play and Satchmo started playing, "When you're Smiling."

Evidently he had seen Louis do his routine before because he had it down pat. He brought out his handkerchief, wiped his brow, the whole nine yards. He would have died if he knew she was watching him. She knew it was one of those rare times in one's life that you get to look right into the soul of a person. He turned the volume up right when Louie was fixing to play some serious trumpet and he picked up the goose he had been working on to use as his make believe horn. He blew the goose like his life depended on it.

She enjoyed his performance immensely. She wished she could have recorded the moment with a camera but, picture or not, she would never forget this uninhibited moment. This was special.

She backed out of sight just as the song was finishing and waited a few seconds before she reappeared.

She said, "Knock, knock" as she entered and asked, "What's up?"

Dave looked half guilty and surprised and asked, "You been standing there long?"

"No, just walked up."

He looked relieved and gave her the cook's tour of the shop. Molly asked a jillion questions and Dave enjoyed her enthusiasm. Some of his dreams and happiest times were spent in the shop. As they walked by the sander where he had been working on the goose Molly couldn't stand it any longer. It was her nature not to let a sleeping dog lay. She picked up the goose and kind of held it by the neck like it was an instrument.

"You know what?" she said smiling.

"What?"

"You play a mean goose!"

Dave turned red immediately and Molly's laughter didn't help matters at all. She put the bill of the goose in her mouth and started humming "When the Saints Go Marching In."

Dave said, "Give me the goose" and he made a grab for it. She wouldn't let him have it and put it behind her back and held it with both hands. He reached around her with his long arms and as he was wrestling her for it, her sweetness overcame him and he kissed her long and hard. She became weak in the knees and the goose dropped to the floor.

Dave suddenly came to his senses and stepped away and said, "I'm sorry, I didn't mean it."

Molly still gasping for air and with hormones exploding replayed his words in her head and after a few seconds said, "Listen Buster! Don't ever kiss me again like that unless you mean it. Understand?"

"Yes." He said sheepishly still weak in the knees himself.

As she was standing there still trying to come to her senses she thought, "Wow! I wonder how he kisses if he really means it." She was at a loss for something to say when she spotted a cage on a shelf over his workbench that had the word MONGOOSE on it in large black letters, also the words, "Caution-Extremely Dangerous," and "Do Not Open" and "Calcutta, India."

"Jim said you had a Mongoose. I thought he was joking."

Dave picked up the cage and said, "He's kind of shy and sometimes doesn't want to come out."

The cage was about two feet long, a foot wide and maybe ten inches high. Half of the cage was boxed in with a single hole that opened into the other end, which was covered with wire screen with about one-quarter inch squares. The bottom of the cage was covered with wood shavings and there was a small water bottle hanging from the side.

Dave started shaking the cage trying to get him to come out. Molly started to try and hold one end of the cage and Dave said, "Don't put your fingers on the wire. They love to bite and they're fast as lightning."

Molly didn't know it but there was a hidden trigger release to the trap door top of the cage.

"Do you see him?" he kept asking and Molly kept getting closer and closer to the cage. When she was just a few inches away, Dave released the trigger and the lid which was attached to the top by a pair of screen door hinges snapped open with a loud bang and the mongoose sprang from the cage directly at Molly's face and she screamed as if a rattlesnake had bit her.

Actually the mongoose that landed on her head was not a mongoose at all but was a coon tail tied to a string that was connected to the trap door.

Molly tried to gain some composure but couldn't and ran all the way from the shop to the house and up the stairs to her room. A little later she came downstairs in a new outfit and said to Jim, "You little stinker! You set me up just perfect on the mongoose. I owe you one and I will get even."

Shortly afterward, Dave returned to the house still smiling and asked, "You OK?"

"Yes, but you scared the H E L L out of me" and said, "Jim, have you ever heard your uncle blow a goose before?"

"No, but one time I heard him blow a screwdriver."

They all laughed and Jim turned on the Rangers. Molly looked at Dave who seemed to be avoiding eye contact for a while and thought about the kiss he hadn't meant. The perfume was potent she decided, and she would definitely use it at a later date. He had tasted the fruit. There would be another time. She would bet on it.

Molly was popular at the bowling alley. One night she bowled a 630 series, which got everyone's attention. Her personality was contagious and she was fun to watch. She almost always drew a gallery.

Over steaks at the bowling alley Dave ragged on her about how she tricked him out of the painting and Molly said, "Jim, did your dad ever tell you about the bet we made that night?"

"No ma'am."

Molly looked at Dave who was turning pale and Jim said, "Know what her brother says? He says don't ever play pool for money with her. He said she beats him like a drum. He said he taught her everything he knew and she passed him. They have a pool table at home and I saw her run the table three times."

"No kidding?"

"Jim" she said, "I could skin you alive for telling him that."

"Why?"

"I was going to win that other painting of me. I like it better than the first one."

"Thanks for the warning Jimbo. What other talents do you have, Miss Molly?"

"A couple!"

"Such as?

"Might show you one sometime if a blue norther rolls in."

When they got back to the farm Dave went to the shop. Molly and Jim went to the east porch and watched the moon come up. She told Jim about her troubles with the insurance company about her car. She said, "Every time

I need to run an errand, I have to ask to use the truck and sometimes he's using it. Last week I met a cute girl in town named Susan and she asked me to come for a visit and a movie. I couldn't go because I didn't have a car. I really miss my freedom."

After a long pause Jim said, "I know a secret."

"Hey, I thought you and I weren't going to have secrets."

"Well, I've got one and I'll probably get in trouble if I tell."

"I've got one too but I was too embarrassed to tell. I'll tell you mine if you'll tell me yours. OK?"

"OK!" Jim said, "You go first."

Molly said, "You know that night your dad showed me the mongoose and I ran to my room."

"Yes mam."

"Well, the reason I ran to my room was because it scared me so bad, I wet my pants and I didn't want anybody to see."

They both had a good laugh and Molly asked, "Now what's your secret?"

"They found your car."

"Who found it?"

"The police."

"What police?"

"The Plano Police Department called. They said they have your car and it was in good shape. All you had to do was show some identification and pick it up."

"How'd they get this phone number?"

"I don't know."

"When did they call?"

"About ten days ago."

"Why didn't he tell me?"

"He was afraid you might leave if you had a car."

"Well, I just might give him a piece of my mind."

"We talked about it together. We don't want you to leave. Dad's going to offer you a job. He's going to match your teacher pay or if you're a gambler he says we can split the pecan crop three ways. He says that everything's working better and growing better since you came."

"Well, my car is worth around twenty thousand. I'd be a fool not to go get it, don't you think?"

"Yes ma'am."

"Did he write the number down?"

"Yes ma'am. It's in the front of the phone book."

"Thanks for telling me. I'll tell him they called again and I got the call. I'll act like it was a surprise. I won't tell him you told me. I think I'll take a bus to Plano tomorrow and pick it up."

Molly couldn't believe she was having this conversation with Jim. He was so mature, so loving and sincere. He was attuned to Dave's thinking and reasoning.

"Know what?"

"What?"

"Dad said if you don't go for plan A or plan B we'll kidnap you and if you try to get away he might try a secret plan."

Molly was loving this conversation and asked, "What's his secret plan?"

"Don't know. He said it was a long shot. He said he had an ace in the hole. What does that mean?"

"I don't know!" she said laughing, "We'll have to try and find out."

Jim said, "I'll give you my share of the pecan crop if you'll stay."

"That's sweet Jim" and she gave him a hug. Inside she was thinking "Wow! Wonder what the 'Pecan Man' would think if he knew that she might be getting two thirds of the pecan crop. This was funny. She might own this farm if she played her cards right."

CHAPTER 14

ENJOY THE GOODIES

M olly had been upset all day. Knowing that Jackie was coming for the
weekend upset her. Nobody seemed to know what to do. Dave knew
that Jackie would be upset that Molly was there. If the nanny was a little old
lady with a wart on her nose it would be OK, but Molly was beautiful. Not
just to him but anybody that saw her, man or woman. He knew he was in
trouble and was going to have to face the music. He was turning into a basket
case.

Jim was also a little fidgety. Kids have a sense that lets them know when
they're not liked. Jackie put up a good front but she had no use for him.

The day dragged on. Jackie had told Dave she would call when she turned
off to the farm road. She hoped to be there by five.

About seven the phone rang and Dave picked it up.

"Hello! Oh hi babe. Where are you?"

"Sorry I'm late. Traffic was terrible; there was a wreck or something. I
should be there in about thirty minutes. I'm hoping we can have a campfire
tonight."

"You bet! We'll see you in a little bit. Drive careful."

Dave turned to Jim and Molly and said that Jackie had gotten tied up in
traffic but would be here in about thirty minutes, she had just dropped off the
Interstate. She's hoping we can have a campfire tonight.

"That's about all she likes about this place." Jim added.

Molly stewed around for about twenty minutes and made the decision
to go for a run. She wanted to meet Jackie but she also didn't want to meet

her. She decided that a good run might get some of her frustrations out of her head. She decided to run till she couldn't run anymore. Some of her clearest thoughts came while she was running. She went upstairs and changed into a running outfit. She came back to the kitchen looking like an ad in a running magazine. She wore a tight fitting jogging bra with a white tee over it. A yellow ribbon in her hair and a pair of running shorts with a little slit up the sides that showed off her perfect legs. It was the kind of outfit that makes men almost run off the road or get a crick in their neck trying to get one more look as they drive by.

Dave panicked when he saw her. "What are you doing? Go put some clothes on. Jackie will kill me if she sees you looking like that."

"Don't worry, I'm going running. I won't be here when she comes" and she was off. She hollered to Jim to hold the dogs because she was going too far for them.

Dave was waiting for Jackie on the front porch and when she drove up he went out to greet her. They exchanged greetings and a quick kiss and started to the house. As they passed the bell she said, "Why don't you get rid of that stupid bell? It's so tacky."

"Ouch!" he thought and he wanted to tell her it was a "happy bell" but he decided against it.

When they got to the front porch she immediately noticed the plants. "The plants look nice, makes it looks like somebody lives here. When did you do them?"

"About a month ago, I had help. Actually, Molly and Jim did them all."

"Oh yes, Molly, the nanny. I want to meet her. She doesn't sound like your normal nanny."

Dave laughed and Jackie asked, "What's so funny?"

"That's an understatement about a normal nanny. She's not normal. She cooks, she sweeps, she washes, drives the tractors, teaches piano, gives computer lessons and is teaching Jim and me how to keep books."

"How much are you paying her?"

"No money, just room and board."

"Something sounds fishy here."

"It's a long story, I'll tell you about it later."

When they got inside the house she noticed the flowers on the hall table. She stopped to admire a vase of about three dozen zinnias.

"Let me guess. The nanny did these."

"Right?"

When they got in the kitchen Jackie pulled out a couple of jars of jalapeno jelly out of her purse. "I made you some more. I figured you were about out"

"You're right! We are out. I need to get that recipe from you. It's really good."

Molly had thought Jackie would be there in time for supper and had set four places at the table. Jackie noticed the good silver and asked, "Is that your grandmother's good silver?" and before Dave could answer she said, "Let me guess, Molly's idea?"

"Yep."

"Well, you better count it before she goes, crazy to use your good silver out here in the boondocks."

"Oh my gosh," thought Dave, "The fur is getting ready to fly."

Jim came in and gave Jackie a hug and told her hello.

"Guess what? We got a computer. Want to see it?"

"Out of the Stone Age, are we?" and she followed him into the study.

Dave had anticipated her going to the study and had taken the two paintings of Molly and turned them backward and placed them in the corner of the room. No use adding fuel to the fire had been his reasoning. He breathed a sigh of relief for having done so. He followed them into the study and when he entered the room he almost had a heart attack.

Both of the paintings were on the easels and facing the room. No doubt who did it. The fur would definitely fly.

"These are beautiful," Jackie said, "Who is she?"

"That's Molly! She's my nanny."

"And where does she sleep?" she asked looking at Dave.

"She sleeps in my room. I've moved in with dad."

"Pandora's Box was open now," Dave thought. "There was no place to hide."

Jim said, "Dad painted this one for us to remember her by when she's gone, but he lost it to her in a bowling match so he painted this one of her singing and dancing for us."

"So she bowls and sings and dances too?"

"Yes ma'am. She's really good. She owes dad twenty-two more dances."

Jim glanced at his dad who quickly gave him a little sign of his finger over his mouth trying to get him to not say anymore.

Jim got the message and stopped talking.

There was a lull in the conversation and Jackie kept staring at the paintings trying to digest all this new information.

Dave said, "What you say we have a campfire?"

"Yeah" Jim answered.

"And invite Molly. I want to meet the nanny that's dancing with my boyfriend."

"She's running right now." Dave answered.

"I'll bet she is. I can't wait to meet her. I want to hear all about her."

When they started down the path to the lake the two dogs came over to pay their greetings and Jackie said, "By God! Don't tell me you've gotten another dog?"

"This is Pudd'n. She's Molly's dog. She always ties a bandana on her collar, because she's a girl."

"Well, keep her away from me; I don't want any dog hair all over these pants."

Dave was glad Jim was going with them. He would help protect him and verify the facts, which he was sure Jackie would ask. Attorneys have a way of getting the facts and Jackie was a good one.

Molly kept mentally kicking herself in the seat of the pants as she ran. What made her put those paintings back up? She knew exactly why he had taken them down. Why did she do it? Her dad had always told her that you get more out of people with a teaspoonful of honey than with a teaspoonful of lemon juice. This wasn't her style. Dave thought she had class. This was not class and it dawned on her that she was picking a fight. She would probably be stepping into the ring tonight. "Damn!" she thought and she kicked herself again.

After about an hour and a half she stopped running. She was out of gas. This was the furthest she had ever run and was surprised when she looked at her watch. It was a long walk back to the farm and by the time she got to the road to the house she had made the decision to take a shower and hit the sack. When she looked toward the lake she could see that the campfire was still going and she said to herself, "Good! I won't have to meet her until tomorrow."

When she went inside Jim was still up and watching "The Man from Snowy River" again.

"How's it going?" she asked.

"OK, dad told me it was past my bedtime so I came to the house."

The phone rang and Molly picked it up and said, "Hello!"

"Molly."

"Yes!"

"Big favor!"

"Sure! What's up?"

"Jackie wants to meet you and I was thinking you could come to the campfire."

"Well, I'm all sweaty."

"That's OK! Could you bring a few things when you come? There's a jar of jalapeno jelly on the sink that Jackie made. Bring some Ritz crackers and my Patsy Cline CD. Oh and a bottle of wine. It's a 91 Monet. Jim knows where it is. Its Jackie's favorite. Oh yeah, and a couple of wineglasses. Do you mind?"

There was a long pause and Molly said, "Give me a few minutes."

"Thanks!" he said and she hung up. It was time to face the music.

Molly bit her lip. Her feelings were hurt. "Bring a couple of glasses! Why not three? Why didn't he get off his lazy rear end and get it himself. This was too much. I told him I would," so she decided to do it.

"Matthew, my friend, I need your help."

"Yes ma'am, what do you want?"

"Get Slick and hook up the travois. Your uncle wants a few things at the campfire and we're going to send Slick on a mission. Your dad said you know where the wine is that Jackie likes."

Jim went to the pantry and there was a whole case and he said, "This is the only kind she likes so dad bought a whole case."

Jim left to hook up Slick and she opened a bottle and took a sip. "Not bad! Not bad at all" she thought and she poured herself a whole glass. She found the apple cider vinegar in the pantry and refilled the bottle up to the full mark and put the cork back in the bottle.

Next she got the pepper jelly and opened it and spread some on a cracker. "Not bad! In fact, damn good!" and she had another. She found the bottle of Tabasco and shook in enough to make a grown man cry and stirred it around and recapped the jar. She put some Ritz crackers in a Ziploc bag. She saw a small dead roach on the windowsill and picked him up with a small piece of paper and started to add him to the bag of crackers. "No," she thought, "I couldn't do that to anybody," and she put him in the trash can.

She got down two wineglasses and put her lips to one of them and left a good lipstick mark. By this time Jim was back and said that Slick was ready to go.

"Wouldn't you like to send Jackie some flowers?"

"No way!"

"Lantana flowers?"

A smile came on his face and he said, "Yes ma'am. I'll go get them" and shortly he returned with a handful.

She wrapped the stems with a damp paper towel and put tin foil around them. She took a whiff. "Phew!" she said, "Bet these will open her sinuses. Don't you think?"

Jim didn't know what they were doing but it was fun.

"Get the Patsy Cline CD."

Jim fetched it and Molly took a nickel that was lying on the counter and scratched the CD.

"Dad's going to skin you alive."

"All's fair in love and war!" she replied, "Now go and get one of your dad's jackets for Jackie."

Jim returned with his favorite blue jean jacket.

"Now go get one of his handkerchiefs."

Jim returned with one of his monogrammed handkerchiefs which she lipsticked and put in on one of the pockets and put her own tube of lipstick in the other.

Then she sat down at the table and wrote a note and put it in an envelope. She put all the goodies in a pack and lashed it to the travois. She attached the note to the pack making sure it would not fall off.

"OK Slick! Let's see how good Jim has trained you. Take it to asshole!"

Slick just stood there and didn't move.

"Oh, you don't know who that is? Go find Dave. Back! Take it to the campfire" and she pointed to the campfire and said, "Back!"

Slick understood and he was off. He arrived at the campfire with enthusiasm. He knew he had done well and Dave was excited to see him.

Jackie told Slick to calm down and not to get her all dirty.

Dave unlashed the pack and they opened it together.

"Oh look!" said Jackie, "Flowers, how sweet!" She picked them up and smelled them. "Wow, they kind of stink!"

Jackie saw the note and picked it up. "Clancy" was written on the envelope.

"Who the hell is Clancy?" she asked.

Dave laughed and said, "It's a nick name Jim has for me."

"Who is Jim?"

Dave laughed again and said, "It's a nickname I have for Matthew."

"Well read the note!"

Dave opened the envelope and read:

Clancy,

Hope this is everything you wanted. Jim picked some flowers for Jackie. He is so thoughtful.

I tasted the pepper jelly because I had never had any before. Wow! Jackie must have a stomach made of iron. It was too hot for me. I put in one of your jackets in case Jackie gets cold. I know how the temperature drops when the sun goes down. I took the liberty of opening the wine because I didn't remember if you had a wine opener in the chuck box. Would have brought these things to you myself but I'm afraid of snakes in the dark. I've kind of got a headache and I'm going to bed early.

Jim is watching the brumbies. I've fed the mongoose, the dogs and the miracle workers.

Enjoy the goodies,
Jessica

P.S.-I lost a game of World to Jim so I'm cooking breakfast in the morning when the birds that sing are on the wing.

"Who is Jessica?" Jackie asked.

"Jessica is Molly."

"I guess that's Matthew's nickname for her, right?"

"Right?"

Dave uncorked the wine and poured each of them a glass. Jackie immediately noticed the lipstick on the glass and said, "You need to start washing better" as she spread some of the jelly on the crackers.

They each tried one of the crackers at the same time and immediately their mouths were on fire and they chased the crackers with a gulp of wine and another frown came to their faces.

"I think the wine has soured" Dave said and he put on the CD and started the music.

It was scratchy and Dave was upset. "That's my favorite CD. Damn!"

Jackie was starting to get cold and Dave handed her the jacket that Molly had sent.

She put it on and said, "This feels much better" and she put her hands in the pockets.

A few seconds later she pulled out a lipstick and asked, "Is this your jacket or Molly's jacket?"

"It's mine."

"Well, whose is this?" and she handed him the lipstick.

"Must be yours."

"No, it's not my brand and I believe this is your monogrammed handkerchief with lipstick on it."

"They must be yours."

"Wrong!" she said. "Something's going on here and I don't like it. Molly's got to go or should I say Jessica's got to go. She's trying to submarine me and I won't stand for it."

"What do you mean submarine?" Dave asked.

"Well for example: bad wine, bad music, bad jelly, stinky flowers, dirty glasses, bad jacket, bad handkerchief and clever little notes. Let me see that note again."

Dave handed her the note, which she read again, and when she was through asked, "What's a brumby?"

"A wild horse."

"This girl is in love with you."

"What are you talking about?"

"This note is too clever. It's full of secrets. She's insulted me. An iron stomach! I don't like it. The little ho has got to go. I won't have her in the same house with you."

"But I need her for Matthew. She's helped him so much already and she's only going to be here for a few more weeks. She's teaching him how to play the piano."

"Well, it's me or her. There is a solution you know."

"What?"

"Marry me, move to New York, become a famous artist and we'll live happily ever after. I can't wait for you forever. Believe it or not there are others who find me attractive."

"What about the farm?"

"Sell the farm."

"You know New York is no place to raise a boy."

"Let Matthew go live with your brother and his wife."

"I can't believe you just said that. Matthew is part of me. He's my son; I've adopted him. My brother can hardly make ends meet. I love the farm and could never leave it. I'm definitely not coming to New York and Molly is not a whore as you have implied. I haven't laid a hand on her."

"I doubt that."

Dave paused a minute and said, "Well, I guess it's time we parted ways. I'll walk you to your car."

"Just like that? It's over?"

"Just like that!"

They walked back to Jackie's car with Jackie looking for snakes the whole way. When they got to the car Jackie said, "Besides being a ho, the girl is a liar."

"How's that?"

"Well, there are no mongooses in the U. S. I know that. They're outlawed in this country. I know that she did not feed the mongoose.

"Well, she's not a liar, I have one."

"I want to see it."

Dave led her to his shop and showed it to her. It didn't take long. Molly had her bedroom window open and heard the scream.

"Nosey bitch!" she thought and she heard the car drive off.

"Adios, Miss Jackie," she said softly and she watched her car lights fade down the farm road all the way to the highway.

CHAPTER 15

MORE DAVE, TALK TO ME

The next morning she was awakened by Jim's, "The Sun is up." She quickly got dressed and went downstairs but he already had breakfast going.

"Hey, I was supposed to cook."

"I know, but I got up early and thought you might like a few extra winks."

"Thanks!" she said as she went over to her purse and pulled out two quarters. She wrote her name on the little dot stickers and dropped them in the cuss box.

Jim smiled and asked, "What'd you say?"

"Can't tell, but I'm doing better. This is my first donation in a couple of weeks."

Dave wandered in and went directly to the coffeepot.

Molly said, "I had the strangest dream last night. I thought I heard a panther scream. I hear they sound like a woman screaming."

"You did! Jackie just had to see the mongoose."

Molly bit her lip to keep from laughing and asked, "How was the campfire?"

"As if you didn't know. You owe me a new CD by the way."

"How did she like the flowers?" Jim asked.

"Cute bud, real cute."

"Did she like the jelly?" Jim asked and he glanced up at Molly who had her finger over her mouth to silence him.

"Your little sabotage plan worked. Jackie's gone for good. Hope you all are real proud of yourselves."

Dave left the room and when he was completely gone, Jim and Molly high fived each other and Molly said, "I believe old Slick did a good job in delivering the goodies" and she slipped him a piece of bacon.

Matthew gave Molly a hug and took off to feed his chickens.

Two days later Dave left before the sun came up on a trip to visit a pecan orchard in Corsicana. He got home about 9:30 that night, and he was on a high. It was a good visit and he got some new ideas for his pecan shelling start up. He saw Molly's car was still here and he was glad. It meant she hadn't left.

Jim met him on the front porch and had an excited look on his face.

"What's up bud?"

"Molly wrote you a note! Come read it. She's somebody, dad! She's somebody!"

"What in the world are you talking about?"

Jim led him to the note and Dave read it. The note read:

Dear Nobody,

I'm at the campfire thinking about the future.
If you feel like putting the whammy on me or clubbing a baby seal, join me.
Wine is optional. A little Waylon and Willie would be nice.

Somebody.

Dave loved the note. He understood every word of it. He was slow to comment and Jim said, "Don't you get it? Your song! Nobody! That's you! She's somebody! Don't you see? She signed it Somebody. She's at the wagon. Go see her. She wants to talk."

Dave said, "I'm going to take a quick shower and shave. Get the small cooler and put some ice in it and get a couple of my Waylon and Willie CD's."

He cleaned up in record time and came back to the kitchen and read the note again. He put a couple of bottles of wine in the cooler. Jim handed him a bag with a loaf of Molly's good bread and the CD's.

Jim said, "Dad, you smell like a French wh____" and he caught himself. "Are you going to put the whammy on her?"

"Might," he answered "If I get the chance. I almost forgot something," and he went to his bedroom and opened the top drawer of his chest of drawers. He took out a small package and put it in his jeans pocket. "Might just need the ace in the hole tonight," he said to himself.

"Why don't you go on to bed? We'll probably talk for a long time."

"Yes sir."

"Where are the dogs?"

"With her."

"Call them in a little while and keep them at the house."

"Yes sir."

Before he started down the path he went to the bell and gave it three quick rings. He tried to rehearse his thoughts on the path about what he was going to say but he was pretty much brain dead. He made a phone call on his cell.

As he approached the campfire he could see Molly sitting on the ground but something didn't look right. There was a shovel stuck in the ground behind her.

As he got closer he could see her face and it seemed to glow from the flames of the fire. She was breathtaking as usual and he wished he had brought his camera. There was definitely another potential painting here.

"What in the world are you sitting on?" he asked.

"This is called a grotto. One summer my brother worked in Destin and this is how they would sit on the beach. You dig a hole that contours to your own derriere. The dirt from the hole turns into a backrest and you build a little mound in front to put your legs over. They're heck to get in and out of, but once you're in, there's nothing more comfortable. Hobbs said they would get in their grottos and put on their sunglasses and watch the chicks. They would purposely place their ice chest a little out of reach and if a good looking chick came by they would ask them a big favor: to hand them a beer. He said it was a great way to start a conversation and of course the girls would want to try the grotto out."

Dave said, "I like your brother more all the time. I believe he could teach me some tricks."

"Probably so" she said laughing.

"How about a glass of wine?"

"I'd love one."

Dave returned with the wine and handed her a glass and said, "That does look mighty comfortable."

She had dug the grotto big enough for two in case he wanted to join her and she covered it with a blanket from the wagon so she wouldn't get her clothes dirty.

Dave put a couple more logs on the fire and asked if he could try the grotto out.

"Sure, I made it a little big" and she asks, "Did I hear my ring a little while ago?"

"Yes."

"Who rang it?"

Dave paused a few seconds and said, "I did."

"Do you love me?"

This is going too fast he thought and he held up his fingers about five inches apart.

"Well thanks, last time your fingers were only about one-half inch apart."

Dave laughed and said, "Darn, I forgot something" and he climbed out of the grotto and put Waylon and Willie on the CD player. He tried to regain some of his thoughts but he couldn't focus. He climbed back into the grotto just as the music started.

"That's more like it!" Molly said smiling, "You must have read my note."

"Yeah, I read it. You said you wanted to talk about the future."

"Yeah" she said, "This has really been fun but I've got to start thinking about getting back. I've got contracts to sign and workshops to attend before school starts."

Dave paused a minute and then said, "I've been thinking about that and I've got an idea. What would you think of staying here next semester?

I'll match your salary and you'll get to see the pecans and the pumpkins come in."

Plan A she thought. She paused a while and said, "That would be fun but I've got a lot of benefits as a teacher: holidays, sick leaves, insurance, retirement. That's a fair offer but I don't know. I'll have to think on it."

Dave decided to offer plan B and said, "Here's another idea. Stay through January and help with the pecan harvest and help us get started in the gift basket business. It could be big and we'll split three ways. You get a third, Jim gets a third and I get a third."

Molly was dying inside. She wanted to laugh so bad. He had no idea that Jim had offered her his third. She'd have two-thirds of the crop for just a few months' work.

"That idea has possibilities but what if the crop is a failure?"

"Well, that's a gamble you'd have to take but the crop looks like it's going to be a bumper year. Your share could be big."

She was dying to say yes to plan A or B but thanks to Jim's inside information she wanted to hear about the "Ace in the hole plan." "I'm not much of a gambler. I'll probably go back home. I love my kids and Ohio's beautiful in the fall."

Dave refilled each of their glasses and they shared some bread. The fire felt good and the grotto was very comfortable.

Dave said, "I don't want you to go."

"What are you going to do? Kidnap me and hide my car." Molly said laughing.

"Well, I kind of tried that and it didn't work."

There was a long pause and Molly pressed on. "Why'd you ring the bell?"

"Because I love you."

"How would I know that? You kissed me pretty good one time and then said you didn't mean it."

"I'd like to try that again" and turned toward her and the rockets went off. When the kiss was over she asked, "Did you mean it?"

"I meant it."

"How would I know you meant it?"

Dave turned away and reached into his pocket and pulled out a small felt bag and handed it to her.

"What's this?"

"Open it."

She did and there were two gold rings inside.

"What's this?"

"They're wedding rings. The small one is yours. Will remembered your size from when Jim bought you the ring. I don't believe in diamonds."

She slipped it on. It was a perfect fit. She slipped the other ring on her thumb and asked, "When do you want to get married?"

"Right now. We'll go to the JP tomorrow. John and Shelley will be our witnesses. The honeymoon starts tonight."

"You don't buy your own wedding ring, Goofus!"

"I didn't, Will lent them to me. I haven't paid him yet. He's got more to choose from if you don't like it."

"No" she said, "It's beautiful. They match. You're kind of full of surprises tonight."

"Yeah!" he said, "Never thought I'd propose lying flat on my back in a grotto. Kind of like a trap you dug and I fell into it."

Molly laughed and rolled over and straddled him sitting right on his belt buckle. She put her hands on his chest and gave him a little CPR like move that kind of took his breath away and asked, "Why would I want to marry you? Give me some reasons."

He loved her spontaneity and the way she made everything fun.

"Because you love me."

"More!" she said.

"Because you want to cook chicken fried toast for me in the morning."

"More!"

"Because you love Jim."

"More!"

"Because you love my dog."

She gave him another little chest compression and said, "More!"

"Because you love the way I blow the goose."

"Wrong!"

"Because you want to cook Buzz Burgers and fix me Blue Bell specials."

"Not hearing what I want to hear."

"Because you want to play World and feed the chickens."

"Wrong answer!"

"So you can paint my toenails."

"Wrong!"

"Because you don't want to turn in your work uniforms if you leave."

"Wrong!" she said laughing.

"Because you love my tractors."

"More!"

"Because you want to live happily ever after."

"More!"

"Because you want me to paint you on red satin."

"Hardly!"

"Because you want to see your plants grow."

"More Dave, talk to me."

He reached up and undid the top button of her blouse and gently grabbed her by the lapels and pulled her closer and said, "Because you'll never find anybody that loves you as much as I do" and he pulled her to him and kissed her with the passion that had been building for the last six weeks.

When they broke for air she pushed him back and said, "That was the reason I was looking for. I accept your offer" and she took his ring off her thumb and slipped it on his finger.

"Now Mr. Nobody, I'd like you to take me to bed in the big house."

They climbed out of the grotto and Dave said, "You sure about this."

"Absolutely sure."

"There's one thing we have to do first," and he got the flashlight and pointed it toward the front gate on the highway. He turned it on and off three times.

Molly was watching him and asked, "What in the world are you doing?"

He shined the light at the gate again and this time there was a return signal of three flashes from car lights.

Molly looked puzzled and asked, "Who's that?"

"Might want to comb your hair, we're fixing to have company."

"Who?"

"The preacher and a witness might as well do this right. I'm going to have to look your old daddy in the eye someday and I don't want him to think I took advantage of his little girl."

Molly laughed and asked, "How'd you know I'd say yes?"

"Your note, it was just about perfect."

They held hands as they watched the car coming down the path and stop at the wagon. John and Shelley got out first and then preacher Bob who was still in his pajamas and wearing a blue robe. They were all smiling. Bob spoke first and said, "Sorry about my dress. Dave said to come in a hurry and I was in bed. Mary stayed at John's and is babysitting the kids. Did we read your signal correctly?"

Dave answered saying; "You did unless she's gotten cold feet."

Molly showed Shelley the ring and she squealed and gave her a hug.

The ceremony didn't take long. John was the best man and Shelley was the maid of honor. Preacher Bob had thought to bring a marriage license and all the I's were dotted and the T's crossed. It was official.

As the car drove off into the night Dave said, "Now I'll take you to bed in the big house."

"What about the fire?" she asked.

"Let it burn."

"My aren't we in a hurry" she said laughing.

"Come on!" he said.

Molly said, "It'll just take a minute; I don't want to get thrown out of the Chuck Wagon Gang and I don't want to see our hay crop burn up."

When they got to the house the dogs were in their boxes and Jim was asleep.

Molly said, "We'll sleep in my room. You go up and get ready and I'll turn everything off."

Dave went upstairs and got in the bed. Molly came up shortly after, locked the door and turned off the light. She came to the side of the bed and began to undress. The moonlight was coming through the window and left nothing to be imagined. As the last piece of clothing fell to the floor Dave said, "Holy shh..." but he caught himself.

"Almost cost you a quarter, potty mouth" and then she said, "I hope this is going to be as much fun as I think it is."

"It won't be if you don't hurry!"

"Are you going to club me like a baby seal?"

"Yes!"

"Well, move over Clancy, I'm coming in."

As he closed his arms around her she said, "Arf arf!"

Molly was first up and got dressed and went downstairs and she was all smiles. Her stallion was even better than she thought he would be. She got the bacon out of the fridge and started the little ritual that Jim had taught her. Two for Dave, two for Jim, two for me, two for Slick, two for Pudd'n, and one for Dave to snitch.

Just as the coffee finished perking, a red bird landed on the kitchen feeder. She went to the east porch and three doves that were on the ground under the St. Francis feeder took off. The sun was just starting to peek its face from behind the trees across the lake and the Martins were doing their morning chirping.

She went back into the kitchen and for the first time sang their silly song. She sang with heart and enthusiasm. The sun was indeed up and the birds that sing were definitely on the wing and singing too. She had already said "Money Money" two times.

Dave came down in record time hoping he would beat Jim to the kitchen so he wouldn't have to explain what he was doing in Molly's room.

"Good morning" he said with a cat bird grin on his face. He came up behind her and put his arms around her and kissed her gently on the neck.

ROY M. PHILP, JR.

She felt herself melting and turned to him and said, "I think I'm pregnant!"

A surprised look came over his face and he asked, "How could you be pregnant?"

She held up one hand and with the other she counted her fingers one through three and said laughing, "How could I not be pregnant? Hell, I might even have triplets."

He laughed and said, "Well, I guess it's possible."

When Jim came into the kitchen Dave was still standing behind Molly with his arms around her and was watching her tend the bacon. They both saw him about the same time and changed their presentation.

Jim instantly felt better seeing them in this lovey dovie mood. Hopefully she had accepted plan A or B or the ace in the hole plan whatever that was. He had said a prayer that she would and another one that his dad wouldn't mess up.

"How was the campfire?" he asked.

"Your dad wanted to talk and kept me up way past my bedtime."

Jim looked at his dad and said, "Dad, you look sleepy."

Before Dave could respond Molly looked at Dave and asked, "What are we going to do today?"

"We could start on some of those new flower beds" Jim answered but he got no response.

Molly looked at Dave and said, "We could play Bear."

Dave looked at her with a puzzled look on his face and she said, "You know, like hibernate."

A smile came to his face and he said, "Sounds good to me."

Jim felt like he might be interrupting something and he said, "I'll be back in a minute, I'm going to feed my chickens" and he left the room wondering what kind of a game Bear was.

When he was gone Dave asked, "What are we going to do with Jim? Are we going to put him in the fox hole?"

Molly laughed and said, "I'll leave that up to you, you're in charge of Jimbo"

After breakfast Molly left the room and Dave said, "Bud, I've almost got her talked into staying but we need to talk a little more, just the two of us. What if you go to the lake by yourself and catch some fish and we'll have a fish fry for lunch. You'll have to do everything yourself; catch the fish, clean the fish, cook the fish, the whole nine yards. Build a fire and maybe cook some biscuits. We'll come down at twelve sharp and join you. If you see her coming with me you'll know she's going to stay. Think you can do it?"

"Yes sir."

"You'll be on a mission. You can't come back to the house. Anything you need you'll have to take with you now. Can you think of anything you'll need?"

Jim thought a minute and said, "I think we need some ketchup" and he got a new bottle from the pantry. He also got some potatoes and said, "I think I'll fry us up some potatoes too."

Molly joined Dave on the front porch and asked, "Where is he going?"

"He's on a mission. We're going to join him at noon for a fish fry. I gave him my watch. We'll tell him the news at lunch."

Molly went back inside and Dave walked to the front gate and watched Jim and the dogs until they were about half way down the path. He went back inside and locked the front door and started toward the kitchen.

Her sandals were at the kitchen table and a few feet further on the floor was her blouse. He turned the corner toward his room and there were her shorts and at the door were her Victoria Secrets as she had called them. The bedroom door was slightly cracked and there was a jar of honey on the floor.

He opened the door a little and the room was dark "What's the honey for?" he asked.

"It's imagination honey! Bears like honey," she giggled and asked, "Do you have an imagination?"

Dave panicked for a moment and went to the den. He picked up the bearskin rug and carried it to the hall. He dropped to all fours and put the rug over his back and the bear head over his own. He crawled to the door and picked up the honey and said, "Grrrrrrrrr! Is that Goldilocks in my bed?"

"Yes!" she said from under the covers and he crawled to the edge of the bed. He saw that she had the covers pulled over her head and said, "Grrrrrrrrrrr" again.

She snapped back the covers and was looking face to face with the bear head about a foot away. She screamed so loud that it scared Dave. It was a Kodak moment.

At the lake Jim got in the boat and put the dogs in the back of the boat and told them to sit. Just as he was about to shove off he said to the dogs. "I should have got some honey for the biscuits. I think I'll go back, it won't take long." He started toward the house but stopped and said, "I think I'll make a cherry cobbler in the Dutch oven instead."

He shoved off and kept talking to the dogs. "Now you all be still. We're going to the other side where the big boys live."

The dogs seemed to understand everything he was saying and watched his every move. When they got to the other side he said, "See that stump! That's her bedroom. I'm going to throw it right in her bedroom and put the whammy on her."

He snapped on the Lucky 13 that Mr. Neel had given him and made a perfect cast. He let it sit until all the ripples were gone and gave it a twitch. There was a tremendous strike and Jim set the hook. The fish came half out of the water and gave a headshake. It was a hawg for sure. Jim put his hand over his heart and tried to hand the rod to Slick. "You reel Slick; I think I'm going to have a heart attack."

As he was extending the rod to Slick the fish did another headshake and the lure came out of his mouth and zinged back toward the boat. Jim reeled it in and said, "Thank goodness he got off, I thought I was going to die."

He put the Lucky 13 back in the tackle box and pulled out a Mudbug. He looked around to see if anyone was watching them and satisfied that they weren't, he snapped it on and told the dogs, "This plug was outlawed in '63. You all have to promise not to tell."

The dogs made a little whimper like they understood.

He rubbed on a buckeye for good luck and made a long cast and started cranking. Wham, he had one and said, "Candy from a baby! I believe we gonna have a fish fry."

QUESTIONS, THOUGHTS, COMMENTS

1. Who was your favorite character?
2. Have you ever tasted mayhaw jelly or gathered mayhaws?
3. Ever baited and run a trotline? Lots of fun!
4. Had the snake not fallen in the boat would Molly and Dave have ever met?
5. Have you ever watched a Carolina wren build a nest? Talk about busy!
6. How did you like Jim's wish to the genie? I thought it was cool.
7. Hope you have seen the movie, The Man from Snowy River. I hope keeping the names straight wasn't too confusing. I worried about that.
8. If you haven't ever smelled the white flower of a butterfly ginger you have really missed something. They are hard to find but definitely worth planting a few.
9. Ever had a quilt like Shelley made for Molly? My grandmother made one for me and it was one of my most prized possessions. We flat wore it out.
10. Wouldn't you have liked to have been there when John gave Jackson the puppy? Nothing like seeing a kid get a first puppy! I know Rudi was also happy.
11. What did you think of Jim's chickens? It was fun writing that part. I'm thinking of getting a few and am in the planning stage now. Don't

know what variety to get. Any suggestions? Are some varieties more fun than others?

12. Have you ever had a whiff of Chanel No. 5? My wife used it on me and I was done. Good stuff!

13. Ever camped in the woods and had a great horned owl give a hoot or two right outside your tent? It will give you goose bumps.

14. Ever had you toenails painted red while taking a nap in a hammock with all your cousins watching? Talk about embarrassing!

15. Ever see a mongoose cage like Dave had in his shop? A guy in a bait shop showed one to my uncle one time and I was watching. My uncle Moodye used a five dollar word. I'll never forget it.

16. How about Herschel giving Jim his tackle box? I liked that part. Have you got a few treasures that need to be passed on? I know I do.

17. When was the last time you had "A Big Dave's Raspberry Doone Special?" That's too long!

18. Was Molly cool or not? How about her palming the egg into Marian's nest or putting the stickers on the eggs! She was also a pretty good note writer don't you think?

19. Hope you will try Aunt Sue's Buzz sauce or her chicken fried toast. They are both A+

20. Hope you have a few lucky buckeyes in your tackle box. If not you need to get some, they really work.

21. Are the fish working in your life? They are working well in ours. Right now Sue and I are using jelly, pickles and Mrs. McGown's cookies as the fish.

22. Hope you are better on your thank you notes than I am. I am always behind. I would like to say thanks to those of you who bought and read the book. Thank you for your time and I hope it was a fun read for you.

23. A special thanks to my longtime friend Tom Bell who designed the cover. Tom is an artist whose specialty is dog portraits and this was his first hoot owl. I think he did a good job.

24. Another special thanks is to a friend, Mildred Elmore who helped in the editing of *The Hoot Owl Man*. Her help was kind and most appreciated. She was very encouraging and suggested that I write a sequel to the book and even gave me several great ideas.

25. Suggestions or comments to me at royphilp2@gmail.com are welcome or by way of Amazon book review. Thanks!

Made in the USA
San Bernardino, CA
28 March 2016